Methodologies for
PRACTICE RESEARCH

Sara Miller McCune founded SAGE Publishing in 1965 to support the dissemination of usable knowledge and educate a global community. SAGE publishes more than 1000 journals and over 800 new books each year, spanning a wide range of subject areas. Our growing selection of library products includes archives, data, case studies and video. SAGE remains majority owned by our founder and after her lifetime will become owned by a charitable trust that secures the company's continued independence.

Los Angeles | London | New Delhi | Singapore | Washington DC | Melbourne

Methodologies for
PRACTICE RESEARCH

Approaches for Professional Doctorates

edited by

Carol Costley
John Fulton

Los Angeles | London | New Delhi
Singapore | Washington DC | Melbourne

Los Angeles | London | New Delhi
Singapore | Washington DC | Melbourne

SAGE Publications Ltd
1 Oliver's Yard
55 City Road
London EC1Y 1SP

SAGE Publications Inc.
2455 Teller Road
Thousand Oaks, California 91320

SAGE Publications India Pvt Ltd
B 1/I 1 Mohan Cooperative Industrial Area
Mathura Road
New Delhi 110 044

SAGE Publications Asia-Pacific Pte Ltd
3 Church Street
#10-04 Samsung Hub
Singapore 049483

Editor: Jai Seaman
Editorial assistant: Charlotte Bush
Production editor: Victoria Nicholas
Copyeditor: Neville Hankins
Proofreader: Jill Birch
Marketing manager: Susheel Gokarakonda
Cover design: Shaun Mercier
Typeset by: C&M Digitals (P) Ltd, Chennai, India
Printed in the UK

Library of Congress Control Number: 2018944687

British Library Cataloguing in Publication data

A catalogue record for this book is available from the
British Library

ISBN 978-1-4739-9159-0
ISBN 978-1-4739-9160-6 (pbk)

At SAGE we take sustainability seriously. Most of our products are printed in the UK using responsibly sourced
papers and boards. When we print overseas we ensure sustainable papers are used as measured by the PREPS
grading system. We undertake an annual audit to monitor our sustainability.

CONTENTS

ABOUT THE EDITORS AND CONTRIBUTORS

Carol Costley is a Professor of Work and Learning and Director of the Work and Learning Research Centre at Middlesex University. She has been Chair of the International Conference on Professional Doctorates (www.ukcge.ac.uk/profdocs) since 2009, Chair of the 'Association of Practice Doctorates' (www.ProfessionalDoctorates.org) since 2009 and a 'Researching Work and Learning' conference series committee member since 1999. Her research interests are in professional doctorates, work-based and work-integrated learning, especially in examining methodologies and epistemologies in work and learning and how they are additional to and support subject-based approaches to knowledge. She works with organisations in the private, public, community and voluntary sectors internationally in the learning and teaching of work-based, taught and research degrees.

John Fulton is a Reader in Practice-based Research and Director of Post Graduate Research at the University of Sunderland. He has over 30 years' experience in teaching and research supervision. He is interested in practice-based research and in particular the methodological approaches which can be used to explore, illuminate and develop practice. He is also interested in social inequalities and their reproduction in education and health, and is involved in a number of social epidemiology studies in sub-Saharan Africa.

Pam Burnard is Professor of Arts, Creativities and Educations at the Faculty of Education, University of Cambridge, in the UK (www.educ.cam.ac.uk/people/staff/Burnard/). She co-convenes the British Educational Research Association (BERA) Special Interest Group Creativities in Education (https://www.bera.ac.uk/group/creativity-in-education). She has, for many years, been a doctoral educator, doctoral supervisor and innovatively managed the EdD (Professional Doctorate) programme in the Faculty of Education. She is an international authority on advancing creativities research and has published widely with 15 books and over 100 articles on the expanded conceptualisation and plural expression of creativities across diverse learning contexts and professional cultures. Pamela is co-editor of *Thinking Skills and Creativity* (www.journals.elsevier.com/thinking-skills-and-creativity) and co-editor of *Transformative Doctoral Research Practices for Professionals* (Sense Publishers).

Heléne Clark is the Director of ActKnowledge, which is a 20-year-old social enterprise with a mission of improving social justice, equality of resources and opportunity, and human rights worldwide. Heléne and ActKnowledge are the leaders in the development and use of theory of change methodology, and she is co-founder of the non-profit Center for Theory of Change. She has taught urban and economic geography, environmental psychology, research methods and theory of change in leading academic institutions. At ActKnowledge, she leads evaluation, policy, planning and capacity building efforts for non-profit partners.

Gill Coleman is Professor of Action Research at Ashridge/Hult Business School, in the United Kingdom, where she teaches and supervises post-experience part-time students in their action research projects for doctoral and masters programmes and has worked with private and public sector organisations on collaborative action research projects in the United Kingdom, United States and Middle East. She has a long-standing interest in action research as a process for learning within higher education, particularly with inquiry-based participative learning for sustainability and corporate social responsibility, and has pioneered its use in supporting a pedagogy for practice-based learning at Ashridge as well as the Universities of Bristol and Bath.

Tatjana Dragovic is a Doctoral Educator and Convenor of the Leadership, Educational Improvement and Development (LEID) research community at the Faculty of Education, University of Cambridge, UK, and a Doctoral Supervisor at the Open University, UK. For the last 25 years she has worked across different disciplines, sectors and industries and is recognised as an international educator, whose interdisciplinary expertise and research interests lie in the fields of creativity, leadership development, coaching and the professional and personal development of educators. Tatjana is a Senior Lecturer in Leadership Development in Slovenia and the co-editor of *Transformative Doctoral Research Practices for Professionals* (Sense Publishers).

Jan Fook has held professorial positions in Australia, Norway, Canada and the United Kingdom, in both social work and education. She is known mostly for her work on critical social work and critical reflection and travels regularly to provide workshops on the latter. Over the last few years she has published several books on critical reflection (including one on researching critical reflection with Routledge (2016)), and is working on several more on learning critical reflection and making organisational changes regarding critical reflection. In January 2019 she is taking up a position as Professor and Head of the Department of Social Work at the University of Vermont.

Catherine Hayes is a Reader in Health Professions Pedagogic Practice at the University of Sunderland and Visiting Professor of Higher Education at both the University of Cumbria and Liverpool Hope. A National Teaching Fellow and Principal Fellow of the Higher Education Academy, she is a supervisor of doctoral and masters theses and holds key responsibilities for curriculum development in the Faculty of Health Sciences and Wellbeing. She also leads pedagogical research for the University of Sunderland's Centre for Enhancement of Learning and Teaching. She is a Founding Fellow of the Faculty of Podiatric Medicine at the Royal College of Physicians and Surgeons (Glasgow) and a Fellow of the College of Podiatric Medicine and General Practice (London). As a Chartered Scientist and Chartered Manager, she has a particular interest in mechanisms of reflection and reflexivity in research-based praxis. She is widely published, her latest co-edited book being *Textbook of Podiatric Medicine* (2017).

Rebecca Heaton is a Senior Lecturer in Education in the Faculty of Education and Humanities at the University of Northampton. She is the curriculum lead for art and design education and a professional practice tutor training teachers through undergraduate and postgraduate routes. She conducts, publishes, presents and reviews research nationally and internationally concerning cognition, art, technology, creativity and education. She is also a a graduate of the EdD course at the University of Cambridge, Faculty of Education.

Kate Maguire is Associate Professor of Professional Practice in the Faculty of Professional and Social Sciences at Middlesex University and head of its transdisciplinary research degree programmes. Her background is social anthropology of the Middle East and organisational psychology both as a researcher and practitioner. Coming into higher education from careers in journalism, political research and trauma studies, she has engaged with anthropologically informed innovative research methodologies and research pedagogy relevant to professional practice research with particular interest in bridging difference, embracing complexity and theorising professional practice to enhance professional learning and organisational change. She has led on fieldwork design and implementation for a number of projects and innovations in the private and public sectors and has published regularly on trandisciplinarity in Springer publications.

T. W. (Tom) Maxwell is an Adjunct Professor in the School of Education, University of New England, Australia. He led the organisation of the first Professional Doctorates conference in Australia in 1996 and continued to be a key part of organising such conferences to 2004. He has published in the areas of professional doctorates, international education (especially in Bhutan), supervision and teacher education. He retired in 2010.

Jill Perry is the Executive Director of the Carnegie Project on the Educational Doctorate (CPED) and a Research Associate Professor in the Department of Administration and Policy Studies at the University of Pittsburgh. Her research focuses on professional doctorate preparation in education, organisational change in higher education, and faculty leadership roles. Her publications have appeared in *Planning and Changing Journal*, *Journal of School Public Relations*, *Innovation in Higher Education* as well as in several books and practitioner journals. She has edited two books and is the editor of *Impacting Education*, the new online journal focused on transforming professional preparation in education.

David Plowright is an experienced lecturer, researcher, programme director, supervisor and examiner at masters and doctoral levels. He is currently a Research Associate in the Department of Curriculum Studies at Stellenbosch University, South Africa. In addition, he also works as a consultant doctoral supervisor for the Centre for Research in Education and Educational Technology at the Open University. Previous appointments have included lecturer in educational leadership and management at the University of Leicester; principal lecturer at Anglia Ruskin University and director of education studies, Norwich City College of FHE. He is currently writing his next publication, *Challenging the Mythology of Methodology: Re-conceptualising Social and Educational Research*, to be published in 2019 by Palgrave Macmillan.

Barry Rogers is a Senior Visiting Fellow at the Department of Psychological and Behavioural Science, London School of Economics and Political Science (LSE). Since 2002 he has led the MSc course Organisational Life at LSE. The course seeks to bridge the gap between theory and practice while addressing emergent issues in the field. Simultaneously he designs and delivers customised executive education programmes working with some of the world's leading organisations. Before life as a pracademic, he spent 17 years working for JP Morgan, Nomura and Morgan Stanley in London, Tokyo and New York. He is currently an EdD candidate at the University of Cambridge, Faculty of Education.

Valerie A. Storey is an Associate Professor in Educational Leadership and Coordinator of the Elementary Education, Lifelong Learning track in the School of Teaching, Learning & Leadership, College of Education & Human Performance, University of Central Florida, Orlando. She is President of the Florida Association of Professors of Educational Leadership. Her research interests are in educational leadership graduate programme design, implementation and outcomes. She designed a reformed EdD programme in Educational Leadership under the auspices of the Carnegie Project on the Education Doctorate (CPED) and chaired both the CPED and American Education Research Association, Division A, Dissertation Committee.

Kath Woodward is Emeritus Professor of Sociology at the Open University. She has published extensively in the fields of gender studies, feminist critical theory and method, and psychosocial studies, with recent empirical focus upon sport and embodied practices, especially in boxing and the Olympics, involving mixed media creative methods of film and auto-ethnographic reflection. Her most recent Arts and Humanities Research Council funded research was into elite performativity and 'being in the zone' and her work on time and temporality in sport (*Sporting Times*, 2012) informed the Olympic Museum Exhibition, 'Chasing Time'. She has supervised and examined a wide range of doctoral students within her research and disciplinary fields and has contributed widely to BSA postgraduate and doctoral seminars and workshops as well as disseminating good practice on getting published to early career researchers and doctoral students, drawing upon her experience of co-editing the *Sociology*, *Leisure Studies* and *Frontiers* journals.

FOREWORD

The editors and authors in this book have taken a step in the right direction seeking first to understand what practice-based research looks like across professional fields, and second to learn what types of methodologies are present in these preparation programmes. In 2007, the US Council of Graduate Schools' Task Force on the Professional Doctorate released a report that sought to distinguish professional doctorates from PhDs. Two important messages came across in this report:

> Graduate colleges should not use one-size-fits-all standards that simply asks why a professional doctorate is not just like a PhD.

> Professional degrees should represent preparation for the potential transformation of that field of professional practice just as the PhD represents preparation for the potential transformation of the basic knowledge of a discipline. (CGS, 2005)

As professional doctorates have flourished around the globe (Perry, 2017), the distinction between them and their sister doctorates (PhDs) has frequently been confused. In particular, this perplexity has focused on the role that research and methodology have in professional preparation. In many programmes the weakening of both has happened where, in fact, they should be strengthened and viewed as tools for improving practice. The more we can understand and distinguish professional doctorates the more we can follow the advice of what the US Council of Graduate Schools describes as preparing professional practitioners to transform their field of practice. We can also learn to distinguish these degrees from traditional doctorates and from each other.

A lesson learned early in the Carnegie Project on the Education Doctorate (CPED) was 'context matters' (Perry et al., 2015), meaning no one education doctorate would work across multiple institutions serving a varied body of educational practitioners. In this same vein, we cannot think of professional doctorates, nor the research preparation, as one size fits all. Each profession has its own needs and expertise. Through his work investigating multiple professional practice doctorates (law, medicine, clergy, nursing, engineering), Lee Shulman, President Emeritus of the Carnegie Foundation for the Advancement of Teaching, discovered that each profession had an individualised means by which professionals are taught 'to think, to perform, and to act with integrity' (Shulman, 2005: 52) thereby learning the habits of mind, hand and heart in their chosen professional field of practice. He called this type of specialised teaching a *signature pedagogy* and outlined three dimensions that describe how it is done:

1. Teaching is deliberate, pervasive and persistent.
2. Teaching and learning are grounded in theory, research, and problems of practice.
3. Teaching helps students develop a critical and professional stance with a moral and ethical imperative for equity and social justice (Shulman, 2005).

The second dimension notes the importance that the theory-research-practice marriage plays in professional preparation. It also supports this book's editors' revival of Frayling's (1993) ideas that research should be performed on practice (research into practice) and practice should be the focus of practitioner research (research through practice).

As preparers of professionals in these practice doctorates, our role is to teach methodology as a signature pedagogy. We must provide our students with the skills and tools to deeply understand and address the problems they face in practice daily – whether they be of medical, schooling, engineering, nursing, etc. origin. In CPED, we call this preparation *inquiry as practice* – professionals are prepared to use data to design and understand the effects of innovation through the ability to gather, organise, judge, aggregate, and analyse situations, literature, and data with a critical lens (CPED, 2010). Such preparation demands that we, as educators, rethink our own practice and consider the dimensions of a signature pedagogy as we design courses. It implies moving beyond the ways in which we have been taught to consider the new ways that professionals will be expected to think, perform and act on problems they encounter.

At the Center for Public Research and Leadership at Columbia University in New York, an effort is underway to re-envision professional education across all fields. Leaders and participants in this effort have come to realise that 'learning to learn will far outstrip the importance of applying the specialized knowledge with which professionals are initially programmed' (Austin et al., 2017: 1). This work suggests that key skills for professionals have become the ability to think critically and creatively, to be flexible and adaptable, and to work effectively in teams (Austin et al., 2017). These skills are equally necessary in the teaching of methodologies as, inquiry as practice. Unlike traditional research performed by academics, research performed in practice is not siloed, nor is it as neat. Professional practitioners work in teams of colleagues, other professionals, and lay people. They work with people who are experiencing real life situations that require immediate or near-immediate solutions that are grounded in evidence that they will work. As preparers of these practitioners, our role is not only to teach research methods and skills, but also to help these practitioners learn to apply them in teams using critical thinking, creativity, flexibility and adaptability.

In short, methodological preparation for professionals needs to look and be different from what has traditionally been taught. The end goal is not to prepare academics who generate knowledge for improved understanding. The goal is to prepare those who apply learning to improve their own practice and those affected by it. In CPED, we call these professionals *Scholarly Practitioners*, someone who:

> blends practical wisdom with professional skills and knowledge to name, frame, and solve problems of practice; uses practical research and applied theories as tools for change because they understand the importance of equity and social justice; disseminates their work in multiple ways; and resolves problems of practice by collaborating with key stakeholders, including the university, the educational institution, the community, and individuals. (CPED, 2010)

This definition frames the idea that methodology in professional preparation is equally as important as content knowledge and should be taught as a tool, in practice-based settings, with others. In this volume, we see a strong effort by the authors to raise the importance of methodological preparation by demonstrating the philosophical underpinnings of methodological preparation, the types of methodologies taught, how they are applied in practice, and the ways in which professional programmes assess the abilities of their candidates before graduating. The editors and authors are to be commended for this comprehensive look that can guide others who grapple with best practices for teaching professionals.

Jill Alexa Perry, PhD
Executive Director, Carnegie Project on the Education Doctorate (CPED)

REFERENCES

Austin, K., Chu, E., & Liebman, J. (2017). Re-envisioning professional education. White paper from Columbia University Center for Public Research and Leadership. New York: Columbia University Center for Public Research and Leadership.

Carnegie Project on the Education Doctorate (2010). *CPED design concepts*. College Park, MD.

Council of Graduate Schools (CGS) (2005). *Task force report on the professional doctorate*. Washington, DC: Higher Learning Commission.

Frayling, P. (1993) Research in Art and Design. Royal College of Art Research papers. http://researchonline.rca.ac.uk/384/3/frayling_research_in_art_and_design_1993.pdf. Accessed 23 October 2018.

Perry, J.A. (2017). The Carnegie Project on the Education Doctorate: Transforming education practice in multiple contexts. In Mok, K.H., Neubauer, D., & Jiang, J. *The Sustainability of Higher Education Massification: Cases from Asia Pacific and the U.S.* New York: Routledge.

Perry, J.A., Zambo, D. & Wunder, S. (2015). Understanding how schools of education have redesigned the doctorate of education. *Journal of School Public Relations, 36*, 58–85.

Shulman, L. S. (2005). Signature pedagogies in the professions. *Daedalus, 134*(3), 52–59.

INTRODUCTION

This book addresses both the underlying principles of practice-based research and methodological approaches appropriate for practice-based research. It is aimed at the professional doctorate candidate, whether a generic professional doctorate, an EdD, a DBA or one of the many professional doctorates on offer. It covers the general principles of practice-based research and is not tied to a particular discipline or professional group.

The professional doctorate is not a recent phenomenon, but one which has a long history. The Doctor of Education (EdD) was offered by Harvard University in 1922 and, in the United Kingdom, the University of Bristol offered the first EdD in 1992. Since then, first in Australia and then followed by the United Kingdom, there have been a proliferation of doctoral programmes and there are now over 40 named doctoral awards. Despite the establishment of the EdD, MD (Doctor of Medicine) and DBA (Doctor of Business Administration) in the United States, it was not until 2000 that the professional doctorate intensified and since then there has been a proliferation of professional doctorate programmes, focused on particular professional groups (Zusman, 2017). Some of the programmes from Australia, United Kingdom, United States, Canada and many other countries are aimed at those preparing to enter a profession, such as the *Doctor of Clinical Psychology*, while others are focused on established professionals, for example the *Doctor of Nursing Science (DNS)* designed to prepare clinicians for advanced roles. Maxwell (2003) identified a third group, namely that of the generic or work-based professional doctorate, for example the *Doctor of Professional Studies (DProf)*, which is not tied into one profession but has a generic focus on work-based practice development.

Common to all professional doctorates is the relation to practice, and most professional doctorates require a final dissertation or thesis which details the focus and original development of an aspect of practice. Research on the impact from graduates of professional practice doctorates is beginning to reveal an alignment with the needs of communities, organisations and professions and how the graduates' research can generate a wide variety of outcomes that have an impact (Wellington, 2013; Costley and Stephenson, 2009). Their ability to transform research into action can meet the needs of employers and society, demonstrate improvements in practice and help society adapt well to the ever-increasing pace of change in the twenty-first century (see e.g. the journal *Impacting Education: Journal of Transforming Professional Practice*, from 2016).

The relationship of the research project to practice can vary. Frayling (1993) identifies three ways in which research can relate to practice: research about practice, research into practice and research through practice. Frayling was discussing design practice, but this conceptualisation has a generic application. Research about practice would mean the researcher examining an issue which may have implications for practice and this may involve carrying out research while not being directly involved with the practice area. It has implications for practice and its findings can then be applied to practice. Research into practice involves carrying out research directly on practice actually in the practice area. Research through practice is, as it implies, using practice as the very focus of the research.

It is apposite that Frayling was in the field of arts, as professional doctorates range over many professional areas, but it is those who are historically steeped in practice, such as nursing and other healthcare roles, teaching and arts, that have led the way in many respects in demonstrating the value of research which has a strong impetus on practice.

This book explores research approaches in the context of practice-based research and as such it covers a very broad area. The focus is on research into practice and research through practice. A key argument is that there is commonality about practice and the development of that practice that transcends disciplinarity. When considering practice, there is great value in approaching research into practice and practice development in a structured and focused manner. This book aims to explore both the underlying principles and the methodological approaches which are relevant to research across the curriculum (often addressing complex, 'real-world' problems) that will ensure a careful, systematic approach.

Practice is both broad and to a degree nebulous, and it is often used in a 'cover-all' way: for example, concepts of practice can differ greatly between work environments. However, comparatively recently there has been an increasing awareness of the ways knowledge can be generated from practice. The increasing popularity of professional doctorates has been an important factor in this development whereby experienced practitioners can develop their professional work to doctoral level.

Practice research can take many forms and much depends on the focus and nature of the practice and practice area which are being explored. This book aims to explore the relevant methodological approaches which will facilitate this, not by presenting an exhaustive list, but rather by a consideration of relevant and commonly chosen approaches. What we aim to do in this book is to explore a range of options and we have purposefully drawn on examples from different disciplines and practice areas. It is also worth mentioning that often practitioners choose methodological approaches which are not valued in their particular area of practice. For example, an engineer wishing to implement a new technique might look to approaches involving human interaction and the management of change involving methods that are sometimes undervalued within a scientific discipline.

In practice-research, the 'self' is important because researchers who are also practitioners are not outside observers but are centrally involved in the research and the research process, possibly carrying out research on themselves. This requires a different skill set from more conventional research approaches (Drake and Heath, 2011).

Practice researchers and practitioner–researchers are often, but by no means exclusively, mid-career professionals, coming to the research with a wealth of experience and a variety of projects already completed. The challenge can be to develop this previous work using reliable methodical approaches that result in useful and rigorously achieved outcomes. This provides challenges for all involved and it is important that researchers position themselves within the research process, which requires a reflective and reflexive ability at a sophisticated level.

Ethical issues are also important and do require much thought as the research often constitutes what is referred to as insider knowledge and part of this is the importance of the positionality of the researcher. Additionally, many ethical committees can classify practitioner research as service improvement where formal approval is not required. However, this is not to say that there are no ethical issues involved as full consent of all involved needs to be gained. There also needs to be some thought to potential ethical problems: for example, in exploring practice, suboptimal or bad practice might be uncovered. Not only at the beginning, but also throughout the process, ethical issues need to be given some detailed consideration. When dealing with practice environments there is almost always the requirement for the co-operation of others and this presents many challenges and requires strategic management.

Acknowledgement of the transient nature of practice is often overlooked. Those in the public sector are aware of the changes in policy and funding cuts which can occur when there are government changes, and they also can happen within the lifespan of a government. This phenomenon is not exclusive to the public sector but also common in the private sector. Strategic management and many skills, often including insider knowledge, are essential in managing the process of research in tandem with changes in policy and practice.

The above discussion serves to emphasise the importance of reflexivity and the need for reflective skills for practice-based researchers. In terms of reflection on and during the research process there is a need to consider the wider contextual factors which can impede the research and for reflective ability and adaptability to alter and develop the process in consideration of the experiences of the researcher. This has important implications for the methodological approaches which are relevant to practice-based research and is a key reason why the choosing of an approach requires detailed consideration. It is also important to emphasise that choosing a methodology is not an exact science and methodological approaches are not mutually exclusive as similar elements may be present in more than one approach. It is more a question of choosing the best fit so that an approach is chosen which will shape and develop the research process in the appropriate manner.

The particulars and themes running throughout the book are around the nature of practice and how the essence of practice can be captured through a research focus. Some recurring points are the need for reflection and for the integration of reflection and often also reflexivity into the research process. Similarly the integration of ethics and ethical principles that relate to practice need to be included in the research process. The transdisciplinary nature of work and practice situations is a theme, as well as the focus of research requiring particular outcomes and recommendations for practice. Also apparent in the choice of research approach are deliberations about the advantages and considerations needed for practitioners who engage in research and have insider knowledge and ontological awareness because of their expert experience.

Although the separate chapters each address issues of practice resulting in similar themes running throughout the book, they are sometimes addressed in different ways. The aim is to explore methodological approaches which are useful ways of framing the research and which ensure rigour and consistency that allow the incorporation of the above principles.

STRUCTURE OF THE BOOK

The book is in two parts.

Part I considers the concept of practice-based research and its philosophical and theoretical underpinnings. The central idea is that there are a number of practice-orientated projects which have used research techniques to develop practice in a unique and systematic way, and there is now a need to pull together and conceptualise these ideas. For example, consideration is given to how the concept of the *Bricoleur*, espoused by Lévi-Strauss, is used to facilitate this process.

The focus is on the position of the researcher and, as such, issues around reflection and reflexivity are addressed. There are also key issues around ethical considerations and the ways in which practice-based researchers and in particular practitioner–researchers need to incorporate ethics in practice research as a strong strand.

Part II examines the methodologies which can be used as an overarching framework for the development of the research programme. These approaches are carefully chosen to reflect the common approaches which are considered by professional doctorate candidates. Each of the authors is a recognised expert in the research methodologies that are explained and discussed and each chapter incorporates real-life examples with exercises and key points.

PART I

Chapter 1 Philosophy and Practice (T. W. (Tom) Maxwell)

This chapter examines the type of knowledge involved in practice-based research and evaluates a growing body of literature examining knowledge that has been characterised as modes 1 and 2. Mode 2 is focused on practice research and emphasises the need for transdisciplinary approaches. Mode 1 is characterised as unidisciplinary in nature and follows the rules and customs of a particular discipline. The key debates and issues are examined in some detail, including the binary that the distinction can set up and the more helpful focus on research in the 'real world' and the transdisciplinarity of more practice-based knowledges.

Chapter 2 Research Approaches in Professional Doctorates (Carol Costley)

One of the main challenges of practice-based research is the difficulty of reconciling quite different philosophical approaches. This chapter examines the claims made for an epistemology of practice in research and the challenges this brings. It considers some of the key elements associated with research that is practice based or practice led, and how such research might be at variance with more established research processes and have a different order of priorities. There are implications of complexity.

Chapter 3 Why Policy Matters Particularly in Professional Doctorates (Pam Burnard, Tatjana Dragovic, Rebecca Heaton and Barry Rogers)

Policy is the mechanism through which values are authored and formulated for society. Policy embodies carefully articulated principles for acceptance and enactment. The practices and policies necessary for resourcing professional doctorates comprise one of their defining features in that they form the background upon which researching professionals engage in shaping practice agendas, leading professional change and, in turn, changing policies. This chapter examines vertical policies that come from legislation or accreditation bodies in top-down ways as compared to or in connection with policies that are more horizontal and 'softer' in character, coming from published materials, traditions or forms of professional dialogue. It also features the accounts of two researching professionals who further illustrate how policy and policy thinking disrupt and reorder their professional doctorate projects.

Chapter 4 Reflective Models and Frameworks in Practice (Jan Fook)

This chapter aims to provide an overview of the different meanings of reflection (and related concepts) in relation to research, and to provide practical guidelines for the use of reflection in research. It discusses how reflection is related to practice-based research and, in particular, how reflection and reflexivity might themselves be used as an approach. Practical examples of specific questions to aid reflection are provided.

Chapter 5 Ethics (John Fulton and Carol Costley)

Here the rationale for any concern for ethical considerations in research is discussed through a short historical review followed by the steps it is usually necessary to take regarding ethics of the research. Consideration is given to the research design, the participants in the research, ethics committees in the university and professional ethics of work situations. The specific characteristics of practice-based research and considerations of research ethics for practitioners who are often insiders in their research fields are given particular attention.

PART II

Chapter 6 Methodology as Personal and Professional Integrity (Kate Maguire)

Moral and ethical domains need to be considered along with the relevant literature and the type of knowledge which is found to be informative and valued by the particular area of practice. The situation for researchers in their professional field involves their position in the field or organisation and the standpoint they take on research integrity in their area of investigation. Researchers in this sense serve a multidimensionality of stakeholders, especially the authority of the university and the professional field or organisation.

Some constructions of research approaches are more concerned with issues of reliability and validity, whereas for others it is trustworthiness and consistency. The personal and professional integrity of the researcher sits at the centre of every action and every choice, thus for professional doctorates where the researcher is more closely connected with the context of the research, the trustworthiness of the research is dependent on the trustworthiness of the researcher and their ability to articulate and account for their choices. This is usually achieved through critical reflection. The chapter lists influences that need to be considered and types of questions to be asked in relation to professional integrity when planning a research design. The approaches to research design raise ethical considerations concerning the choice of what to research, why it is to be researched and how.

Chapter 7 Capstone Design (Valerie A. Storey)

This chapter explains how a dissertation or thesis changes in methodology, format and impact to become a dynamic document guiding change to help resolve a complex problem of practice. Alternative dissertation models are discussed and the Dissertation in Practice (DiP) as a model for practice doctorates is recommended.

Chapter 8 Auto-ethnography (Kath Woodward)

This chapter explores auto-ethnography as a research methodology and a set of methods which are increasingly popular as a way of getting 'inside' the field. The chapter draws upon work in sport, including one of the editor's work on the Olympics and a range of boxing auto-ethnographies to evaluate the approach drawing upon psychosocial and feminist theoretical perspectives.

Chapter 9 Action Research (Gill Coleman)

The strengths, and challenges, of action research are explored, through this often misunderstood approach (rather than a method) that combines action and systematic reflection. The key principles to action research are explored: it is highly participative; it places the researcher as always present in the research, as co-participant and/or facilitator; and it is messy and emergent. It is therefore appealing to practice-based researchers, who want simultaneously to advance their understanding and their capacity to enact that understanding in their day-to-day work.

Chapter 10 Case Study (Catherine Hayes)

This chapter explores case study methodology within the context of a practice-based professional doctorate. Definitions of case studies are considered and a definition pertinent to practice is established. The variety of approaches to the design of a case study is given detailed consideration: empirical–theoretical, single or multiple, explanatory or descriptive, as well as specific or general approaches are considered. The combination of research methods and how they can be used to address issues of practice development and ways in which the data can be combined are explored.

Chapter 11 Mixed Methods Research (David Plowright)

The chapter introduces an alternative mixed methods approach, an integrated methodology, that is an innovative way of addressing many of the conceptual and design issues associated with a more traditional mixed methods perspective. It provides a coherent and easily applied framework for planning and implementing small-scale research aimed at evaluating and improving practice located in a professional context.

Chapter 12 Translational Research (John Fulton)

This chapter considers translating research findings into practice. Using examples from health and education it considers ways of ensuring the reliability and validity of original research. The chapter concludes with a consideration of the ways in which translational research can structure a postgraduate research project.

Chapter 13 Theory of Change (Heléne Clark)

This chapter introduces theory of change as a methodological approach which can shape and focus a professional doctorate. Theory of change is a well-used and often demanded process nowadays in social change, social research and philanthropy. The chapter outlines the principles of theory of change and gives a step-by-step guide as to how it can be used to shape a practice-based research study. Some useful addendums help to expand understanding of theory of change.

REFERENCES

Costley, C., & Stephenson, J. (2009). Building doctorates around individual candidates' professional experience. In D. Boud & A. Lee (eds) *Changing Practices of Doctoral Education* (pp. 171–87). New York: Routledge.

Drake, P., & Heath, L. (2011). *Practitioner Research at Doctoral Level: Developing Coherent Research Methodologies*. New York: Routledge.

Frayling, C. (1993). *Research in Art and Design, Royal College of Art Research Papers*, http://researchonline.rca.ac.uk/384/3/frayling_research_in_art_and_design_1993.pdf. Accessed 27 January 2018.

Impacting Education: Journal of Transforming Professional Practice (2016 to present). http://impactinged.pitt.edu/ojs/index.php/ImpactingEd. Accessed 16 June 2018.

Maxwell, T. W. (2003). From first to second generation professional doctorate. *Studies in Higher Education*, 28(3), 279–92.

Wellington, J. (2013). Searching for 'doctorateness'. *Studies in Higher Education*, 38, 10.

Zusman, A. (2017). Changing degrees: creation and growth of new kinds of professional doctorates. *Journal of Higher Education*, 88(1), 133–61.

PART I

Underlying Principles

PHILOSOPHY AND PRACTICE – WHY DOES THIS MATTER?

T. W. Maxwell

INTRODUCTION

Those who are approaching (or doing) practice-based research need to understand the tradition, the philosophical underpinning, of that work. This is especially the case where the neophyte researcher is most likely to think of research in the most common tradition of unidisciplinary work governed by laws, as is the case in the vast majority of PhDs. As will be discussed below, one way of understanding this is to think of such research as mode 1 (see below). In contrast, professional doctorate (PD) research is more often mode 2 and as such is transdisciplinary. Each has its own philosophical tradition.

The work of Gibbons et al. (1994) was an important breakthrough for many interested in doctoral education as it clarified and crystallised the otherwise implied distinctions between the PhDs and the PDs that were being addressed in the early years (1990s). However, recent research by Flood (2011a), discussed below, has shown that the work of Gibbons et al. can be thought of as one of the more recent developments of a long-standing and important thread in philosophical thought.

The rise of PDs in Australia and elsewhere in the last two decades or more has led to a reconsideration of the nature of doctoral education and an interest in practice-based research. There is not always clarity about the nature of PDs despite their being on the scene for more than 20 years. For example, Scott et al. (2004) in their UK-based study of PDs in three professions found four kinds: disciplinary, technical rational, dispositional and critical. Of these the first two are more usually linked to the PhD and the latter two to the PD. In Australia, despite a 'crisis discourse' on the PhD (e.g. Cuthbert and Molla, 2015) and the critique of the place of PDs in doctoral education (e.g. Evans et al., 2005), PDs are in a reasonably healthy state. For example, Kot and Hendel (2012) report the emergence and growth of PDs in Canada, the United States and the United Kingdom as well as in Australia. However, in Australia, there has been a decline in awards associated with the standard professions, for example the EdD, and a phenomenal increase in niche PDs (Maxwell, 2011). Clearly, though, PDs are part of the higher education landscape (Lee et al., 2000; Kot and Hendel, 2012; Costley, 2013).

PDs, then, are an important arena for doctoral research in the professions. PDs are also an important addition to university awards because they provide the site for practice-based research at a high level. Practice-based work is embodied in professional practice sometimes producing new knowledge which Gibbons et al. (1994) term mode 2 knowledge production. Mode 2 knowledge is generated through addressing problems or issues which occur in practice and as such it tends to draw from a range of disciplines and approaches. An exploration of these concepts form the first sections of this chapter which is followed by an outline of the relevant Flood (2011a) research on ancient to recent philosophical bases for PD work. The chapter concludes with a consideration of some implications that follow from this line of reasoning. Firstly we should clarify some definitions.

KEY DEFINITIONS

The relevant definition of 'profession' in the *Concise Oxford Dictionary* (COD) is 'vocation or calling especially one that involves some branch of learning or science' and this is consistent with both the definitions of PDs that follow. However, it is important to note that the COD definition appears quite narrow in the face of the recent growth of cutting-edge professional work involving more than one kind of professional knowledge (see niche doctorates, Maxwell, 2011). In Australia the definition of the PD is taken as follows:

> A program of research, scholarship and advanced study which enables candidates to make a *significant contribution to knowledge and practice in their professional context*. In doing so, a candidate may also contribute more generally to scholarship within the discipline or field of study. Professional Doctorate students should be required to apply their research and study to problems, issues or other matters of substance which produce *significant benefits in professional practice*. (CDDGS, 1998, 1; my emphasis)

The definition in the United Kingdom is as follows:

> A Professional Doctorate is a programme of advanced study and research which, whilst satisfying the University criteria for the award of a doctorate, is designed to *meet the specific needs of a professional group* external to the University, and which develops the capability of individuals to work within a professional context. (Hoddell, 2002: 62, in Costley, 2011: 11; my emphasis)

There are similarities and differences here. For example, both identify the university as the quality control institution. The former identifies professional practice (twice) whereas this is implied in the latter (see italics) and both mention 'advanced study' and 'research'. Personal capacity building is explicit in the latter and implied in the former. Both give a clear view of what is required. Practice- and work-based doctorates (Costley and Lester, 2012) would fall into this group. First-degree doctorates, such as the Doctor of Medicine in the United States, are not considered PDs.

Activity

Thinking about your own professional practice, think about the types of knowledge that are most valued and by whom.

Consider for example: uni-disciplinary knowledge; transdisciplinary conceptualisations of knowledge; purely practice-based or practice-led thinking about knowledge; practical situations and practice based problems; theoretical knowledge; and an evenly balanced mixture of theory and practice.

In the development of your research how will this structure your thinking in the generation of your ideas?

Consider the ways in which this might present particular challenges.

'Professional practice' links two concepts that are difficult to define. Indeed the former has clearly changed in meaning, particularly over recent times. Green (2009: 1–6) discusses these and related concepts (see also Kemmis, 2009: 22–3) but lack of space precludes rehearsing Green's discussion. Ultimately, Green (2009: 6–7) suggests four senses to assist in the understanding of 'professional practice':

a. practising of a profession (medicine, education, and so on);
b. practising professionalism (enacting what it is to be a professional);
c. professional practice evokes a moral quality (doing what is right for others); and
d. practising as a professional implies a fee for service (a service that cannot be done by the uninitiated).

Green goes on to point out (7–9) the importance of authentic activity and how experience can grow out of practice. 'Experience' here means more than length of time in practice and implies improvement of some kinds over time usually relying on reflection. He also points out that practice is always contextualised, as he put it: '"context" needs to be thought of as *part of practice*, as inscribed in it' (8). This leads us to the consideration of mode 2 knowledge production wherein context is critical.

MODES 1 AND 2 KNOWLEDGE PRODUCTION

Historically, Gibbons et al. assisted the conceptual development of PDs with their publication of *The New Production of Knowledge*. While there have been critiques of the Gibbons et al. conceptualisation (see e.g. Scott, 1995; Fuller, 1995), their work has been useful. Lee et al. (2000: 124) used Gibbons et al.'s ideas to explicate their model for PD development. The central feature, where professional work leading to a doctoral award should be placed, they argued, was at the confluence of the workplace, the profession and the university. The model was useful at that time because it pointed to the centrality of the workplace, an important idea for academics at the time (Maxwell, 2003). At about the same time David Boud developed a curriculum model for work-based learning that focused more on the individual and brought together the workplace and the profession, the 'university' not being required in the general model (Boud, 2001, in Costley and Lester, 2012). Boud's focus upon the student is appropriate in PD learning and research since it is the capacity building of the person and the research questions that are developed by the person in the thoroughly contextualised research process that are central to the development of the PD work. Implied here is the idea that a university-based supervisor/adviser cannot usually provide the research questions to the PD student as is commonly the case in much unidisciplinary research.

Lee et al. (2000) argued, as others have done since, that mode 2 knowledge production underpins research of professional practice. Usher went a little further. She argued that mode 2 knowledge is a more appropriate conception for the 'knowledge economy' (Usher, 2002: 147). 'Knowledge economy' has an implication of immediacy. Seddon (1999) made a more general point than Usher (2002): mode 2 knowledge is more likely to be useful in its own right. This is not to say that mode 1 knowledge production is not worthwhile, but rather that mode 2 knowledge has its own warrant, namely the production of useful knowledge by the professional in the workplace in association with others in community. In similar vein, Lee et al. (2009: 9) put the issue succinctly that PD education, potentially, could be underpinned by 'the generation of a different knowledge distinguished by an overall practice rationality'. Consequently mode 2 knowledge production, when thought of from this perspective, contrasts strongly with mode 1.

Mode 1 knowledge is more typically associated with the PhD rather than the PD. Mode 1 knowledge is generated in a disciplinary context: that is, in universities or affiliated institutions. It arises from an academic agenda, is usually discipline focused but sometimes multidisciplinary and is accountable to the academic community. In many respects, we can say that mode 1 knowledge production is more associated with academic knowledge, and so disciplines, as areas of study. Its project is to produce knowledge governed by laws. Hamilton (2005: 287) put it this way: 'Theoretical science refers to detached forms of inquiry, contemplative forms of reasoning and the establishment of necessary, eternal and unchanging truths.'

So, mode 1 contrasts strongly with mode 2 knowledge production. Reviewing their work of the previous decade, Nowotny and colleagues identified the key features of mode 2 knowledge production as:

a. generated in the context of application;
b. transdisciplinary – 'the mobilization of a range of theoretical perspectives and practical methodologies';
c. produced at a greater variety of sites due to technological advances;
d. highly reflexive; and
e. subject to novel forms of quality control, not all of which are desirable (Nowotny et al., 2003: 186–8).

It is worth noting the distinction that Nowotny et al. (186) make regarding mode 2 knowledge production and applied research.

'Mode 2' knowledge is generated within a context of application. This is quite different from the process of application by which 'pure' research, generated in the theoretical/experimental environment, is 'applied', technology is 'transferred', and knowledge is subsequently 'managed'. The context of application, in contrast, describes the total environment in which scientific problems arise, methodologies are developed, outcomes are disseminated, and uses are defined.

We can see then that mode 2 knowledge results from practitioner agency and/or reflection and/or research *in* practice. Research sites are geographically widespread (workplaces) which contrast greatly with distributed but focused places of mode 1 research, the universities, where problems '[are] set and solved in context governed by academic interests of specific communities [characterised as] discipli-nary; homogeneous; hierarchical and form preserving; accountable to discipline-based notions of methodologically "sound" research practice' (Lee et al., 2000: 124).

Lee et al. (124) also note that there are overlaps between the two modes, that is they are not discrete, and this is consistent with the Maxwell and Vine (1998) conceptualisation.

AN IMPORTANT PHILOSOPHICAL THREAD

J. Bernard Flood completed his EdD portfolio in 2011 with Dr Joy Hardy and myself as co-supervisors. His was not a practice-based doctorate but was, rather unusually, theoretical. It might have been a PhD but the research issues addressed underlay professional practice. Paradoxically, his research was quintessentially mode 1. Flood established an important and definite thread in philosophical think-ing in practical reasoning starting with Aristotle (384–322BP). Flood, like Hamilton (2005: 287), pointed out that Aristotle made a distinction between the practical and theoretical sciences. This is a distinction that is followed in this section which relies heavily on Flood's work (Flood, 2011b: 6–26).

Ultimately what we want in a professional person is practical wisdom, someone who has experience enough to recognise the points of significance in the chosen field of practice. This involves the confluence of real problems in real places, in real time and with real people and real resources. For Flood the starting point is Aristotle's *phronesis*. Flood understood the debates around *phronesis* over the last two decades and concluded on this with a quote from Natali (2001: 188, in Flood 2011b: 6): 'there is wide agreement among interpreters in characterising *phronesis* as practical knowledge. … *Phronesis* brings about agreement of reason and desire that finds expression in good deliberation.' Here there is already the moral sense and deliberation that were identified above about professional judgement. 'For Aristotle, then, *phronesis* involves deliberation, leading to (moral) choice and that leads to action. The choice is rational and is linked with deliberation' (Flood 2011b: 8). Reflecting on *phronesis*, Dunne (1997: 368) wrote it 'is precisely the kind of reason which, as including practical *nous*, has developed an "*eye*" (Aristotle) or a "nose" (Wittgenstein) for what is salient in concrete situations'. Thus *phronesis* concerns practical wisdom and is rational and ethical, associated with the right action in real situations. And, according to Flood, such practical wisdom resides in a *phronimos*, the person who has 'an initial aptitude cultivated and developed by experience' (Guthrie, 1998: 346, in Flood, 2011b: 9). A *phronimos* is close to what we understand as an experienced person in the full sense of 'experienced'.

Flood argued that *phronesis* was further developed by Aquinus (1325–74) as *prudentia* which goes beyond our common understanding of the term 'prudence'. Flood (2011b: 18), interpreting Aquinus, argued that *prudentia* applied to all decision making, not just to ethical decisions thus extending Aristotle. Three stages were required:

a. weighing up possibilities around the means to the good desired;
b. judging which means is the best; and, lastly and most importantly,
c. executing/implementing the results of that deliberation (18).

Here the moral sense is retained ('good desired') as is the intellect and action. Flood (19) also points to the importance of experience in acquiring *prudentia* as seen in *phronesis*. *Prudentia* 'is the outlook or disposition which enables the agent to arrive at the right application in the particular situation and to perform it' (Westberg, 1994: 190, in Flood, 2011b: 20). So there is an emphasis on the particular situation and action.

John Henry Newman (1801–90) extended both of the above conceptions as the illative sense. Newman's conceptualisation allows insight and intuition along with rationality from many sources of data (Flood, 2011b: 20–30), though it should be said that Newman depended heavily on Aristotle's *phronesis* (Dunne, 1997: 33–8). Aquino points to the contribution made by Newman and in so doing explicates the illative sense:

> Newman's project focusses upon the informal and tacit dimension of reasoning, shaped by experience and personal insight. ... The illative sense sifts, evaluates, and integrates various pieces of evidence into a synthetic judgement and furnishes concrete answers to specific questions. ... The illative sense connects various pieces of data, its manner of concluding does not follow a strictly rule-governed process of inquiry. (Aquino, 2004: 5, in Flood, 2011b: 21)

Note particularly the addition of the 'informal and tacit' in the illative sense.

Newman was concerned with the epistemic rather than the statistical probability (Flood, 2011b: 23). This phenomenology of mind approach draws criticisms but Newman 'appeals to the normal operation of the mind in concrete matters which are too subtle, minute, delicate and intricate to be put into logical rules or forms' (Flood, 2011b: 22). Moreover, decisions made using the illative sense in these complex situations are made with certitude not certainty (22–3) since the illative sense does two things. It:

a. brings together *all* arguments, however subtle; and
b. determines their worth separately and in combination (27).

This leads to a decision to act with certitude and, like the philosophers before him, Newman contended that the illative sense was concerned with the practical.

Flood (2011b: 31–2) then added an important dimension. He critiqued the three philosophers' primacy given to the individual and individual thought. Flood used Macmurray's (1891–1976) 1953–4 Gifford Lectures to shift the centre of reference from the person in thought to thought in action. Kilpatrick (1989: xi, in Flood, 2011b) put it succinctly thus: 'the essence of the self is that of an agent in action rather than a thinker in thought'. For Macmurray action was more central to existence than thought since action is embedded in human experience which is shared. This also resonates with Aquino's (2004, in Flood, 2011b: 30) position that the illative sense is communal: that is, guaranteed only through communities of informed judgement. Kemmis too pointed out that 'practice has a number of extra individual features that need to be elucidated. These include such features as being formed and conducted in social settings, shaped by discourses, and being dramaturgical and practical in character' (2005: 394).

These ideas and much recent neo-Aristotelianism thinking challenge modernist, goal-oriented propositions about scientific management (Hamilton, 2005: 287). One could say too that this is precisely what the mode 2 PDs, and particularly the practice-based doctorates, are doing in doctoral education. Green (2009: 5) identifies Alasdair MacIntyre, Stephen Toulmin, Hans-George Gadamer and Joseph Dunne as key thinkers in this area. To these we can add Wilfred Carr, Stephen Kemmis and Bill Green himself. Even Donald Schön, especially in his extended critique of technical rationality (Schön, 1983: 21–49) and his 'Research and practice' chapter (307–25), gives early attention to the relationship between rationality and practice from the practitioners' point of view. Claude Lévi-Strauss could also be included. His 'The science of the concrete' and, in particular in the chapter where he addressed the *bricoleur/bricolage* (Lévi-Strauss, 1962: 16–22), provides a French anthropologist's view. Not least has been the recent leadership by Gibbons and Nowotny through their work on mode 2 knowledge production. All were writing in the 'rough ground' of knowledge production.

In summary, the philosophical thread attended to here shows there is a long tradition of thinking that we can call practical wisdom that is separate from, or at least different to, the presently dominant scientific reasoning. Here, then, is the warrant for research on professional practice. The argument for research *in* practice is strong. The earliest version, *phronesis*, focused upon intellectual virtue in practical ethical matters being developed centuries later in Newman's illative sense of 'informal and tacit dimension of reasoning, shaped by experience and personal insight' (Aquino, 2004: 5, in Flood, 2011b: 21). The illative sense is applicable to reasoning about all concrete matters leading to the right action (Dunne, 1997: 37). Practical wisdom is gained through (critical reflection in and on) experience. Practice-based research by the practitioner enables precisely the researcher's phenomenology of mind to engage in the research process and to communicate the results to the relevant community. Hamilton's summary is elegant:

> Practical science … aims to develop and improve practical reasoning, recognising that such activities are both morally and contextually informed. In practice, then, there is a necessary association between the practical, the ethical and the contextual. (2005: 287)

Activity

Before reading the next section, write down the implications you think Hamilton's 2005 quote above might have for the development of your practice.

If you have a research project in mind, consider also its implications for the development of that project.

IMPLICATIONS

There is a range of issues that follow from this way of thinking. Firstly, the complexities of practice in the everyday real-life setting of real people, places, timings and funds mean that PD research cannot normally be addressed by a neophyte. One reason for this is that, unlike in mode 1 knowledge production where the researcher is typically guided by a university supervisor/adviser/mentor, the mode 2 knowledge producer works on questions identified out of their practice usually geographically elsewhere from the university. Gaining supervision/advice/mentoring off-campus for PD work, while not as direct as on-campus, can easily be facilitated by modern technologies. Moreover, the complexities of the workplace mean that PD research demands the knowledge of practice complexities (*phronesis*) and nuances (*techne*). That knowledge opens opportunities for significant questions to be asked. This is no easy task, certainly so for the neophyte. In short, professional, and even worldly, experience is essential. Such experience means that the 'student' is usually more in control of the research process from the point of view of its supervision.

Complexities and nuances are more pointed as the research is undertaken *in*, not on, the workplace. Political niceties need to be negotiated carefully over time. This is especially so since the researcher/employee does not exit the research site but is embedded in it. Additionally, challenges to custom and practice through the research processes and outcomes can be personally and professionally challenging both to the researcher and for other workers. Moreover, the status of different people is likely to be challenged in such an environment. New identities might be formed. Indeed, PD work is clearly a process that facilitates the development of a professional identity. More research is needed on this (see Trede et al., 2012). Studies with PD students like that of Mantai (2015), who used interviews of 30 PhD students on their becoming researchers, would be useful though preferably using a mixed methods approach. PD research in the workplace contrasts starkly with the 'armchair' deliberation of much mode 1 research on the workplace by an outsider who – although this is not always straightforward – more simply negotiates access, implements the research plan and then departs.

There are also implications for the university. Clearly a new market for students has developed. This is an important consideration in the present market economy that universities, at least in the United Kingdom and Australia, currently face. As

Costley (2013) has argued, there is also a demand for higher education graduates who have more work-related skills including research skills. But more than this, universities should be employing PD graduates for the expertise and experience that they would bring to the supervisory/advisory process. Alternatively, an adjunct from a relevant workplace may be engaged as part of the supervisory team. As indicated above, this process has some considerable differences as compared to much PhD supervision.

Such differences evolve from the idea that workplace research, in the heat of action, requires judgements that are 'good enough' (Flood, 2011b). The concept of 'good enough' comes from Winnacott (1971, in Flood, 2011b: 35) and is extremely useful in the real world. Winnacott, a London psychologist, was working with mothers who were concerned whether their mothering was adequate. Rather than aim for perfection and always be thwarted, Winnacott advised they aim for their mothering to be good enough and be relaxed in that. The idea of 'good enough' is essentially consistent with professional work: decisions are made and monitored; modifications can be made if required. Such deliberations and actions contribute to the formation of a professional identity and are based in reflexivity which is 'representative of a growing maturity and self-reflexivity' (Barnard, 2011: 56) desired of the professional and in PD work.

It follows from the reasoning immediately above that another implication is that workplace research includes practical reasoning. Such practical reasoning can be developed over time, that is from experience (see above). It may be formalised in a PD. The development of practical reasoning intended in undertaking a PD is analogous to the development of research skills as one of the major outcomes of a PhD. Thus the award of a PD gives the workplace researcher a licence to research, independently of supervision/advice, in the same sense that a PhD does.

The final implication is that the subject, the body, is very much present in professional practice research. The researcher is more than an insider but *inside* the research. Green and Hopwood (2015: 5) put it this way: 'This is thinking with and through the body, in the very course of practice, as a primary mode of being and becoming.' This contrasts greatly with typical mode 1 research which maintains an avowedly 'hands-off' or detached stance. The PD practitioner also finds an authoritative voice (Reid and Green, 2009) through the research. Armsby and Dreher (2011: 75) concluded: 'We think of the outcomes of a PD ... as being embodied in the candidate, now and in the future; located in the context of the research and development work; shaping professional knowledge and practice or a combination of all these three.'

CONCLUSION

PDs, including those identified as practice-based doctorates, have become an important part of the higher education research scene over the last 25 years. This is especially the case in Australia and the United Kingdom. The work of Gibbons and colleagues highlighted the important distinction that now is aligned with PD work: unlike applied research, mode 2 knowledge production is generated in the context of application which 'describes the total environment in which scientific problems arise, methodologies are developed, outcomes are disseminated, and users defined' (Nowotny et al., 2003: 186). Such PD research is undertaken *in* not *on* the workplace. Flood (2011b) showed, ironically using mode 1 knowledge production, that the idea of knowledge production in context has a proud philosophical history beginning with Aristotle (*phronesis*), then through Aquinus (*prudentia*) and Newmann (the illative sense). Later writers such as Dunne, Hamilton and Gibbons and colleagues have added to our understanding. Being clear about these philosophical ideas is essential for those undertaking PD research and its supervision. Understanding the long philosophical tradition underpinning professional and practice-based research gives the researcher confidence.

Several implications were drawn. The argument was made that experience, in the full sense of the term, is necessary to undertake PD work successfully. Research in the workplace means that political *nous* has to be brought to bear, identities shaped and practical reasoning developed, the latter being akin to the development of research skills in the successful PhD. Following Schön, deliberation in and on action, together with reflexivity, mean that workplace research can be 'good enough' and is embodied in the person of the practitioner. The ultimate outcome is for the professional to become a 'wise practitioner' (Flood, 2011b).

Key Points

- Professional practice can produce new knowledge which is generated in the context of application.
- Professional practice knowledge in this sense is not what has been called applied knowledge because it 'describes the total environment in which scientific problems arise, methodologies are developed, outcomes are disseminated, and users defined' (Nowotny et al., 2003).
- Workplace research undertaken by practitioners themselves brings with it practical reasoning. Such practical reasoning can be developed over time, that is from experience, and this is a significant source of knowledge.

ACKNOWLEDGEMENT

My thanks are due to Dr Bernie Flood for his helpful comments. Any errors are mine.

ANNOTATED BIBLIOGRAPHY

Costley, C. (2013). Evaluation of the current status and knowledge contributions of professional doctorates. *Quality in Higher Education*, *19*(1), 7–27, DOI: 10.1080/13538322.2013.772465.

The status and knowledge contributions of professional doctorates (PDs) undertaken by practising professionals is centre stage in this article. It gives a good introduction to PDs worldwide via an extensive literature review and is illustrated with a research project. Additionally, individual chapters in Storey, V. A. (ed.) (2016) *International Perspectives on Designing Professional Doctorates: Applying the Critical Friends Approach to the EdD and Beyond* (London: Palgrave Macmillan) provide a country-by-country breakdown of PD development.

Flood, J. B. (2011a). Towards the philosophy of education in the NSW Clinical Pastoral Education (CPE) Movement. Unpublished EdD portfolio, University of New England.

Flood established an important and definite thread in philosophical thinking in practical reasoning starting with Aristotle (384–322BP). Flood argued that Aristotle's *phronesis* was further developed by Aquinus (1325–74) as *prudentia*. John Henry Newman (1801–90) extended both of the above conceptions as the illative sense. Flood then used Macmurray's (1891–1976) 1953–4 Gifford Lectures to shift the centre of reference from the person in thought to thought in action. His work leads to the conclusion that experience, in its fullest sense, is necessary to undertake PD work successfully and that workplace research can be 'good enough'.

Gibbons, M., Limoges, C., Nowotny, H., Schwartzman, S., Scott, P., & Trow, M. (1994). *The New Production of Knowledge: The Dynamics of Science and Research in Contemporary Societies* (London: Sage).

The work of Gibbons and colleagues was an important breakthrough for many as it clarified and crystallised the otherwise implied distinctions between the PhD and the PDs. Their work was an accessible and timely way in the philosophical debate for which Flood has given the history of the key thinkers. Their conception of mode 1 and mode 2 knowledge production was key. The latter was later refined by Nowotny, H., Scott, P., & Gibbons, M. (2003) Mode 2 revisited: the new production of knowledge. *Minerva*, *41*, 179–94.

Green, B. (ed.) (2009) *Understanding and Researching Professional Practice*. Rotterdam: Sense Publishers.

A number of useful chapters can be found here, especially Green's Introduction. Read and Green's chapter concerning the practitioner's voice places the practitioner at the centre of the research. The article by Trede, F., Macklin, R, & Bridges, D. (2012) Professional identity development: a review of the higher education literature. *Studies in Higher Education, 37*(3), 365–84. DOI: 10.1080/03075079.2010.521237 develops the complementary notion of professional identity development.

REFERENCES

Aquino, F. D. (2004). *Communities of Informed Judgment: Newman's Illative Sense and Accounts of Rationality*. Washington DC: CUA Press.

Armsby, A., & Dreher, H. M. (2011). Towards a metric for measuring the value of professional doctorates. In T. Fell, K. J. Flint & I. Haines (eds) *Professional Doctorates in the UK 2011* (pp. 71–9). Lichfield: UK Council for Graduate Education.

Barnard, A. (2011). Professional doctorates for social science. In T. Fell, K. J. Flint & I. Haines (eds) *Professional Doctorates in the UK 2011* (pp. 55–61). Lichfield: UK Council for Graduate Education.

CDDGS (Council of Deans and Directors of Graduate Studies) (1998). *Guidelines: Professional Doctorates*. Unpublished paper prepared by Terry Evans, Adrian Fisher and Wolfgang Gritchting. Adelaide: Council of Deans and Directors of Graduate Studies.

Costley, C. (2011). Professional doctorates and the doctorate in professional studies. In T. Fell, K. J. Flint & I. Haines (eds) *Professional Doctorates in the UK 2011*. Lichfield: UK Council for Graduate Education.

Costley, C. (2013). Evaluation of the current status and knowledge contributions of professional doctorates. *Quality in Higher Education, 19*(1), 7–27. DOI: 10.1080/1353 8322.2013.772465.

Costley, C., & Lester, S. (2012). Work-based doctorates: professional extension at the highest levels. *Studies in Higher Education, 37*(3), 257–69. DOI: 10.1080/03075079.2010.503344.

Cuthbert, D., & Molla, T. (2015). PhD crisis discourse: a critical approach to the framing of the problem and some Australian 'solutions'. *Higher Education, 69*, 33–53.

Dunne, J. (1997). *Back to the Rough Ground: Practical Judgment and the Lure of Technique*. Notre Dame, IN: University of Notre Dame Press.

Evans, T. D., Macauley, P., Pearson, M., & Tregenza, K. (2005). Why do a 'prof doc' when you can do a PhD? In T. W. Maxwell, C. Hickey & T. D. Evans (eds) *Professional Doctorates: Working Towards Impact* (pp. 24–34). Proceedings of the 5th International Professional Doctorates Conference, Geelong: Deakin University.

Flood, J. B. (2011a). Towards the philosophy of education in the NSW Clinical Pastoral Education (CPE) Movement. Unpublished EdD portfolio, University of New England.

Flood, J. B. (2011b). Educating the wise practitioner. In J. B. Flood, *Towards the Philosophy of Education in the NSW Clinical Pastoral Education (CPE) Movement*. Unpublished paper #6, EdD portfolio, Armidale: University of New England.

Fuller, S. (1995). Is there life for sociological theory after the sociology of scientific knowledge? *Sociology, 29*(1), 159–66.

Gibbons, M., Limoges, C., Nowotny, H., Schwartzman, S., Scott, P., & Trow, M. (1994). *The New Production of Knowledge: The Dynamics of Science and Research in Contemporary Societies*. London: Sage.

Green, B. (2009). Introduction: understanding professional practice. In B. Green (ed.) *Understanding and Researching Professional Practice* (pp. 1–18). Rotterdam: Sense Publishers.

Green, B., & Hopwood, N. (2015). The body in professional practice, learning and education: a question of corporeality. In B. Green & N. Hopwood (eds) *The Body in Professional Practice, Learning and Education: Body/Practice?* (pp. 15–33). Dordrecht: Springer.

Hamilton, D. (2005). Knowing practice. *Pedagogy, Culture and Society, 13*(3), 285–90.

Hoddell, S. (2002) *Professional Doctorates*. Staffordshire: UK Council for Graduate Education.

Kemmis, S. (2005). Knowing practice: searching for saliences. *Pedagogy, Culture and Society, 13*(3), 391–426.

Kemmis, S. (2009). Understanding and researching professional practice: a synoptic view. In B. Green (ed.) *Understanding and Researching Professional Practice* (pp. 19–38). Rotterdam: Sense Publishers.

Kot, F. C., & Hendel, D. D. (2012). Emergence and growth of professional doctorates in the United States, United Kingdom, Canada and Australia: a comparative analysis. *Studies in Higher Education, 37*(3), 345–64. DOI: 10.1080/03075079.2010.516356.

Lee, A., Brennan, M., & Green, B. (2009). Re-imagining doctoral education: professional doctorates and beyond. *Higher Education Research and Development, 28*(3), 275–87.

Lee, A., Green, B., & Brennan, M. (2000). Organisational knowledge, professional practice and the professional doctorate at work. In J. Garrick & C. Rhodes (eds) *Research and Knowledge at Work: Perspectives, Case-Studies and Innovative Strategies* (pp. 117–36). London: Routledge.

Lévi-Strauss, C. (1962). *The Savage Mind (La pensée sauvage)*. London: Weidenfeld & Nicolson.

Mantai, L. (2015). Feeling like a researcher: experiences of early doctoral students in Australia. *Studies in Higher Education, 42*(4), 636–50. DOI: 10.1080/03075079.2015.1067603.

Maxwell, T. W. (2003). From first to second generation professional doctorate. *Studies in Higher Education, 28*(3), 279–92.

Maxwell, T. W. (2011). Australian professional doctorates: mapping, distinctiveness, stress and prospects. *Work Based Learning e-Journal International, 2* (1); downloaded from http://wblearning-ejournal.com.

Maxwell, T. W., & Vine, K. (1998). The EdD at UNE: the view through conceptual bifocals. In T. W. Maxwell & P. J. Shanahan (eds) *Professional Doctorates: Innovations in Teaching and Research* (pp. 73–81). Proceedings of the Conference 'Professional Doctorates: innovations in teaching and research', Coffs Harbour. Armidale: University of New England.

Nowotny, H., Scott, P., & Gibbons, M. (2003). Mode 2 revisited: the new production of knowledge. *Minerva, 41*, 179–94.

Reid, J.-A., & Green, B. (2009). Researching (from) the standpoint of the practitioner. In B. Green (ed.) *Understanding and Researching Professional Practice* (pp. 165–84). Rotterdam: Sense Publishers.

Schön, D. (1983). *The Reflective Practitioner: How Professionals Think in Action*. London: Maurice Temple Smith.

Scott, D., Brown, A., Lunt, I., & Thorne, L. (2004). *Professional Doctorates: Integrating Professional and Academic Knowledge*. Maidenhead: Society for Research into Higher Education & Open University Press.

Scott, P. (1995). *The Meanings of Mass Higher Education*. Buckingham: Society for Research in Higher Education and Open University Press.

Seddon, T. (1999). Research, recommendations and realpolitik: consolidating the EdD. *Australian University Researcher, 26*, 1–14.

Trede, F., Macklin, R., & Bridges, D. (2012). Professional identity development: a review of the higher education literature. *Studies in Higher Education, 37*(3), 365–84. DOI: 10.1080/03075079.2010.521237.

Usher, R. (2002). A diversity of doctorates: fitness for the knowledge economy. *Higher Education Research & Development, 21*(2), 143–53.

RESEARCH APPROACHES IN PROFESSIONAL DOCTORATES: NOTES ON AN EPISTEMOLOGY OF PRACTICE

Carol Costley

Pragmatism: a philosophical stance that takes the position that human experience is best viewed in terms of practical outcomes and achievement.

Bricoleur: the notion of the *Bricoleur* as coined by Lévi-Strauss, constructing things using whatever materials are at hand, in the research context. Rather than drawing from one approach, a variety of methodological approaches are used to address an issue or answer a particular question.

Habitus: as termed by Bourdieu, the disposition of an individual which is composed of individual characteristics and the experience and class position of the individual.

Power: Foucault used the notion of power in particular ways and for him it was not a top-down power, but rather it was exerted in different ways on all in society often by their own self-regulation.

Transdisciplinary: the use of a variety of disciplinary approaches which creates a new and novel focus which is more than the sum of individual components.

Epistemology: the philosophy of knowledge.

INTRODUCTION

The emergence of professional and practice-based doctorates in the academic land-scape since the 1980s has transformed conventional approaches to research by positing a new epistemological relationship between education, research, industry and the public sector and which can be seen in the wider knowledge arena in the thinking about how knowledge is produced and accessed (European Commission, 2012). Research sparked by professional/practice doctorates that themselves have grown across a range of disciplines sits at the nexus of different epistemological traditions leading to the greater interrelation of different forms of knowledge. The practice-based nature of the range of professional doctorates has also revealed a commonality in the way knowledge and the research that informs such knowledge are understood. The influence of the disciplines with the interrelation of knowledge and the focus upon practice with its concern for creative and useful outcomes has implications for academic cultures, doctoral programme design and doctoral peda-gogy leading to the focus of this chapter, which is a further note on the epistemology of practice in relation to research approaches.

What is argued here is that professional doctorates do tend to use established research approaches such as case study, action research and mixed methods, but they have extended and enlarged upon the approaches, making them more purpose-ful. Approaches such as auto-ethnography and translation research are also becoming more in-use as appropriate approaches for someone engaged in research-ing their own localised practice.

Looking at a broad range of professional doctorates, it appears that these exten-sions or enlargements to some extent have more in common within professional or practice-based doctorates than they do within any given discipline area, so for example research approaches used on an EdD may have more in common with a DBA than they do with a PhD in Education (Costley, 2013). This is because the key methodological interest is in a practice situation and the aim is often to enhance or create good practices. Practice has a situated and contextual relevance to the knowledge being created and used. In turn the focus upon practice gives rise to dif-ferent forms of knowledge.

DIFFERENT FORMS OF KNOWLEDGE HAVE LED TO EPISTEMIC CHANGES

Different forms of knowledge arising from the work of professional people under-taking creative and innovative practices through doctorate learning challenge the traditional epistemological and ontological foundations for doctoral research. Professional doctorates often merge knowledge production, knowledge management and research processes within a context of application. They need to be responsive to a more adaptable and practice-led character of knowledge creation. Barnett, for example, has called for 'a heightened *epistemic flexibility* within curricula' (2014) and before him Schön called for a more reflexive role for knowledge (1987). Flexibility here can mean a matter of the ways in which disciplines might open themselves to each other in transdisciplinarity or pluridisciplinarity and at different levels of knowledge production. For example, the European Commission is envisaging new forms of research collaboration across Europe so as to form a 'European Research Area', to become 'a byword for creativity, excellence and efficiency – and the catalyst for a new Renaissance in the way we think, act and research globally'. More efficient local and global networks are changing the world and transforming traditional approaches to research with a continuous innovation chain linking education, research and industry and the public sector. At policy level, a 'European Research Area' would drive integrated science, from basic research and scientific training, to more innovative and practice-focused research (European Commission, 2012).

Research in practice and practice knowledge are not new ideas and have conceptualisations that have been with us throughout the ages. Some might cite Aristotle for his work on practice. There is often mention made of the American philosopher and educator John Dewey, who was a founder of the philosophical movement known as pragmatism which he also called 'instrumentalism'. His work on the power of experience (Dewey, 1938) has resonance today.

Then there were the post-structuralist thinkers from the 1970s. For example, what is now being developed has some similarities with Lévi-Strauss's (1972) notion of the *Bricoleur* whereby approaches to the research of practitioner–researchers are grounded, useful, creative and have application to work practices, critical application and possibilities for agency. Lévi-Strauss's *Bricoleur* is an approach with a strong theoretical background and relevance for today's practitioner–researchers. The *Bricoleur* is engaged in practice and for Lévi-Strauss (1972: 18) this involved a first 'practical step', a 'retrospective' detailed examination of 'similarities and differences' in signs mediating the use of material artefacts.

Bourdieu's (1977) concept of the habitus negotiates between objective structures and practices, transcending the dichotomies that had previously shaped theoretical thinking about the social world. Foucault (1979) described power, which is an important issue for most theorists when discussing human actions that depend on shared skills or understandings, as a web of relations of force among individuals where subjects learn to self-regulate their practices. Giddens' (1984) theory of structuration found a connection between agency and structure, expressed in the term 'duality of structure' in that people make but are constrained by their environment. Feminist scholars have shown how women's different experiences to that of men bring about different practices for which there has been unequal treatment, multiple systems of domination making it challenging to confront oppressive power structures (Harstock, 1997).

Social structure puts constraints on practice that exists through human agency, causing both agent and structure to be involved in interpenetrating, interdependent and shifting practices. It follows that we can only understand actions within their specific practical contexts.

Scholars have drawn on these thinkers and others to analyse how research inquiry can be shaped in the context of professional practice. In 2001 Schatzki et al.'s book on the practice turn gave a clear message that high education had a more engaged focus on practice, but that to turn practice and theory into a dualism was unhelpful. Given all of these powerful theorists having written and many more on practice, it is hard to explain why it is still a matter of such debate. Simply put, it seems that throughout the twentieth century scientific methods were worked out that had clear and certain processes that should be followed. This gave research a set of rules and guidelines that could be followed with some assurance that results would be correct. These guides and structures are still in place and provide us with a backdrop of well-worked-through ideas and concepts.

Then along with a great deal of other scholarly arguments about practice research and not to mention an argument on the value of qualitative research that had been raging since the 1970s, Schön set out an argument for an epistemology of practice in a well-known text that is worth citing here again:

> The research university is an institution built around a particular view of knowledge. ... In the varied topography of professional practice, there is a high, hard ground overlooking a swamp. On the high ground, manageable problems lend themselves to solution through the use of research-based the-ory and technique. In the swampy lowlands, problems are messy and confus-ing and incapable of technical solution. The irony of this situation is that the problems of the high ground tend to be relatively unimportant to individuals or society at large, however great their technical interest may be, while in the swamp lie the problems of greatest human concern. The practitioner is con-fronted with a choice. Shall he remain on the high ground where he can solve relatively unimportant problems according to his standards of rigor, or shall he descend to the swamp of important problems? (1995)

The debate between so-called rigour and relevance comes from what some call technical rationality, which generates epistemologies that have formed the modern research university. Schön points to professional concerns that are fraught with such things as uncertainty, complexity, uniqueness, conflict and deal with the more instrumental problems of practice that had not been included and did not count as appropriate. It is these relevant and real-world issues that tend to be the subject of professional doctorate research and we might argue that research methodologies have been originally constructed to deal with the issues on Schön's 'high ground'.

THE MODERN APPLICATION OF PRACTICE-BASED RESEARCH APPROACHES

Since these words, much has been challenged, much has changed and much has stayed the same. Some see it as a divide between qualitative and quantitative approaches and some do not. What may be fair to say is that there is more flexibility in the way research is approached and many researchers now carefully draw upon a range of methods that may have more traditionally been confined to particular research approaches. Schön's point that 'research' as it was understood as relating to a particular view of knowledge that is only concerned with his metaphorical 'high ground', has now been circumvented by applying research approaches to his metaphorical 'swamp' activities. It might be argued that it should not be beyond the intellectual capacities of those in academia, where there is great knowledge of research, critique, literature, theory, and so on, that this expertise be applied to a rethinking of research in areas of practice. After 20 years or so of scholarship in this area, some advancement has been made as this chapter later demonstrates.

Doctorate programmes that specialise in practitioner-led research are developing research approaches that are more conducive to the facilitation of knowledge production in practice. Giving greater primacy to practice knowledge has caused new developments in doctoral education. Doctoral learning that seeks to enhance practice and develop benefit to communities and organisations in professional contexts is leading to different understandings of the wider knowledge contributions of doctorates by creating and providing useful and innovative contributions to professional work (Costley, 2013; Lester, 2012).

An example of how this expansion of knowledge has impacted doctoral education and doctoral outcomes can be seen in the criteria used for examining doctoral theses by some universities in the United Kingdom. The UK Quality Assurance Agency has a helpful set of doctoral characteristics (QAA, 2015) while Wellington (2013) pulled together a more detailed selection of the contributions of doctorates that are judged against in the final viva. Below is an extract from Wellington's paper, which constitutes a synthesis of the criteria used by a sample of universities and how he analysed the criteria to reveal the kind of knowledge that was being recognised as doctorate level.

'Originality'? 7 possibilities

- BUILDING NEW KNOWLEDGE:
  - e.g. Building on or extending previous work. Putting a new brick in the wall
- USING ORIGINAL PROCESSES OR APPROACHES
  - e.g. New methods or techniques applied to an existing area of study. New methods or techniques applied to a new area
- MAKING NEW SYNTHESES
  - e.g. Connecting previous studies
- NEW CHARTING OR MAPPING OF TERRITORY
  - e.g. Opening up new areas (e.g. that were taboo) or neglected areas

(Continued)

(Continued)

- NEW IMPLICATIONS
  - For practice. Policy or theory
- RE-VISITING A RECURRENT ISSUE OR DEBATE
  - e.g. Bringing New evidence OR New thinking to bear
- REPLICATING OR REPRODUCING EXISTING WORK
  - e.g. work from elsewhere in a new geographical context, or a new time context or with a new sample

(Wellington, 2013)

In the past doctoral criteria for passing a doctorate would have been more about the examiners' judgement of whether or not the work constituted an original contribution to knowledge and of course that the work had been rigorously researched. Wellington's examples show that the knowledge definition has been broadened and this breadth of definition of new knowledge is more able to encompass the outputs of professional doctorates.

A widening concept of knowledge is understood as emanating from, developed in and providing change for professional contexts. Professional doctorates provide a way of addressing knowledge that is to an extent outside disciplinary cultures and can offer alternative views and values that have resonance with practice, thereby engaging higher education more coherently with learning at work.

Knowledge in practice can, Kemmis (2005) argues, be constituted in the reflexive processes of the practitioner, the discursive and material processes of the particular context and the socio-political setting. This knowledge may not fit into disciplines but it does have agreed value. Research in work situations has subject matter and the subject matter is not necessarily a centralised disciplinary activity. Breaking away, but only to some extent, from the disciplinary knowledge that has confirmed the status and quality of higher education for more than a century has brought about some concerns in relation to the breakdown of traditional notions of objectivity and validity and how knowledge can be said to have a sound epistemological basis and be reliable. A problem for practice-oriented research is that disciplinary knowledge results in 'weakly contextualised knowledge'. More strongly contextualised research data is more able to produce 'socially robust knowledge' (Nowotny et al., 2003). Reliable knowledge has always been reliable within boundaries but the boundaries have changed to take on the wider social context that professional doctorates generate.

Having made this case, it can be unhelpful to separate practice-oriented doctorates from those that are understood as theoretically oriented. It is the case that many doctorates engage with more practice-focused approaches, but the theoretical outcomes of the research undertaken by researchers was often separated from what was (and still is) counted as 'applied' research. The traditional use of the word applied is not the same as what we now understand as research in practice. Applied was more a case of applying an existing theory rather than for example what in action research is called 'living theory' or the notion that some researchers put forward where theory can be drawn out of practice rather than the other way round.

There is no doubt that doctorate degrees internationally are becoming more engaged with knowledge production in practice settings and the industrial PhD is an example (Armsby et al., 2017). Pedagogies have changed to accommodate doctorates that have deliberately chosen to focus their doctorate candidates through their practice. These doctoral pathways have developed their research approaches more in relation to a 'practice turn'. Education is reflecting changes in society in an advanced technical and information age. The desirability of a 'knowledge economy' in which knowledge is generated and applied to foster social and economic impact has also been critiqued (Peters, 2001) and during this time of change it is crucial that critique is acknowledged and receives a response. One response relating to how the situation is more complex than a simplistic dichotomy between academic and professional knowledge comes from Drake and Heath (2011), who state that there appears to be a range of different knowledges produced through professional doctorate degrees, each underpinning power relationships which exist between different knowledge frameworks. From this it can be considered that there is 'a move towards more inclusive and respectful acceptance that learning and knowledge production takes place in a variety of contexts, including the academy' (Drake and Heath, 2011).

An example of the way research approaches are generally explained can be found in a Society for Research in Higher Education workshop (SRHE, 2018) on 'Research approaches and methods'. The workshop

> aims to clarify the different approaches to research to aid in the selection of methodology, design and techniques appropriate to given research problems. It covers: Choice of overarching paradigm or philosophy, and how this might be determined by discipline. (SRHE, 2018)

That the workshop aims to take an approach appropriate for a given research problem indicates that the workshop would be suitable for a range of researchers in different areas of research and that, as we probably all agree, the approach, methodology, methods, and so on should be the right ones to address the given research problem.

Whoever runs such a workshop may have particular experience and views on what a research problem might look like, what the scope of a research problem should be (e.g. if the research ends when the data has been analysed and evaluated or for example when recommendations have also been set out in detail or perhaps when a reflective account of the research has been added). Is the research linked directly to practice, immediate change or making change as the research is progressed in some way? The workshop convenors would probably say that yes, it could be that as well, and the following areas that the workshop covers would not preclude this:

- How this determines research questions or hypotheses;
- The range of possible research designs, building in strength to combat inevitable weaknesses;
- The selection of appropriate and coherent techniques;
- A review of different data types and their implications;
- When and what to consider about analysing your data. (SRHE, 2018)

Will the workshop address ethical considerations from the perspective of a practitioner? The convenors could say that the ethical considerations should be appropriate for the research being undertaken. Will it address transdisciplinary qualities in the research? This seems unlikely as it is already stated that the overarching paradigm or philosophy is likely to be determined by a discipline. Will they talk about practical outcomes and recommendations to different sets of stakeholders? They could do this if the attendees raised this as something that should be part of their research outcome. Will they consider approaches to research that require insider knowledge, ontological insight and a developer's awareness of current practice? This seems unlikely but again it would probably not be dismissed as unworthy and the convenors are likely to know of texts that can be referred. Will they address a critical research-minded grasp of methods and epistemology? It seems likely that this will be addressed. My set of questions and answers about this workshop are drawn solely from my own and colleagues' experience. The point to be made is that existing conventional approaches are still relevant to producing different forms of knowledge but they are often set down and explained in ways that do not fully cover the practice-based, often both practical and creative, goals of practitioner research. Plowright makes similar points in Chapter 11 in this book in Table 11.1.

Doctoral research undertaken by practitioners themselves in the context of their own practice has undergone significant developments. A more practice-conscious understanding of the nature of knowledge, its justification and the rationality behind how it is believed by those in the field is more prevalent. The approaches to practitioner-led research often nurture the creation and application of knowledge needed to solve complex societal problems involving heterogeneity of stakeholders. Although there have always been doctoral researchers who have undertaken practice-oriented research, some areas of doctoral education have now developed pedagogies and curriculum innovations that better facilitate the development needs of knowledge production in practice situations. Many of these more recent developments involve inter- and transdisciplinary approaches to doctoral education. Transcending boundaries in research is now more prevalent and accepted, for example interdisciplinary research is encouraged by research councils. Transdisciplinarity as an approach that overcomes the structure of disciplinary differentiation in academia has become more recognised.

Activity

List the key features which you associate with developing your practice.

Spend some time on this and compare your points with the subsequent text.

TOWARDS AN EPISTEMOLOGY OF PRACTICE

Out of all of this, the rise in practitioner research at all higher education levels and also project-based research has led to a closer scrutiny of acts of research and picking out practice-oriented differences that might lead us to a careful look at research approaches used in practice that constitute an epistemology of practice. The practitioner research that features in most professional doctorates has a constant set of concepts. These involve approaches to knowledge that embrace a wide practice-based contribution to knowledge, approaches to learning and teaching that place the learner as having practice expertise and the 'teacher' as facilitator of that expertise and experience and emphasises learner-centred and reflective practice. On professional doctorate awards students undertake practice-led research into areas of their own professional knowledge, often within an organisation and engaging with academic and professional communities of practice. The interplay between 'real-world' focus and scholarly research approaches leads often to a new conceptualisation of the nexus between theory and practice in research.

In relation to modes of knowledge production fostered by many practice-led doctorates and the research approaches that are used, they draw on an epistemology that demonstrates a subtle yet significant move and/or change in that they require a different order of priority to and reconceptualisation of knowledge claims. Here are some of the elements that have a different, often nuanced approach:

- an acknowledgement of context and situatedness;
- ethical considerations that may prioritise values and consider a range of 'truths';
- some transdisciplinary qualities, such as a more considered set of practical outcomes and recommendations to different sets of stakeholders;
- an approach to research that requires insider knowledge, ontological insight and a developer's awareness of current practice; along with
- a critical research-minded grasp of methods and epistemology.

CONTEXT AND SITUATEDNESS

The nature of high-level professional practice has led to approaches to postgraduate training and research activities that include the development of appropriate methodologies for practitioner-led research which address highly contextualised knowledge within situated practices. Knowledge produced in the context of application is at the same time conceiving knowledge as a means of advancing practice with utilitarian benefits and underpinning practice with critical discourse on existing knowledge. The frontier of the higher education knowledge base is then extended and the benefits of higher education are more directly applied to work settings. Doctoral candidates are free to make sense of their context and, in this sense, agency, position and situatedness are key factors. Situatedness (Lave and Wenger, 1991) is the development of individual intelligence requiring both social and cultural influences. It arises from the interplay between the researcher, the situation (the particular set of circumstances and the researcher's position within it) and context (where, when and the background that provides the multiple perspectives needed for understanding). Organisational, professional and personal contexts will affect the way a piece of research and development is undertaken (Bouck, 2011).

The focus outside of the academic community provides new and informed analysis about what is held as important, useful and high-level doctoral learning. Professional doctorate learning demands knowledge of professional contexts informed by a more wide-ranging knowledge of the area.

TRANSDISCIPLINARY QUALITIES

Changes in approaches to the way higher education interprets and researches knowledge production in communities have been developed in practice, theory and through policy changes. For example, researchers working in transdisciplinary teams (a practice that started in the field of environmental sustainability) support research that springs from different professional cultures and disciplinary subfields. It encompasses both the subject-orientated knowledge the students want to acquire and the idea of a socially distributed, practice-oriented, transdisciplinary knowledge, that involves multiple stakeholders (Costley and Pizzolato, 2017), 'an infusion of transdisciplinary curriculum and research into academic affairs [is] an inevitable consideration' (Hyun, 2011).

Drawing upon conceptualisations in relation to new modes of knowledge (Nowotny et al., 2003) find that the reflexivity, eclecticism and contextualisation of transdisciplinarity make it inherently transgressive. It transcends disciplinary boundaries, reaching beyond interdisciplinarity, causing university structures to become less relevant. Producers of research are not only scientists. Research has moved into society itself so the nature of research now investigates a wider range of activities.

CRITICAL AND RESEARCH MINDED

Practitioner–researchers need to understand a range of research approaches and become 'research minded'. They need to interpret the results of research as well as develop their own practitioner research. They need to embrace both new and more traditional approaches to research. Take for example the research strategy of 'maximising variation': instead of the 'representative sample' that might be selected by an independent researcher, the insider knows the areas where the variation is more prevalent and can focus upon these. The practitioner–researcher is not making a random choice but because the researcher knows different cases relating to the research that have different anomalies and cover more of the variation, the researcher thereby maximises differences based on what is already known. The researcher must make dynamic interpretations and wise judgements which are ideally made on the basis of a collective wisdom that can provide complex insights and sophistication of argument. The report of the Walden University Professional Doctorate Working Group requires the professional doctorate research to be 'Amenable to Scientific Study' in that it will need to contain a scholarly, systematic method of inquiry to be applied to address the problem (Walden University, 2012).

INSIDER KNOWLEDGE, ONTOLOGICAL INSIGHT AND A DEVELOPER'S AWARENESS

Practitioner–researchers undertaking doctorates are often acknowledged as experts in their fields by their peers in their professional areas based on practice and expertise.

The context of practitioner research has to be clarified in each given situation; institutional conditions, events, narratives and images may be relevant. Interpretations involving social values are the subjective views of the practitioners. Networking and forming relationships across professional and academic cultural boundaries are ways to consult with others and overcome individualised perspectives both within practice situations and often between practice and research communities. There can be helpful and informative links between organisations and academia and a dialectics between text and context.

Insider knowledge and know-how for the practitioner–researcher is, in research terms, thought of as both strength and weakness. The impartial, objective stance of the researcher is challenged, yet conversely the in-depth understanding of the insider, communicating the context, involves the judgement of an insider to provide in Geertz's terms the 'thick description' – context similarity then brings us to generalisation a 'thick', i.e more in-depth and nuanced, interpretation. The scope of the topic and breadth of the researcher's conceptualisation of the topic will affect the degree to which the researcher translates the research into recommendations for practice.

Those doctorate candidates who are researching their own practice usually gain ontological insight into their research and this is generally encouraged by tutors. Doctorate candidates who are researching their own practice need to consider their own positionality in their research situation. Considerations around ontology lead to epistemics as the candidates consider their research approaches.

REFLECTIVE PRACTICE

Professional reflection and reflexivity is now used widely. There have been critiques about its use, for example that much reflective practice is too focused upon the individual instead of group/teamwork orientations that are not situated understandings of practice (Boud, 2010; Talbot, 2012). Inevitably professional doctorate candidates usually engage in a reflexive process as they already put themselves into the frame of the research because of their expertise in the field as developers of current practice. As they reflect upon their own practice and the practice of others, they can come to an interpretation through a range of texts that includes relevant knowledge and information found in practice situations and can gain an appreciation of the different lenses through which texts can be viewed.

A CONSIDERED SET OF OUTCOMES

The intent of many of the research degrees that focus upon practitioners who are not wishing to engage in an academic career tends to give more credence to imparting the results of the research to non-academic audiences because their working environment is where they are rooted and there is a need to be recognised, reviewed and trusted by peers (Storey, 2016). This creates the need for credibility not only for sharing, presenting research findings, but also as a credible colleague in the field. Such notoriety is a key factor in implementing the outcomes of the research. Practitioner–researchers find themselves needing to provide compelling and persuasive arguments to a range of audiences. For these reasons there is a need to plan for the research which is often an innovative change or addition to a work setting that makes an enhancement, as part of the research proposal. As well as good standing in the community, the nature of the research then also has issues of value where considerations of time, implementation and purpose also enter into overall considerations of the research to a greater extent.

ETHICS, VALUES, TRUST AND POWER

The positionality of doctoral researchers engaged with their own practice has ethical considerations (Govers, 2014). Widening concepts of knowledge in practice contexts are purposive to specific contexts that are more socially and vocationally oriented and these purposes come in addition to the 'culture' of academic knowledge seeking 'truth' for its own sake.

A move away from the prime concern being that of truth and merit towards ethics that prioritise values and utility have implications that change the rank order of more established views on research ethics in academia. It comes about because practitioners as researchers need to make the right judgements and decisions to act, based upon a deep knowledge of people and organisational protocols; their colleagues require an insider's persuasiveness to secure action. The object of this persuasive rhetoric is judgement and judgements are made within a framework of human values, trust and power. See also Chapters 5 and 6 regarding ethical considerations in professional doctorates.

Overall, some of the elements that contribute to an epistemology of practice that engenders practice-oriented research approaches must embrace situated and contextual research that can be messy and complex, especially if the researcher is already embedded in that practice. Integral to practice research is the exploration of the phenomenon from a range of perspectives. The various perspectives needed for understanding a particular research problem in practice are usually connected with context. If the researcher is an 'insider' in such contexts, their situatedness within that context is based upon the positionality of the researcher and the set of circumstances at that time. These factors can constitute differences in the way research is conducted, the perceptions of the researcher and other stakeholders such as colleagues that need to be taken into account in the research. Constraints of real-time research, availability of resources and workplace permissions such as access to people may or may not be at the disposal of the researcher. There can be issues of ethics, values, trust and power that have specific connotations when subjects of the research are known to the researcher, where reputational issues involve professional and research issues. That the outcomes of the research can produce valued purposes and products that make personal and professional differences to a specific community is a value that practitioner–researchers can bring with them throughout the research process and beyond.

CONCLUSION

Recent work addressing philosophical issues raised by the category of practice are pushing the boundaries of where suitable research and development approaches to the work of professional doctorates are being developed. Research undertaken as part of a professional doctorate has become a way to enhance practice and to develop benefit to particular professional groups and organisations.

It is likely that the peers who are best placed to make judgements about whether the research is needed, whether it is appropriate and is undertaken using appropriate methods and approaches to the gathering of data and meeting the considerations of the practitioners are both academics and professionals in the field who have a close connection with the professional sphere in which the research is undertaken.

Key issues for professional doctorates are that a widening concept of knowledge is understood as emanating from, developed in and providing change for professional contexts. Professional doctorates provide a way of addressing knowledge that is to an extent outside disciplinary cultures and can offer alternative views and values that have resonance with practice, thereby engaging higher education more coherently with learning at work. A key issue is therefore the nature of course design and candidate support that provides flexible patterns of research and development. Professional doctorate programmes need knowledge of constructing and evaluating doctorates in their specific context and physical location and how the experience and expertise of doctoral candidates together with an appropriately supported approach to research, critical engagement and critical reflection can better support them.

Considerations should be given to the nature of high-level professional practice and how higher education can support developments with its expertise in research, critical thinking and a whole range of pedagogical practices that can be of benefit to individuals and communities outside or on the periphery of higher education networks. For example, approaches to postgraduate training and research activities can include the development of appropriate methodologies for practitioner-led research which addresses highly contextualised knowledge within situated practices. Recent work addressing philosophical issues raised by the category of practice are pushing the boundaries of where suitable research and development approaches to the work of professional doctorates are being developed.

Key Points

- There is a long tradition of knowledge being derived from practice which goes back as far as Aristotle.
- Recently there has been an increased focus on the value of practice and practice-based research.
- This 'turn' towards practice-based research calls for a new relationship between theory and practice.
- Key issues to consider are:
  - including a developer's awareness of the research aims;
  - an imperative to communicate results of the research to non-academic audiences;
  - transdisciplinarity;
  - criticality;
  - the reflective stance of the researcher;
  - ethics, values, trust and power.

ANNOTATED BIBLIOGRAPHY

Boud, D. (2010). Relocating reflection in the context of practice. In H. Bradbury, N. Frost, S. Kilminster & M. Zukas (eds) *Beyond Reflective Practice: New Approaches to Professional Lifelong Learning*. London: Routledge.

This chapter addresses professional reflection at work and makes the point that we work in teams so that individual reflection, which appears to be most prized by universities, may need a different or additional dimension when reflecting on professional practice. We all know that problem solving and change making in work situations bring about the best results when done collaboratively. Many other chapters in this book are well worth reading, so if you get the whole book have a look through the different perspectives.

Kemmis, S. (2005). Knowing practice: searching for saliences. *Pedagogy, Culture and Society*, 13(3), 391–426. www.gu.se/digitalAssets/1224/1224587_Kemmis_knowing_practice.pdf. Accessed 19 June 2018.

In this paper Kemmis highlights spheres of knowledge mostly found in professional practice. He points out that professional practice takes place in social settings, shaped by discourses, and is dramaturgical and practical in character. This helps us gauge how change in practice is not just a matter for practitioners or practitioner–researchers but creates the need to change discourses in which practices are constructed and the social relationships which constitute practice. Practitioners need to network and prepare collaboratively for change in their practices, making a case that legitimises change and changes minds.

REFERENCES

Armsby, P. M., Costley, C., & Cranfield, S. (2017). The design of doctorate curricula for practising professionals. *Studies in Higher Education*, Published online: 25 April.

Barnett, R. (2014). *Conditions of Flexibility*. York: Higher Education Academy.

Bouck, G. M. (2011). Scholar-practitioner identity: a liminal perspective. *Scholar-Practitioner Quarterly*, 5(2), 201–10.

Boud, D. (2010). Relocating reflection in the context of practice. In H. Bradbury, N. Frost, S. Kilminster & M. Zukas (eds) *Beyond Reflective Practice: New Approaches to Professional Lifelong Learning*. pp.25–36. London: Routledge.

Bourdieu, P. (1977). *Outline of a Theory of Practice*. Cambridge: Cambridge University Press.

Costley, C. (2013). Evaluation of the current status and knowledge contributions of professional doctorates. *Quality in Higher Education*, 19(2), 7–27.

Costley, C., & Pizzolato, N. (2017). Transdisciplinary qualities in practice doctorates. *Studies in Continuing Education*, 40(1), 30–45.

Dewey, J. (1938). *Logic: The Theory of Inquiry*. New York: Holt, Rinehart & Winston.

Drake, P., & Heath, L. (2011). *Practitioner Research at Doctoral Level: Developing Coherent Research Methodologies*. London: Routledge.

European Commission (2012). The new Renaissance: will it happen? Innovating Europe out of the crisis. Third and final report of the European Research Area Board, EUR 25269. *Luxembourg*: Publications Office of the European Union. DOI: 10.2777/84667.

Foucault, M. (1979). *Discipline and Punish: The Birth of the Prison*. Harmondsworth: Peregrine Books.

Giddens, A. (1984). *The Constitution of Society: Outline of the Theory of Structuration*. Cambridge: Polity Press.

Govers, E. (2014). An analysis of ethical considerations in programme design practice. *Journal of Further and Higher Education*, 38(6), 773–93.

Hartsock, N. (1997). Comment on Hekman's 'Truth and method: Feminist standpoint theory revisited': Truth or justice?' *Signs*, 22(2), 367–74.

Hyun, E. (2011). Transdisciplinary higher education curriculum: a complicated cultural artefact. *Research in Higher Education Journal*, www.aabri.com/manuscripts/11753.pdf. Accessed 19 June 2018.

Kemmis, S. (2005). Knowing practice: searching for saliences. *Pedagogy, Culture and Society*, 13(3), 391–426.

Lave, J., & Wenger, E. (1991). *Situated Learning: Legitimate Peripheral Participation*. Cambridge: Cambridge University Press.

Lester, S. (2012). 'Creating original knowledge in and for the workplace'. *Studies in Continuing Education* 34 (3), 267–280.

Lévi-Strauss, C. (1972). *The Savage Mind*. London: Weidenfeld & Nicholson.

Nowotny, H., Scott, P., & Gibbons, M. (2003). Mode 2 revisited: the new production of knowledge. *Minerva, 41*, 179–94.

Peters, M. (2001). National Education Policy constructions of the 'knowledge economy': towards a critique. *Journal of Educational Enquiry, 2*, 1.

QAA (2015). Doctoral Degree Characteristics. *Gloucester: Quality Assurance Agency* www.qaa.ac.uk/docs/qaa/quality-code/doctoral-degree-characteristics-15.pdf?sfvrsn= 50aef981_10. Accessed 23 July 2018.

Schatzki, T., Cetina, K. K., & Von Savigny, E. (eds) (2001). *The Practice Turn in Contemporary Theory*. London: Routledge.

Schön, D. A. (1987). *Educating the Reflective Practitioner*. San Francisco: Jossey-Bass.

Schön, D. A. (1995). Knowing-in-action: the new scholarship requires a new epistemology. *Change*, November/December, 27–34.

SRHE (2018). Society for Research in Higher Education events. www.srhe.ac.uk/events/. Accessed 28 January 2018.

Storey, V. A. (ed.) (2016). *International Perspectives on Designing Professional Practice Doctorates*. New York: Palgrave Macmillan.

Talbot, J. (2012). Beyond introspective reflective learning: externalised reflection on a UK University's Doctor of Professional Studies programme. *Work Based Learning e-Journal International, 2*(2), 1–2. http://wblearning-ejournal.com/archive.php. Accessed 28 January 2018.

Walden University (2012). Professional doctorates: literature, history, and recommendations. Walden University Professional Doctorate Working Group, http://scholarworks.waldenu. edu/white_papers/2/. Accessed 28/01/2018.

Wellington, J. (2013). Searching for 'doctorateness'. *Studies in Higher Education, 38*, 10.

WHY POLICY MATTERS PARTICULARLY IN PROFESSIONAL DOCTORATES

Pam Burnard, Tatjana Dragovic, Rebecca Heaton and Barry Rogers

KEY TERMS

The researching professional: a professional who is undertaking a professional doctorate to enhance the quality of professional learning and to improve professional education more generally.

Impact: research which brings a demonstrable contribution to professions, professional practice or professional learning in the form of benefits to individuals, institutions, organisations and/ or society and the economy.

Policy impact: this is an important part of research impact involving a number of ways in which research can achieve policy impact and resources available to assist researching professionals.

INTRODUCTION

Policy is translated through institutional and workplace forces that lead us to think and act in certain ways. Policy involves the ongoing production of reports, texts, mission statements and curriculum and practice requirements. The underlying principles of policy are played out in the politics of institutions and the learning cultures in which, for researching professionals, the doctoral supervisor is a key player

(Kamler and Thomson, 2006: 22). The confluence of these interrelated factors determines the policy issues that characterise both the doctoral programme and the researching professional's practice and project. What this means is that policy is very much to the fore and the background against which professional practice and professionally engaged learning, and, subsequently, professional doctorates, operate (as illustrated in Figure 3.1).

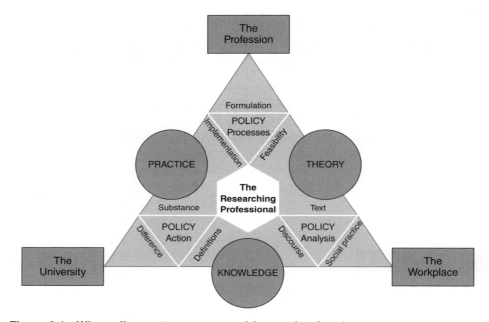

Figure 3.1   Why policy matters to researching professionals

In this chapter, we begin with Stephen Ball, the British educational sociologist who argues, 'the meaning or possible meanings that we give to policy; [because] it affects "how" we research and how we interpret what we find' (1993: 10). We explain how policy thinking shapes practice and how policies are the mechanisms through which values are authored and argued; how their vocabularies are formed and spoken about as conditions of acceptance and enactment. We discuss how researching professionals need to be concerned with long-term movements in policy development – themselves processes – which can be examined by exploring policy formulation, implementation and feasibility, interests of which inform the professional doctorate programmes in that they form the background upon which the researching professional engages in shaping policy action involving practice substance, difference and delimitation. We examine the use of policy analysis of vertical policies that come from legislation or accreditation bodies in top-down ways as compared to or in connection with policies that are more horizontal and 'softer' in character coming from published materials, traditions, or forms of professional dialogue that are largely underexplored. Researching professionals from two different fields (art and business) voice their practical experiences with policy and policy thinking as contributors to their professionally engaged, policy-changing practices. The chapter ends with: a reiteration of the arguments that require a shift in how we think about policy and how we value it as part of professional doctorate programmes; a discussion of how epistemological issues concerning researching professionals' knowledge and policy contexts matters; and how knowledge and policy contexts inform each other; and, finally, a policy discourse from which to drive not only the mobilisation of professional knowledge, but also wider changes in society.

Our argument for 'why' researching professionals need to amplify policy usage as processes, action, analysis and change in relation to practice, theory and knowledge (creation and mobilisation) paves the path for transformative practice and therefore determines change agendas for researching professionals in their professional workplace (see Figure 3.1). The imperative of policy work for the researching professional is, then, to make policy changes on meta, macro and micro levels. The key question, then, is why do professional doctorate programmes need to acknowledge and expand engagement with policy proper for researching professionals?

THE IMPERATIVE OF WHY POLICY MATTERS TO THE RESEARCHING PROFESSIONAL

Policy often tends to represent a model of unidirectional mandates of non-linear relationships between research and policies: that is, rarely are government policies, for instance, influenced by professional practice, theory and knowledge(s). Policy operates *upon* practice, theory and knowledge(s), in ways that shape them (at best), or limit and constrain them, or (at worst, and more often) undermine them, while the relationship of the researching professional's project to practice may vary and may well move from research *about* practice and research *into* practice to research *through* practice. In reviewing research practice, Pollard (2015) observes that research users, such as policy makers, appear to prefer the terms 'research-informed' and 'evidence-informed', but an even closer relationship between researching professionals and policy makers is significant and central to driving evidence framing and underpinning the macro and micro levels of policy change on social actions.

It is as if the spinning wheels of practice, theory and knowledge (as shown in Figure 3.1) generate connections that lead to policy change. Greater participation in policy processes and action is imperative if policy analysis and change are to shift to a system of multidirectional contributions. While practice and theory can inform the direction and advancement of a profession and its field (Schneider and Ingram, 1997) – and this is our point – the political relevance and dual determination of all shades of policy are central to the context and maintenance of values in professional doctorate research and the positioning inherent in the reflexivity and framing of the researching professional's own enterprise.

There are significant influences on and implications for researching professionals about how to proceed with professional doctorate research in terms of what policy means, to others, and particularly what policy, for the research professional, holds as their own theoretical uncertainties about the meaning of policy, policy processes, action and analysis. But to the question of 'what is policy?' some meanings can be nuanced as follows. Firstly, there is the view that professional doctorates involve the kinds of methodologies that frame practice research, which means that *policy as text* and *policy as discourse* can be articulated and understood in terms of policy processes as well as in terms of policy action. Secondly, we must take into account the influence and emphasis on situated perspectives and specific context (such as in a profession, workplace and university) including the meta-, macro- and micro-level processes and action that take account of people's perceptions and experiences. Thirdly, it can be necessary to go beyond optimism about the possibilities of developing theories of change and their application in practice and policy. We can and should do more, in this context, than just garner useful findings and articulate and test theories of change; rather, new practices must be developed that activate the mechanisms of change and policy change.

According to Ball et al. (2011), everyone who encounters policy texts *remakes* them through their beliefs, goals and histories and interpretative practices. Thinking, doing and action, in policy terms, are part of the work of researching professionals who, critically, do much more than merely revisit their 'practice', assumptions and values. Researching professionals generate entrepreneurship where collaboration allows for the formation of more complex, sustainable and innovative workplace action that marks a community of practice; they develop perspectives on, and inter-organisational co-ordination in, their own workplace; and they create professional agencies which become multiple, flexible and changing. Therefore, if we accept and understand policies as 'textual interventions into practice' (Ball, 1993: 12) then a clear pathway for active policy participation, policy action and policy change is paved for the potential 'impact' of professional doctorates which can be outcomes in the context of new knowledge creation and mobilisation. We argue that, in the context of such action and change, and as the researching professionals' positioning changes in the course of time, across multiple and discrete phases of research, they develop into critically reflexive researchers who are asking work-based/policy-based and workplace/policy-place questions. Thus, policy 'matters: it is important, not the least because it consists of texts which are (sometimes) *acted on*' (Beilharz, 1987: 394). For researching professionals, this represents the 'doing', 'studying' and 'being' change agents theorising professional practices in the context of their own policy processes, policy action and analysis (see Figure 3.2 below).

ON SETTING PARAMETERS THAT LEAD TO POLICY ANALYSIS AND CHANGE

Understanding the many forms of policy, as well as policy analysis procedures, is essential for researching professionals. Educational leadership and the management literature (Ball, 2009) offer key insights into how we can become more *policy savvy*, making use of policy as tactics for employing ideas such as controlling meeting agendas and decision-making processes, practising co-optation, developing listening and diplomacy skills, the strategic application of data, asking critical questions, employing government language, expanding policy into alternative conceptualisations of influence and change, and the use of policy discourse.

According to Ball, a theorist who has written extensively on politics and policy making, policies are 'both systems of values and symbolic systems' that are 'ways of representing, accounting for and legitimating decisions' (1994: 124). So, we need to become more skilled at analysing policy positions, constructing imaginative policy and reforming policy practice. A phrase coined by Bolman and Deal (2008: 216) called *'mapping the political terrain'* requires that researching professionals need to understand the complexity of policy and engage strategically with its potential.

So, understanding the many forms of policy work is central. This process starts with policy appropriation being the 'creative interpretative practice' that occurs when 'a policy that was formed within one community of practice meets the existential and institutional conditions that mark a different community of practice' (Levinson et al., 2009: 782). What this means, for researching professionals, is mapping how policy is created in their own workplace (e.g. organisation, business, local government, institution, state government). Policies are regularly interpreted and remade by all those who encounter them. Each of us acts and thinks in policy terms within each community of practice we meet, contribute to or work within. We all have policy-related discussions, use policy discourses, and appropriate or interpret and expand or reframe them in our practice as professional researchers and doctorate educators. We see evidence of this in the language which comes to constitute the *discourses* we adopt.

To exemplify this challenge, we consider the CRAC report commissioned by the Higher Education Funding Council for England (HEFCE), published in 2016 to depict the current landscape of professional doctorate (PD) provision by English higher education institutions (HEIs).

The language of this report sets parameters that have led to particular kinds of policy debate and contestations. Most problematically – apropos of our argument – PDs remain contested sites, regarded as being in tension with PhDs, and devalued as serving as a proxy for practice ('applied') research rather than academic ('pure') research (Flint and Costley, 2010: 2). We argue that, as with the blurring of boundaries between disciplinary and practicum knowledges (and between the discipline and the profession), the exciting intersection of the symbiotic domains of policy, practice and research needs to be more explicitly positioned. Thus, if PDs are to deliver the multidirectional movement of both policy and practice, an outcome which they potentially and uniquely promise (Flutter, 2016: 11), then we must be very clear: policy matters.

The CRAC report shows how public policy matters to researching professionals from the quality and conditions of workplace settings, to the employment practices and the change agendas set within professional practice by the researching professional. The study of public policy matters, having a direct relevance to professionals and professional practice.

What we also learn from reading the CRAC report is that researching professionals share a unique relationship to industry in co-creating knowledges which the economy requires, knowledges which HEIs legitimise. The success of policy makers to force an effective and 'profitable' relationship between higher education and employment can be demonstrated through the Quality Assurance Agency for Higher Education (QAA) 2014 review of engagement between higher education and industry. The recommendations from these reports and other reviews become embedded into higher institution curricula (another type of policy document).

Policy cannot be farmed out to others or relegated as something that sits outside the purview of researching professionals. Policy change forms part of the outcome of impact agendas. So, how does, or might, this look in PD and researching professionals' practice?

Figure 3.2 attempts a more detailed elaboration of Figure 3.1, showing the PD as a collaborative enterprise with central structures for sustainably supporting the 'doing', 'studying' and 'being' of new 'researchers' and 'practitioners' to co-constructing reflexively the paradigm in which they are working as 'researching professionals'. Here we see that the interconnectedness of policy thinking can create strong learning spaces within and between the workplace and the university and between practice and theory, which is not unidirectional but is, rather, multidirectional: the university does not provide the theoretical framework through which PD students can analyse the situation and act as a catalyst of change in their own and their community's practice, but, rather, active policy participation in professional learning communities engages with policy thinking and activism to shape action and impact the nature and extent of impact of transformative change. While PD learning communities also operate within this plane, the relationship between the different spheres, for us, needs to be more of a collaborative enterprise – *as equals* – operating in PD learning communities which form more of a 'professional' network with a greater synergy between agencies.

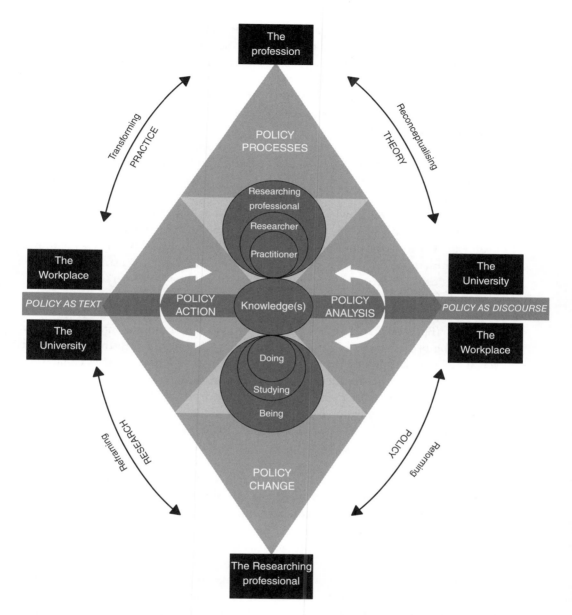

Figure 3.2 How policy matters as a defining parameter of the professional doctorate

SO, HOW SHOULD RESEARCHING PROFESSIONALS GO ABOUT POLICY ANALYSIS?

Document analysis is a form of qualitative research in which documents are interpreted by the researcher to give voice and meaning to a topic. Types of documents include: (a) *public records* (including mission statements, annual reports, policy manuals, student handbooks, strategic plans and syllabi); (b) *personal documents* (including calendars, emails, scrapbooks, blogs, Facebook posts, duty logs, incident reports, reflections, journals and newspapers); and (c) *physical evidence* (including flyers, posters, agendas, handbooks and training materials; these are useful/essential for reviewing policy documents such as curricula with situated practices in local contexts) (O'Leary, 2014).

The term 'discourse' often refers to the way people *use* spoken and written language, as well as methods or habits of operation and action ('modus operandi') – representing as well as constructing a certain understanding of an object or phenomenon.

For *discourse analysis*, which is essential, both as a means of framing organisational research and in order to interrogate issues in the workplace concerning professional knowledge and practice (Bowen, 2009), analysis of policy as text and policy as discourse (involving spoken and written language) is central (Ball, 1993).

Ball reflects on the context of policy research and how, even if researching professionals feel 'safely ensconced in the moral high ground', policy research is always in some degree 'both reactive and parasitic' on the prevailing and changing moral economy (Ball, 1997: 258). All of this involves a continuing interrogation by researching professionals of how different forms of policy fit into the context and social action underpinning their research. We know that **vertical** policies come from legislation or accreditation bodies in top-down ways. In contrast, policies that are more **horizontal** are 'softer' in character coming from published materials, traditions, or forms of professional dialogue. Both kinds of policy are subject to and produce different policy discourses (Schmidt, 2017: 15). Hence, again understanding the complexity of policy is an imperative, as Ball argues:

> There is a basic and apparently irredeemable tension at the heart of education policy research. A tension between the concerns of efficiency and those of social justice … Individual researchers must address, or try to resolve, the tension as they see fit: although it just may be that some of one side has to be sacrificed to achieve more of the other. (1997: 271)

Discourse analysis explores how language changes over time rather than just focusing on what is said. Since texts are constructed with specific contexts such as workplaces, there can be no single, correct, authoritative interpretation of a document. So, discourse analysis involves looking at the text from different perspectives to examine the researcher's own underlying assumptions, intentions, beliefs and values. Since the 'meaning' of any text is constructed in the gap between the reader and the text, reflection on our own assumptions and our relationship with ourselves as politically positioned individuals and as collectives is needed.

The **discourse theory** of Laclau and Mouffle (2014) offers a good starting point for the particularities of discourse analysis, clarifying methodological implications and concretising strategies for the analysis. Theories of professions form the other main strand of literature that informs the theoretical framework. The idea of uniting discourse theory and perspectives on professions in a theoretical frame may be very important to the overall stance of seeing the social world as discursively constituted, in order to secure coherence. The status of the discourses in terms of how they incorporate theoretical notions needs to be visible. The socially constructed discursive formations, which limit and form what is *sayable*, what can be *spoken about*, what is *conserved*, what is *remembered*, what is *reactivated* and what is *appropriated*, in and across professions and professional discourse, are complex and need to be carefully developed. For these reasons, the policy and curriculum documents selected or omitted need to be methodologically justified along with, crucially, the policy stance of the researcher (Jorgensen and Phillips, 2011).

So, what kinds of **policy analysis** might potentially play a significant role – from legislation to practice? How should researching professionals position themselves for policy analysis? What are the specific policy initiatives that place PD educators as targets of policy directives? If we accept that 'policies are the mechanisms through which values are authoritatively allocated for society', as is argued by Schneider and Ingram (1997: 2), then how might policy analysis translate into PD methodologies? How might researching professionals engage with and enact change agendas, providing conditions and legitimacy that will impact and inform policy changes on a macro level?

Dryzek (2006: 200) characterises the main task of policy analysis as 'speaking truth to power … analysts become interlocutors in a multidirectional conversation, not whisperers in the ears of the sovereign'. This sees *policy analysis* engaged through multiple forms such as texts, practices, symbols and discourses that define and deliver values. These will include a set of practices which exemplify regulations that direct ways to engage with others and mediate how we practise, how goods and services (including how cultural and educational development) are delivered, and disclosures on how income and status are viewed and experienced.

Often, we equate policy with unidirectionality rather than considering how it can be redefined or rethought as multidirectionality. Researching professionals, because of the unique nature of the PD, are capable of doing more than merely closing implementation gaps between a policy's intended outcome and its actual impact. The interconnectedness between policy and practice is what makes PDs full of potential. Researching professionals can be, and should be, **policy practitioners**, creating and challenging, and facilitating the mobilisations of new knowledge and learning (this is a practice which is already at the centre of policy formation). Why should researching professionals live at the margins of policy? Closer engagement with policy is imperative for researching professionals because policy is the realm within which their vision, research questions, aims and vision can be enacted.

All of this requires reconsideration of today's PD literature, the teaching about policy processes and the expectation that policy analysis be addressed as an imperative by researching professionals. We need to see positive signs of real and differentiated policy work and discourse in PD programmes which stress policy issues in terms of divergent approaches that include portfolios, blogs, podcasts, audio diaries, live presentations, visual presentations and artefacts as part of dissertation writing, recalibrating conceptions of PD assessment and supervision.

Examples such as these that follow for researching professionals show us that policy thinking can help in shaping new approaches to professional change and consequently to professionally engaged, policy-changing practices. This message is largely absent from PDs.

METHODOLOGIES FOR CONNECTING PROFESSIONAL DOCTORATES AND POLICY/IES

Gordon Kirk from the University of Edinburgh captured the purpose of PDs in a simple but effective way: 'The PhD is to understand the world. The Professional Doctorate is to change the world' (Perry, 2016). The researching professionals' journeying starts with an awareness that there is a need for change in their workplace, profession, discipline and sometimes even in policy; it is not surprising that such a starting point initiates divergence from traditional approaches to research.

ADKAR, defined by its developer Hiatt (2006) as a model for change in business, government and our community, emphasises the importance, as a crucial prerequisite, of having an **Awareness** of the need to change, the **Desire** to participate and support the change, **Knowledge** of how to change, the **Ability** to implement the change and **Reinforcement** to sustain the change (see Figure 3.3).

A	**Awareness** of the need for change
D	**Desire** to support and participate in the change
K	**Knowledge** of how to change
A	**Ability** to implement the change
R	**Reinforcement** to sustain the change

Figure 3.3   ADKAR model for change (Hiatt, 2006)

The PDs (with their ongoing reflective process) seem to be an appropriate approach for acting upon raised Awareness of the need for change. The researching professionals choose the PD path due to their Desire to support and participate in change, to be change agents in their own professional contexts, communities of practice or even society – 'our community' as Hiatt puts it. The university provides Knowledge and engages in a capacity-building process that leads to the researching professionals' Ability to implement the change and achieve impact. Reinforcement to sustain the change may be needed not only from decision makers within the workplace, but also from professional bodies and authorities.

The researching professional pursuing the PD path steps into the role of a change agent and therefore cannot afford to be focused only on 'doing things right' (Bennis and Nanus, 1985) – for example, on 'playing by the book' and on following strictly defined methodological approaches – but first and foremost on 'doing the right things': that is, achieving their ultimate goal – change and impact – through designing creative, different, unique and most effective methodological approaches for the context in question.

The following examples of creative methodological approaches might inspire a need for richer interactions in real time between policy and sometimes daring and ground-breaking PD methodologies which champion the very essence of practice research – Awareness of a need for change and Desire for impact.

EXAMPLE 1: 'A RESEARCH EXHIBITION' BY RESEARCHING PROFESSIONAL REBECCA HEATON

Rebecca Heaton, Senior Lecturer in Art Education and a Doctor of Education researching professional, applied a true change agent's approach while analysing challenges of, and solutions for, a misalignment between a need for change in her practice and limitations of existing methodological frameworks.

In Table 3.1 below, Rebecca reflects on her journey towards 'doing the right things': that is, achieving her ultimate goals – of change and impact – through reflection on multi-layered methodological approaches involved in the process. As an artist, art educator, researching professional and a change agent, Rebecca clearly demonstrates that challenges of 'walking her talk' (i.e. carrying out research that is embedded in her professional practice as an artist and educator) need to be overcome by introducing change into the research methodology itself. Policy might benefit from being informed equally by the process of reshaping methodological approaches and by the process of reshaping researching professional's practice.

Table 3.1 Aligning the desire for change and research frameworks (by Rebecca Heaton)

REFLECTIONS on 'HOW to do the right things'	CHALLENGE	SOLUTION
A **portfolio is art**, it is research and it is educational practice. It is therefore relational and so aligns with Bourriard's (2002) concept that art practice is steeped in cultural influence and socialisation. The portfolio encompasses writing, listening, publishing, making, exhibiting, blogging, disseminating, connecting acts/processes and outcomes/products of articles, book chapters, posters, artworks, conference contributions, lectures and teaching experiences	Documentation	Exhibition
A **research exhibition**, as art journals do (Scott Shields, 2016), presents artefacts that move beyond data representation; they dialogue with concepts, data and ideas through a living performance that connects theory with practice	Accessibility	Auto-ethnography

(Continued)

Table 3.1　(Continued)

REFLECTIONS on 'HOW to do the right things'	CHALLENGE	SOLUTION
A **portfolio** is a purposeful body of work that reflexively stories a student's journey to academic achievement, in a formative or summative manner (Cry and Muth, 2011). Portfolios are criticised for their ability to show deep knowledge (Wasley, 2008). They are time consuming to generate, can lack clarity and are challenging to assess (Cry and Muth, 2011)	Document, convince, exemplify	Connect and map theory, practice, research, acts and outcomes
Research portfolios are also criticised for presenting what Costley (2013), in relation to doctoral education, terms discipline-based knowledge because of heavy associations to practice. A significant benefit of a portfolio, and another reason for exhibition selection as research in this thesis, is that exhibitions can expose learning cognition (Bransford et al., 1999)	Research value	Exposure
Cognition is the main concept underpinning this exhibition and is exposed by communicating a reflexive learning journey, through a body of multi-textual research, which exemplifies artist teacher cognition. The exhibition, as research, as a portfolio, demonstrates a profession. It exposes an artist teacher's skill set and models personal, professional and academic growth, components that Cry and Muth (2011) outline as advantages of assessed portfolios	Capturing growth	Voices, truth, reflexivity, acts and outcomes

The university, as illustrated in Figures 3.1 and 3.2, provides Knowledge of how to, and Ability to, change. PD students and/or researching professionals are encouraged proactively to inform themselves about and analyse relevant policy/ies (e.g. Higher Education Policy, Graduate Students Supervision Policy) in order to co-create a platform for pursuing and later for sustaining impact and changes in their professionally engaged, policy-changing practice. Doctoral supervisors play a pivotal role in contributing to Knowledge and Ability to change in the researching professional's professionally engaged, policy-changing practice.

If Rebecca's use of exhibition, exposure, connective/mapping theory, practice, research, acts and outcomes gets disseminated and transcends changes and impacts in her own professional practice (micro level), it can contribute to the reshaping of vertical and/or creation of **'horizontal'** policies.

Rebecca's creative visual narratives are illustrated below by:

(a) Exhibit 1: Perspectives (on multi-sensory culture), collaborative art (pen on paper) 2014; and

(b) Exhibition of Doctor of Education (EdD) Collection: *An auto-ethnographic to artographic lens on artist teacher practice* that was on show at the Beyond Surface Exhibition, The Glass Tank Gallery, Oxford Brookes University (Figure 3.4). Images (left to right): Interdisciplinarity, Cognition, Aesthetic discourse, Digital practice, Social justice, Artist teacher voice, Performativity and Artography.

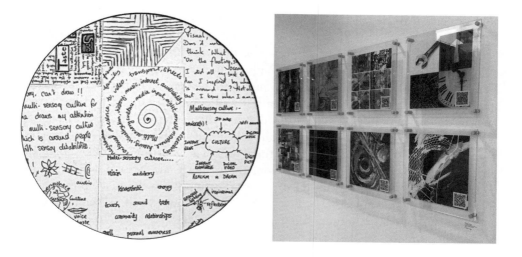

Figure 3.4   (a) Exhibit 1 and (b) Exhibition of EdD Collection (Rebecca Heaton)

Rebecca's account of how policy matters in her professional doctorate project

In the context of my professional doctorate, that is a thesis structured as an exhibition examining artist teacher cognition (Heaton, 2018), policy has influenced formation on several levels. Policy has shaped practice through alterations in curriculum content taught, as a university academic training teachers, in the way I deliver or teach such content and in the way I conduct and disseminate research in art education as a curriculum area. These practices have directed and instigated professional change, on conscious and subconscious levels and in inward and outward ways. For example, consciously I have gained confidence as an academic in voicing a cognitive voice informed by policy in a professional subject area. In doing so, subconsciously I have expanded my ability to be critical and to afford myself the opportunity to reveal vulnerabilities. These conscious and unconscious acts are inward alterations to practice because they affect the self directly. But the acts also have influence on practice outwardly: confidence to project a cognitive voice in art education has led to the dissemination of research and subject-related concepts at academic conferences, in publications, for practitioners and academics (Heaton and Crumpler, 2017), and in teaching and exhibitions (Heaton, 2017). These practice alterations influenced policy in a top-down and bottom-up direction, thus illustrating again the case of textual interventions which, as Stephen Ball argues, can change things significantly through 'the complexity of the relationship between policy intentions, texts, interpretations and reactions' (Ball, 1993: 13).

To exemplify policy influence, I use the current marginalisation of art education in the United Kingdom as a contentious context (Payne and Hall, 2017), a subject central to the theme of study in my professional doctorate. The professional doctoral study I embarked on is informed and shaped by the policy legislation in art education I have referenced, policy in this case being national subject reports and inquiries, curriculum documentation (Department for Education (DfE), 2013) and professional and institutional policies. Research questions and data collected have manifest and been interrupted by time, space and movement in policy legislation, production, dissemination and use. In a softer way the materials I have constructed, published and disseminated have connected with policy by interrupting aspects of them – such as questioning why a focus on digital technology appears omitted from the primary art National Curriculum (DfE, 2013), using policy aspects to generate cognitive webs of connectionism (Naidu, 2012) like connecting policy with academic theory and personal practice and by ensuring research undertaken is timely, relevant and of use to progress the field. Policy connection has been used to form professional dialogue around issues and practices such as the influence of neoliberal agendas on artist teacher practice and art education, to form partnerships and most importantly, I feel, to create ripples of change like contributions to the reinstatement of value towards the recognition and worth of cognitive practice in art education. Policy mobilisation in professional doctorates can influence subject disciplines and professional doctoral participants as shown.

Rebecca's account clearly shows that her PD has been informed and affected by policies while her awareness of the need for change inspired her to develop methodologies and research designs that engage in policy-changing practices.

Activity

Think about your own professional research. How have you already considered policy in the research process? What influence has this had on your personal practice and outwardly to society?

    Possible areas for consideration might be:

1. Whether you have used policy to interrupt, alter or reform the research approaches you have adopted.
2. The challenges faced in your research and the solutions you have used to overcome them.

Once you have done this, draw and label a web that connects you with your research, practice, key policies, intentions, challenges, solutions, changes and impacts. This may help expose the complex relationships you have with policy that Ball (1993) speaks of.

EXAMPLE 2: POLICY-INFORMED DOCUMENTS AND 'STORYBOARDING' BY RESEARCHING PROFESSIONAL BARRY ROGERS

Barry Rogers, Visiting Senior Fellow of the London School of Economics and Political Science, and a Doctorate of Education student, researching the impact of temporal context on behaviour, acts as a leader of change in a business context. As his PD study involves the production of a visual tool to be used and tested in a business context, Barry faced the unique situation of needing to:

(a) prepare a 19-page Research Agreement based on Research Ethics Policy but heavily redefined, reshaped and adapted for the business professional practice; and

(b) negotiate an extra document for Intellectual Property based on Intellectual Property Policies for Universities but also heavily redefined, reshaped and adapted to the context of a professional doctorate bridging the worlds of academia and business.

Barry's case clearly indicates how strongly PDs need to be supported by existing policy/ies and at the same time how the impactful-in-real-time nature of PDs can inform, expand, redefine and reshape existing, and create new, policy/ies. The researching professionals are thus leading the transformative change in all three circles: at the workplace, in their own profession, at the university. This comes together in policy as their own transformation from practitioners to researching professionals expands to a role of policy changers.

True to his research and desire to develop a visual tool to introduce changes in his own professional context, Barry also integrated 'visioning of his visual tool' as part of his unique research portfolio. His use of storyboards, a form of sequential art where illustrations are used (on big boards) and arranged so that they visualise the story (Figure 3.5), achieved effective visualisation, memorability, empathy and engagement.

Barry's account of how policy matters in his professional doctorate project

As an educator I design and deliver customised learning experiences inside organisations. The holy grail within my field concerns the transfer of learning to the workplace (Cheng and Hampson, 2008). The challenges associated with 'transfer' are long standing and seemingly intractable (Blume et al., 2010). My professional doctorate project seeks to broaden the debate by developing the work surrounding the context to transfer (Evans et al., 2010). In particular it explores the role of non-linear time in practising learning commitments after a learning programme. As part of a Mixed Methods Action Research project I am developing a visual coaching tool.

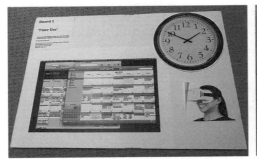
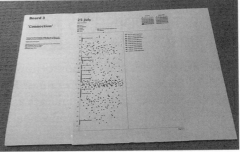
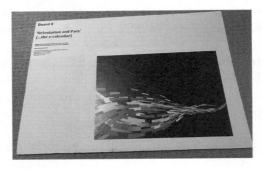

Figure 3.5 'Storyboarding' of Barry Rogers' Professional Doctorate in Education

I had a significant issue ahead of my Registration Viva, a midway milestone oral examination required of the professional doctorate at this university. Writing and talking about the visualisation of non-linear time sounded very abstract. I felt constrained by the traditional format of a standard registration document. The policies and procedures underpinning this written format did not do justice, I felt, to the visual nature of my study or my desire to create something practical and useful.

In the end I opted for a mini-portfolio approach. I designed a set of storyboards aimed at capturing the visual essence of the temporal dimension within the tool and submitted these alongside my registration document. During the viva I used the boards to outline the potential elicitation and enabling qualities of the tool as well as the underlying temporal concepts. The boards prompted a lively, constructive discussion while modelling the potential creativity – and practicality – of the tool.

This experience highlights a fundamental issue surrounding the ability of the researching professional to shape change. The professional doctorate has a unique quality in affording the scope for distinct, non-traditional approaches to the research process (Burnard et al., 2016). Be it negotiating a multi-layered research agreement or addressing intellectual property rights, many of the issues I faced forced me to test the existing policy framework inside and outside the academy.

Ultimately the complexity of our everyday practice situations challenges researching professionals to reflect on how we make sense of, and explain, what we do (Jarvis, 1998). This is increasingly important in a world where the perceived gap between theory and practice is ever present (Vermeulen, 2007). My experience, I feel, highlights the role of the researching professional as *sense-giver*, sitting *between* the worlds of research and practice (Sutcliffe and Wintermute, 2006). In this middle space we are forced to be creative in making the phenomena we research relevant and engaging to those outside our realm of everyday experience. Storyboards were a small attempt to bridge this gap. I suspect they touch upon the broader role of the researching professional as change maker in wider society.

Barry's account highlights, on one hand, 'testing' of the existing policy framework through negotiating a lengthy Research Agreement and, on the other hand, the use of an unconventional 'storyboarding' approach, thus proving the ability of the researching professional to shape change.

Both accounts reinforce the argument that policy is one of the defining features of the PD as it provides the foreground for and background upon which the researching professional engages in driving professional and wider changes in society by doing the doctorate differently and changing policies on the way.

Activity

Think about your own professional research. How have you had to 'test' existing policy as part of your research process? What impact has this had in shaping change within your personal research and practice, as well as within a wider societal setting?

Possible areas for consideration might be:

1. Where current policy has acted as a potential 'roadblock' to the intended approach, and direction of your research.
2. Where a mix of stakeholders defines the policy background for your professional research. (Note that a stakeholder here is defined as anybody who has a meaningful role in influencing your relationship with policy.)

Once you have done this, take a sheet of paper and draw a circle in the middle – this is you! Then:

(a) Locate the key policy stakeholders as bigger or smaller circles around you, depending on your assessment of their importance in shaping your policy setting.
(b) Draw a line between you and each stakeholder. Think of your role as a *sense-giver* to each of these stakeholders in helping to shape change in the emerging policy environment. Consider also to what extent this is a mutual sense-giving process.
(c) Then draw a line between stakeholders and 'see' how they act as *sense-givers* to one another.
(d) Finally, consider how your collective action may have an impact on your wider societal setting.

(Continued)

(Continued)

As shown in Figure 3.6, this process may help to display the complex relationship you have with your policy environment (Ball, 1993).

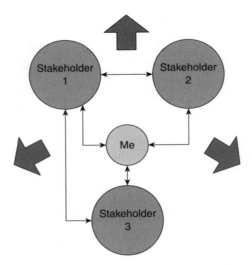

Figure 3.6   Mapping a complex relationship to the policy environment

DRIVING PROFESSIONAL AND WIDER CHANGES IN SOCIETY: DOING THE DOCTORATE DIFFERENTLY

In the above, the researching professional is a change agent and, to use a metaphor from the leadership literature, a 'shaker and mover' (Nicholls, 1987: 17) – the one who raises awareness of the need for change, has a burning desire to carry it out and then 'shakes and moves' orthodoxies on different levels (meta, macro and micro) of the work place, the profession, the university and policy by knowing how to, by being able to and by wanting to sustain the change.

The PD's temporal element enables changes and impacts events on the way, thus empowering researching professionals to 'do the right things': to do the doctorate differently in order to exercise three types of change leadership (Nicholls, 1987: 24):

(a) in the micro dimension, that is in the context where the researching profession-
     als first observed and raised Awareness of the need for a change – where they
     start their doctoral journey;
(b) in the macro dimension, that is 'shaking and moving' whole organisations (in
     intern and multi-professional practice) so that they acquire and co-create

Knowledge and Ability to cope with change in the future and achieve results and impact; and

(c) in the meta dimension, that is relating individuals/change leaders/researching professionals to their wider environment/our community/society/policy through 'visioning' – a complex interaction of observation, articulation, conviction and empathy with or without the use of power or authority (Nicholls, 1987: 16) in order not only to initiate and influence transformational change in wider society, but also, most importantly, to sustain it.

CONCLUSION – SO WHAT FOR PROFESSIONAL DOCTORATE EDUCATION?

Following the kind of policy tracing and policy work suggested in this chapter is challenging. Researching professionals and their doctoral supervisors have their own capacities and their own agendas, shaping their responses and adaptations to the policies and practices that are in place. Policy makers, researching professionals and doctoral supervisors are members of the 'What works?/What matters?' industry. Policy frameworks provide a way of thinking about, monitoring, reviewing and adjusting policy in the context(s) of practice. We cannot escape the importance of practice, theory *and* policy. However, the exhilarating emphasis on and amplification of the context of policy and the context(s) of practice need to be central to the idiom and critique of professional doctorates. Policy applies as much to what can be done and known as it does to what can and should be changed.

Our arguments for why policy matters in this chapter are further, related distinctions which are centrally useful for researching professionals doing practice research in workplace conditions of uncertainty and diversity. Here, researching professionals need to be particularly attentive to the context(s) of practice, mechanism, intended and unintended outcomes, and processes of human adaptation.

What bears strong resonance for the researching professional is having a role to play not only in shaping and navigating the researching professional's own experiences and professional development, but also 'in signaling the wider, societal potential of the professional doctorate as a catalyst for **transformative change**' and for '**knowledge creation and knowledge mobilization**' (Flutter, 2016: 11).

We have some encouraging signs that professional doctorates, as Flint and Costley (2010: 12) argue, are being seen 'as an emerging dialogical approach to learning, for, in and through work' by means of advancing researching professionals' leadership through policy. We argue, however, nearly a decade on, that researching professionals can serve as policy makers. We see policy mattering a lot more in the future expectation and assessment of researching professionals.

It is time for the professional doctorate learning communities to do more than just *think* in policy terms. It is time to challenge the centralised and hierarchical forms of *policy action*, to understand the ways in which researching professionals engage with the *policy process* as they create and respond to policy, and to share effective ways for researching professionals to step into policy and change it.

We see policy mattering a lot in the future expectation and assessment of researching professionals as being involved in the development of policy and not just weighing in on the value or effectiveness of a policy after it has been developed.

We also see policy mattering as an imperative for researching professionals and their supervisors to build into the initial doctoral proposal and registration documents opportunities to analyse, interpret and contribute to policy agendas. The ongoing engagement with policy, as a way forward in the change agendas and facilitation stakes, constitutes an imperative for researching professionals to achieve impact.

Activity

Use the following exercises and questions, based on what has been outlined in this chapter, to begin framing your own approaches to policy thinking and analysis:

1.   Think about your own areas of focus. What are today's most hotly contested policy issues and policy debates driving them, and what is at the core of these contemporary political agendas? How do these trends and developments matter?
2.   Consider how you will begin to frame your research with past and present policy issues and debates. Pay particular attention to the key concepts of education policy, economic necessity and education reform and how these inform your context.
3.   In Stephen Ball's seminal book *The Education Debate* he presents a useful concept which he calls 'policy technologies'. These involve the calculated deployment of forms of organisation and procedures, and disciplines or bodies of knowledge, to organise human forces and capabilities into functioning systems:

    these technologies are devices for changing the meaning of practice and of social relationships. They provide a new language, a new set of incentives and disciplines and new set of roles, positions and identities within which what it means to be a teacher/student/learner, parent, and so on are all charged. (Ball, 2009: 50)

Reflect on and write critically about the specific policy technologies underpinning your research.

4.   What are the vertical and horizontal strands of policy that inform your inquiry? Locate them and position where policy reform will feature in your inquiry methodologically.
5.   How will you go about document and/or discourse analysis in your inquiry methodologically?

Key Points

- Policy is the mechanism through which values are authored and formulated. Policy embodies carefully articulated principles for acceptance and enactment.
- Policy is one of the defining features of the professional doctorate in that they form the background upon which the researching professional engages in shaping practice agendas, leading professional change and, in turn, changing policies.
- This chapter has examined vertical policies that come from legislation or accreditation bodies in top-down ways as compared to or in connection with policies that are more horizontal and 'softer' in character, coming from published materials, traditions, or forms of professional dialogue.
- Both (kinds of) policy and professional doctorates should inform each other and engage in creating a common platform for discussion and partnership in order to drive not only professional change but also wider changes in society.

ANNOTATED BIBLIOGRAPHY

Ball, Stephen. J. (2009). *The Education Debate*. Bristol: Policy Press.

In this enthralling book, Stephen Ball guides us through the flood of government initiatives and policies that have been introduced over the past 20 years, including beacon schools, the academies programme, parental choice, foundation schools, faith schools and teaching standards. He looks at the politics of these policy interventions and how they have changed the face of education, 'joining up' policy within a broader framework of initiatives, turning children into 'learners' and parents into 'consumers'. Ball's sociological approach to analysing and making sense of current policies and ideas around education uncovers issues of class, choice, globalisation, equality and citizenship, as well as the conflicting needs of children and families on the one hand and the economy and the state on the other. This book invites you to reflect on and enter into dialogue with policy as text and policy as discourses. It provides essential tools and insights on various forms of policy analysis essential to doctorate programmes.

Burnard, P., Dragovic, T., Flutter, J., & Alderton, J. (eds) (2016). *Transformative Doctoral Research Practices For Professionals*. Rotterdam: Sense Publishers.

This book shares the lived-through debates, deliberations, challenges and experiences of a group of professional (practitioner) doctorate students, their supervisors and lecturers. The critical perspectives and examples explored offer a wealth of insights on the distinct practices and unique journeying of researching professionals embarking on professional doctorates. The volume invites you to reflect on and enter into dialogue with your peers and professional learning and research communities about the distinctiveness of the professional doctorate.

Levinson, B. A. U., Sutton, M., & Winstead, T. (2009). Education policy as a practice of power: theoretical tools, ethnographic methods, democratic options. *Educational Policy*, 23(6): 767–95. DOI: 10.1177/0895904808320676.

This article outlines some theoretical and methodological parameters of a critical practice approach to policy. The article discusses the origins of this approach, how it can be uniquely adapted to educational analysis, and why it matters – not only for scholarly interpretation but also for the democratisation of policy processes as well. Key to the exposition is the concept of 'appropriation' as a form of creative interpretive practice necessarily engaged in by different people involved in the policy process. Another crucial distinction is made between authorised policy and unauthorised or informal policy; it is argued that when non-authorised policy actors appropriate policy they are in effect often making new policy in situated locales and communities of practice.

REFERENCES

Ball, S. (1993). What is policy? Texts, trajectories and toolboxes. *Discourse: Studies in the Cultural Politics of Education*, *13*(2), 10–17.

Ball S. (1994). *Education Reform: A Critical and Post-structuralist Approach*. Buckingham: Open University Press.

Ball, S. (1997). Policy social and critical social research: a personal review of recent education policy and policy research. *British Education Research Journal*, *23*(3), 257–74.

Ball, S. (2009). *The Education Debate*. Bristol: Policy Press.

Ball, S., Maguire, M., Braun, A., & Hoskins, K. (2011). Policy subjects and policy actors in schools: some necessary but insufficient analyses. *Discourse: Studies in the Cultural Politics of Education*, *32*(4), 611–24.

Beliharz, P. (1987). Reading politics: social theory and social policy. *Journal of Sociology*, *23*(3), 388–406.

Bennis, W., & Nanus, B. (1985). *Leaders: The Strategies for Taking Charge*. New York: Harper and Row.

Blume, B. D., Ford, J. K., Baldwin, T. T., & Huang, J. L. (2010). Transfer of training: a meta-analytic review. *Journal of Management*, *36*(4), 1065–1105.

Bolman, L. G., & Deal, T. E. (2008). *Reframing Organizations: Artistry, Choice, and Leadership* (4th edn). San Francisco: Jossey-Bass.

Bourriard, N. (2002). *Relational Aesthetics*. Dijon: Presses du reel.

Bowen, G. A. (2009). Document analysis as a qualitative research method. *Qualitative Research Journal*, *9*(2), 27–40.

Bransford, J. D., Brown, A. L., & Cocking R. R. (1999). *How People Learn: Brain, Mind, Experience and School*. Washington, DC: National Academy Press.

Burnard, P., Dragovic, T., Flutter, J., & Alderton, J. (eds) (2016). *Transformative Doctoral Research Practices for Professionals*. Rotterdam: Sense Publishers.

Cheng, E. W. L., & Hampson, I. (2008). Transfer of training: a review and new insights. *International Journal of Management Reviews*, *10*(4). https://onlinelibrary.wiley.com/doi/abs/10.1111/j.1468-2370.2007.00230.x.

Costley, C. (2013). Evaluation of the current status and knowledge contributions of professional doctorates. *Quality in Higher Education*, *19*(1), 7–27.

CRAC (2016). *Provision of Professional Doctorates in English HE Institutions*. Cambridge: The Career Development Organisation.

Cry, T., & Muth, R. (2011). Portfolios in doctoral education. In P. Maki, N. Borkowski, & D. Denecke (eds) *The Assessment of Doctoral Education*. Herndon: Stylus Publishing. (pp. 215–38).

Department for Education (DfE) (2013). *Art and Design Programmes of Study: Key Stage 1 and 2. National Curriculum in England*. www.gov.uk/government/publications/national-curriculum-in-england-art-and-design-programmes-of-study. Accessed 19 June 2018.

Dryzek, J. (2006). Policy analysis as critique. In M. Moran, M. Rein & R. Goodin (eds) *The Oxford Handbook of Public Policy* (pp. 190–206). New York: Oxford University Press.

Evans, K., Guile, D., Harris, J., & Allan, H. (2010). Putting knowledge to work: a new approach. *Nurse Education Today*, 30(3), 245–51.

Flint, K., & Costley, C. (2010). Critical perspectives on researching the professional doctorate. *Work-based Learning e-Journal*, 37(3), 257–69.

Flutter, J. (2016). Fields and oceans: helping professional doctorate students to orientate themselves and navigate through their practitioner research journeys. In P. Burnard, T. Dragovic, J. Flutter & J. Alderton (eds) *Transformative Doctoral Research Practices for Professionals* (pp. 30–14). Rotterdam: Sense Publishers.

Heaton, R. (2017). *Artist Teacher Cognition* [8× Digital Photographs]. Beyond Surface Exhibition, Oxford Brookes University, The Glass Tank Gallery, June/July.

Heaton, R. (2018). Autoethnography to artography: cognition in artist teacher practice. EdD thesis, University of Cambridge.

Heaton, R., & Crumpler, A. (2017). Sharing mindfulness: a moral practice for artist teachers. *International Journal of Education and the Arts*, 18(26). www.ijea.org/v18n26/. Accessed 19 June 2018.

Hiatt, J. M. (2006). *ADKAR: A Model for Change in Business, Government and Our Community*. Fort Collins, CO: Prosci Learning Center Publications.

Jarvis, P. (1998). *The Practitioner-Researcher: Developing Theory from Practice*. Chichester: Wiley.

Jorgensen, M., & Phillips, L. (2011). *Discourse Analysis as Theory and Method*. London: Sage.

Kamler, B., & Thomson, P. (2006). *Helping Doctoral Students Write*. London: Routledge.

Laclau, E., & Mouffle, C. (2014). *Hegemony and Socialist Strategy: Towards a Radical Democratic Politics*. London: Verso Books.

Levinson, B. A. U., Sutton, M., & Winstead, T. (2009). Education policy as a practice of power: theoretical tools, ethnographic methods, democratic options. *Educational Policy*, 23(6), 767–95. DOI: 10.1177/0895904808320676.

Naidu, S. (2012). Connectionism. *Distance Education*, 33(3), 291–94. DOI: 10.1080/01587919.2012.723321.

Nicholls, J. (1987). Leadership in organisations: meta, macro and micro. *European Management Journal*, 6(7), 16–25.

O'Leary, Z. (2014). *The Essential Guide to Doing Your Research Project* (2nd edn). Thousand Oaks, CA: Sage.

Quality Assurance Agency for Higher Education (QAA) (2014). The frameworks for higher education qualifications of UK degree-awarding bodies. Gloucester: QAA.

Payne, R., & Hall, E. (2017). The National Society for Education in Art and Design (NSEAD) Survey Report 2015–2016: Political reflections from two art and design educators. *International Journal of Art and Design Education*. DOI: 10.1111/jade.12142.

Perry, J.A. (2016). The Scholarly Practitioner as Steward of the Practice. In V.A., Storey and K.A., Hesbol (eds) *Contemporary Approaches to Dissertation Development and Research Methods, Hershey: Information Science Reference*. ICI Global. (pp. 300–313).

Pollard, A. (2015). Achievement, divergence and opportunity in education: some outcomes and challenges of REF 2014. *Research Intelligence*, 126(Spring), 10–11.

Schmidt, P. (2017). Why policy matters: developing a policy vocabulary within music education. In P. Schmidt & R. Colwell (eds) *Policy and the Political Life of Music Education* (pp. 11–36). New York: Oxford University Press.

Schneider, A., & Ingram, H. (1997). *Policy Design for Democracy*. Lawrence: University Press of Kansas.

Scott Shields, S. (2016). How I learned to swim: The visual journal as a companion to creative inquiry. *International Journal of Education & the Arts*, *17*(8).

Sutcliffe, K. M., & Wintermute, T. P. (2006). Commentary: Gladwell as sensegiver. *Journal of Management Inquiry*, *15*, 404–405. DOI: 10.1177/1056492606294865.

Vermeulen, F. (2007). 'I shall not remain insignificant': adding a second loop to matter more. *Academy of Management Journal*, *50*(4), 754–61.

Wasley, P. (2008). Portfolios are replacing qualifying exams as a step on the road to dissertations. *Chronicle of Higher Education*, 11 July, Education Research Complete EBSCOhost. Accessed 30 April 2017.

REFLECTIVE MODELS AND FRAMEWORKS IN PRACTICE

Jan Fook

INTRODUCTION

Reflection is an important aspect of any research project and it is particularly relevant in practice-based research. Key considerations are: why we choose to undertake a research study; what this means in practice; what issues there are which need to be considered; and what the practical constraints are. When we bring about change in practice things seldom go according to plan and there are often too many other factors involved, not least from the other people who are involved. We need to reconsider and often refocus; this is an element which is implicit and indeed runs throughout many of the research studies. This chapter will outline ways in which reflection can be integrated into research studies and what this means within the research context.

There is quite a push nowadays to be reflective and also to include reflection in many academic and professional endeavours. It occurs across a range of disciplines and professions (Moon, 1999) and also more recently in the field of leadership (Pellicer, 2008). Students may be required to demonstrate reflective abilities, either in assignments and in practical experiences such as placements, or in professional portfolios. So we are very familiar with reflection from a learning perspective.

What we are less familiar with is the use of reflection in the research field, especially in the practice of research (Fook et al., 2016). Nonetheless doctoral candidates are being asked to demonstrate it in their research design or implementation, and it is often seen as mandatory to include a section on reflexivity in the doctoral thesis, regardless of the research design. Unfortunately it is not necessarily clear how reflection and reflexivity are related, and, indeed, what reflection even means, especially in practice. Because these ideas are used in many different disciplines and professions, often without reference to other usages, the meaning is compounded. In addition, it is not necessarily easy to transfer meanings between learning and research traditions.

In this chapter I attempt to give an overview of the meaning and use of reflection (and related terminologies), taking into account the different usages of the term, and illustrating it with practical examples, so that readers might gain a more discerning and critical understanding of how to design and conduct their research in a more sophisticated way with the use of reflection. I begin by discussing reasons for the renewed interest in reflection and the implications for research. I then move on to clarify different concepts and terms associated with reflection, drawing out the different theoretical frameworks used to illuminate different approaches or models. I then come back to draw a clearer distinction between 'reflection' (a term more associated with learning traditions) and 'reflexivity' (a term more associated with research traditions) and outline in more detail the important implications for researching professional practice. I then develop a practical model which integrates core ideas about reflection and reflexivity. In the last two sections I outline some major approaches to using reflection in research, and illustrate with practical examples drawing on the earlier integrated model. I then finish with a discussion of some of the practical issues which might arise for researchers.

REFLECTION AND ITS RELATIONSHIP TO RESEARCH

Although the concept of reflective practice is widely used in professional education, and its contemporary usage is often attributed to the work of Donald Schön (1983) relatively recently, the concept of reflection is actually written about by authors in many diverse fields, and goes back much further. Some argue that the idea of reflection goes back to Socrates, who spoke about 'the examined life for ethical and compassionate engagement with the world and its dilemmas' (quoted in Nussbaum, 1997). Why then is there a renewed interest in reflection?

It seems ironic that we in academia and the professions should be becoming increasingly interested in reflection (which is often associated with looking inwards) when the turmoil, division and fragmentation which is happening on a global scale threaten to tear down the very values with which reflection appears to be associated. Yet there is something about these frighteningly divisive times, I think, which forces us to recognise the importance of different peoples' experiences in different contexts. From this flows the idea that personal experiences need to be taken into account when trying to explain, interpret and understand situations. This forms the backbone of a type of knowledge revolution, often associated with postmodern thinking, where we now recognise that there may be many different perspectives on a situation, and that these may be contradictory. No longer is it acceptable to search for the 'one truth'.

We have also been forced to recognise that what might pass as 'the truth' may simply be what is asserted as 'the truth' by more powerful people or groups, and that in fact disempowered or marginal people might have perspectives which are just as legitimate (but which might simply not have been heard or have been discounted). Foucault (1972) of course has given us a framework for understanding the connections between knowledge and power. This is widely used as an underpinning framework in many, what might be loosely termed, 'postmodern' approaches to an understanding of knowledge creation. In this framework, it is acknowledged that what counts as legitimate knowledge is often not necessarily a matter of the objective 'truth', but more a matter of 'whose truth' is believed and privileged. In this sense, the more powerful groups in society tend to have their own understanding or perspective asserted (often at the expense of less powerful groups). The 'discourse' (ways of talking about and labelling an issue) of the more powerful groups tends to be the one which is accepted as generally true, and in this way the perspective of more powerful groups is maintained. A good illustration of this is what happens after a war, when it is normally the perspective of the victors which is dominant.

This sort of analysis leads us to question the immutability of ideas, by drawing attention to the interests and social functions which are served by specific ideas, and sets of ideas. In this way, it is useful, as researchers, to be able to analyse the social functions supported by certain sets of ideas (discourses). (This is a concept at the heart of critical perspectives (Agger, 1998; Brookfield, 2005).) Foucault's concept of discourse (Purvis and Hunt, 1993), which allows us to trace how particular ways of speaking about social phenomena (and actions and cultural ways of being which are related), can maintain certain knowledges and the power imbalances which are created by them. This type of thinking means that we now recognise the importance of learning about how people make their knowledge, what it is about their experiences which shape it, and how an awareness of it can help us arrive at more complex, and perhaps more balanced, understandings of social phenomena. This is where reflection comes into its own

Activity

Thinking of your own profession or occupation, identify what can shape the central themes and ideas.

Reflection, in its most basic sense, can be seen as *learning from experience* (Dewey, 1933). What is learning and experience and how the process happens are all open to debate. However, in its simplest sense, 'learning from experience' encapsulates the idea that people think about their experience, in order to make meaning of it and to take lessons which they can apply to future living (e.g. Boud et al., 1985). What constitutes reflective thinking (as opposed to any type of thinking) is something I will address further on. What is important to note here is that recognising the importance of reflection also involves recognising that people's own knowledge-making, from their own personal experience, is something which must be taken into account. Reflection therefore becomes important as a way of making knowledge. Now, of course, if you see research as involving the making of knowledge, then reflection is crucial to research.

What needs further thought is *how* and *whose* reflection is taken into account. It makes a difference of course if we are talking about research participants' reflections as opposed to researchers' reflections. And, crucially, how reflection is defined and practised will also make a big difference. These issues are heavily influenced by the theoretical frameworks used to inform reflection, and the sorts of practical models which are used. These are addressed in the following discussion.

THE CONCEPT OF REFLECTION AND RELATED CONCEPTS

The concept of reflection is difficult to pin down, partly because there are so many different perspectives on it, but also because different disciplines and professions write about it differently and separately, for the most part making little reference to each other. Earlier I mentioned some of the diverse fields which include reflection in their professional education programmes. What I did not mention in detail was other disciplines which do not necessarily educate for professional practice, but which also include reflection as a significant concept. These include writing about spirituality (Hunt, 2016). An easy starting point to help differentiate between these different perspectives is to view 'reflection' as being on a continuum ranging from relatively superficial to more deep-seated understandings. At one end of the continuum, the changes aspired to be brought about from reflection might be relatively minor and limited to professional practice only, whereas at the other end the changes might be relatively fundamental and lead to transformative changes in general living. These sets of changes are of course not mutually exclusive – superficial changes will also be part and parcel of more transformative changes. Also, changes in professional practice are assumed to be part of broader life changes.

Conceiving the continuum in this way helps us understand the differences in meanings *as they relate to the stated purpose of reflection*. Where reflection is more instrumentally conceived (perhaps as in some types of professional education), the purpose will be seen as about improving professional practice (e.g. Schön, 1983). This might be the case in many of the professions, especially those where more pragmatic and measurable outcomes might rule, such as in some health professions (Collington and Ross, 2016). In professions and disciplines where a moral or value aspect is also seen as important (e.g. social work) the purpose of reflection might be conceived as being about the development of an ethical stance. Similar processes might be used, but obviously if outcomes are conceived radically differently, then how they are identified may differ broadly, and may be more open to contention.

In the remainder of this section I will outline the usages of some of the different terminologies and will draw on the framework outlined in this continuum to make these points more clearly.

The concept of reflection is that it is often conflated with some commonly used other terms, such as 'reflexivity', 'reflective practice' and 'critical reflection'. In addition, different theoretical frameworks may be used to underpin different approaches to reflection (Fook et al., 2006). Below I outline some of the major terminologies and frameworks.

I begin with the term 'reflective practice' because it is perhaps the one in most popular usage, and is also perhaps the least complex one. As mentioned earlier, it derives from the work of Donald Schön, an American engineer who was bold enough to write about the gap between theory and practice and posit that this gap came about because the theory taught in universities was perhaps out of touch with the changing demands of professional practice. He contends that professionals do in fact create theories when they practise, but that these theories may often only be implicit and may remain embedded in what people do, rather than be openly articulated. This difference between 'espoused' and 'enacted' theory, for Schön, lies at the heart of the gap between 'theory' and 'practice': that is, theory is what is often espoused, but practice incorporates the theory we really believe (as evidenced by what we do). This led him to posit that a process of reflecting on the assumptions underlying practice (or the theory implicit in our actions) would allow practitioners to unearth their 'enacted' theory and bring it more into line with their desired or 'espoused' theory. Reflective practice was thus the ability to reflect on embedded assumptions in practice, and to improve practice by making it more congruent with the beliefs or thinking which the practitioner held to be right or desirable. A major contribution of Schön's work therefore has been to remind us that our deeper underlying assumptions, of which we may be largely unaware, are highly influential, and therefore in order to improve what we do, we need to unearth and examine them.

Reflective practice, in this sense, is a term and concept related to the education of practising professionals and has become a byword in their fields. Ultimately, however, it is limited to its application in practice within professional fields, and can be criticised for these limitations, especially since it may not necessarily lead to fundamental changes, and can remain relatively superficial. Nonetheless, researchers are also professionals who practise research, and a reflective practice approach, whereby researchers unearth assumptions they make about research practice, can be very effective in contributing towards improved research practice.

'Reflection', on the other hand, is not limited to the education of practising professionals, but, as mentioned earlier, goes back to Socratic times, and is written about in many of the non-professionally oriented disciplines including philosophy and theology. Reflection in a broad sense relates to how we live our lives as human beings and is seen to be a characteristic or ability required for 'human flourishing' (Ghaye, 2010). This cuts to the chase about what it means to be human. Of course you can now start to see why philosophers and theologians might be interested in reflection, and also why it might be difficult to pinpoint what reflection is, how it happens, and what its outcomes are supposed to be.

Educationalists, especially adult educationalists, have written extensively about reflection (e.g. Boud et al., 1985; Brookfield, 1995; Moon, 1999; 2004). As mentioned above, reflection is often defined according to Dewey's definition as 'learning from experience'. Many authors tend to include the idea that learning includes the reformulation of guidelines for practice or living (e.g. Boud et al., 1985). In this sense, reflection can be seen as a broader activity than reflective practice. Reflective practice may be limited to improved professional practice, but reflection should help develop guiding principles for life (which would of course encompass professional practice). Reflection should touch on deeper values which of course guide professional practice, but also have implications for daily living.

What then is *critical* reflection? In the most basic meanings, there are two ways of understanding the critical aspect of reflection. Firstly, reflection can be critical because it cuts to a significant depth, enabling a fundamental change of thinking or behaviour. In some ways it might be argued that all effective reflection is critical, if it allows us to reformulate our general principles for living. Mezirow's *transformational learning* (2000) relies on this very fundamental reflection, in which very deep assumptions are examined and changed, leading to 'transformational' changes in actions.

Secondly, though, reflection is also 'critical' when a critical theory perspective is applied, making a connection between the ideas unearthed through reflection, and how these ideas have a role in creating power. An understanding of how and why ideas are created, and the social and power functions ideas perform (whether or not the people who hold them are aware of them), is therefore integral to this understanding of critical reflection. (For further elaboration, see Brookfield, 1995.) This perspective on critical reflection is related to concepts of consciousness-raising (Hart, 1990) in which people become aware of the political functions of the beliefs they hold. This is the first step in becoming aware that not all beliefs are inherently true or false, but that there may be other psychological, social or political reasons for believing in their truth or falsity. This of course is a step along the way to being able to question and change beliefs (and behaviour based on them). This aspect of the 'critical' in critical reflection reminds us that there are strong theoretical and sociological analyses which underpin some concepts of reflection. In this sense, it is important to recognise and understand what types of theoretical frameworks underpin your approach to reflection. The work of Foucault and other deconstructionists is an example of one of the major ways of theorising the relationship between knowledge creation and power as an underpinning of critical reflection (e.g. Fook, 2016; Morley, 2014).

Where does the concept of 'reflexivity' fit? Unlike the ideas of reflective practice and critical/reflection, the idea of reflexivity seems to have originated from the social sciences, and was written about especially in relation to research. It is particularly relevant in disciplines like anthropology, where it is crucial that researching anthropologists do not make ethnocentric interpretations of the cultures they are studying. This is vital if little is known about the culture under study.

Reflexivity, in simple terms, refers to 'turning inwards' (Steier, 1991) and is often likened to 'looking in the mirror'. In practical terms it means the ability to factor in the influence of oneself into what one sees, and the interpretations one makes of one's world (Fook, 1999). On the face of it, this might appear to be a relatively simple concept. However, when we factor in *all* aspects of ourselves – who we are physically, psychologically and socially (including influences of gender and sexuality) – as well as the numerous contexts which influence who we are (historical, cultural, geographic, political, economic), being reflexive becomes a quite complex matter. There are of course many different and more complex ways of understanding reflexivity (Alvesson and Skoldberg, 2009: 8), especially from the perspective of sociological research, which I will not go into here. Suffice to say that in essence it refers to the ability to analyse and understand one's world (and therefore research it) recognising the particular lenses and influences which one brings to it by virtue of who we are as human beings in the social context. This means that being able to recognise the influence of contexts (and changing contexts as well of course) is an important aspect of being reflexive.

Reflexivity, however, as a concept has been transferred to other disciplines, and is a term often used roughly synonymously with 'reflectivity' (Fook, 1999). The original emphasis on research draws attention to the knowledge-making process, and therefore the role of self, especially in determining what knowledge is privileged and how it is interpreted. This then means that everything about us as researchers – our blind spots, our decisions, our biases, our methods, the way participants respond to us, our reactions within our own contexts – becomes a crucial aspect of the research process, and unavoidably frames how our research is conducted. With this in mind, it is easy to see the parallels with reflection, which focuses on the deeper assumptions we make, of which we are largely unaware. The concept of reflexivity allows us to see, with much more complexity, the types of assumptions we make which emanate from who we are as individuals and social beings within particular contexts. Reflexivity can also be critical when the critical perspective, as discussed above, is applied. That is, if an analysis of how our own selves and the knowledge we create is linked to an understanding of how power operates in society, then the reflexivity is critical.

REFLECTION AND REFLEXIVITY

How do the two concepts of reflection and reflexivity integrate in relation to research?

From the above discussion you will have seen how both reflection and reflexivity are useful ideas in how we understand knowledge-making, perhaps coming at it from different angles. Reflection on our own experience is a form of learning from experience in order to formulate new principles. Reflexivity involves a reflection on ourselves and our experience in order to articulate and understand how we influence the knowledge we create. In the process of reflection, the emphasis is perhaps on how the in-depth learning about oneself translates into better ways of living. With a process of reflexivity, the emphasis is perhaps more on how knowledge of oneself translates into better research. Both involve similar processes and commitments, if perhaps theorised differently. I would argue that both processes can be transferred between contexts. A commitment to reflecting on research practice can use an understanding of reflexivity to enhance practice by developing better guidelines for research practice. A commitment to being reflexive in research can generalise to better practice in all relations where knowledge creation is a key component of interactions. Neither approach nor concept is mutually exclusive.

There is a great deal of literature on the use of reflexivity in qualitative research in particular (e.g. Newton et al., 2011; Day, 2012). Some authors argue that reflexivity is absolutely essential to qualitative research, especially in experiential research (Shaw, 2010). However, it is vital in all qualitative research, given the need for a degree of researcher subjectivity in interpreting findings.

In reviewing the different meanings of reflection and related concepts, I have come to develop a more integrated understanding, which I outline below.

AN INTEGRATED UNDERSTANDING AND PRACTICAL MODEL OF CRITICAL REFLECTION

I now define reflection as: initiated by a process of unearthing and examining deeply held assumptions embedded in experience, in order to redevelop the meaning of this experience and reformulate new guiding principles (more congruent with fundamental values) for practice. This in turn should enable a more ethical and compassionate engagement with the social world.

This definition combines all the elements we have discussed above, but the specifics of what the practice of reflection looks like will differ according to the theoretical framework used (Fook et al., 2016). Also, I should reiterate that not all reflection will necessarily focus on developing a 'more ethical and compassionate engagement with the world'. The focus might be restricted to whatever the particular purpose at hand is. In a research context, for example, the focus might vary between ensuring that the method/design is congruent with the deeper purpose of the research. Or the focus might be on ensuring that research participants are treated ethically. In this model I utilise all the concepts outlined above: namely, an understanding and process of reflective practice; a concept of reflexivity; a postmodern approach to knowledge-making; and a critical perspective on power and its operation. Lately I have also introduced notions of spirituality (Gardner, 2011; Fook, 2017), to acknowledge the broader meaning-making and aspirations towards 'human flourishing' aspects of reflection.

What is difficult with critical reflection is to translate these many diverse and broad aspirations into a practical model with which most of us can readily engage in our day-to-day work as professionals and researchers. Below I outline a practical model which I have developed over several years and which integrates the elements discussed above. I designed the model so that it can be modified for different situations (Fook, 2002; Fook and Gardner, 2007; 2013; Fook et al., 2016). In this chapter I have focused on practical examples from research settings, but the process was originally designed for learning across a whole range of different professions and practices.

The process is conducted in two stages and is based on using critical incidents (an example of a significant experience that the reflecting person wants to learn from). The first stage focuses on unearthing deep assumptions so that the person can examine them. The second stage focuses on making new meaning and guidelines from the learning which results from unearthing and examining these assumptions. This is all done within an ethical learning climate, that is a safe and non-judgemental environment, designed to support vulnerability and to encourage openness and readiness for self-examination. Critical reflection can be conducted in small groups, in one-to-one interaction, or as self-reflection. The main principles should be followed in all instances. I have used research examples below, but the questions can be asked/modified for other settings.

In stage 1, after the person presents their critical incident, reflective questions are used to help unearth assumptions that are implicit in it. These questions are formulated from different theoretical frameworks: *I wonder what you were assuming about other people; what were you assuming about your own responsibility or the responsibility of other researchers/managers; what are you assuming that interviewees will feel able to tell you?* (reflective practice framework). *What are you assuming about how the research participants will see you?* (reflexivity question). *How do you think research participants will see your power as the researcher?* (critical reflection and reflexivity question). *What is it about you that led you to make that interpretation?* (reflexivity and postmodern question).

The aim of the questions at this stage is to open up thinking and to help delve into what is behind the thinking, especially ideas or beliefs about which the person is relatively unaware. Questions can be asked of the person reflecting (by other people in the group if a small group, or by a partner if in a one-to-one situation), or by the person themselves (to themselves if self-reflection). At the end of stage 1, the person should be able to identify some assumptions that they were not aware of before, and that they want to consider further.

In stage 2 (which should be conducted after a break of at least a day or so), the person focuses on their further reflections (i.e. what they think some of their underlying assumptions were); how they want to change what they think and what they do; and how they would label their new approach to practice. Questions at this stage are still reflective, but aimed at helping the person to recreate their thinking/practice on the basis of their reflections. The focus is not on having the answers, but on a process of crafting new ideas and actions. Labelling a new approach is an important aspect of developing new guidelines for action.

AN EXAMPLE

I have constructed a hypothetical example of a critical reflection on research practice below, to help illustrate the process.

THE CRITICAL INCIDENT

This is from Syra, a researcher who specialises in researching professional practice. In Syra's words:

> This happened to me a few years back. I was invited to submit an application in response to a call for a small amount of funding to conduct some practice research for a government organization. I was aware that there was another researcher, Steve, who was interested in securing the funding from this call. I contacted Steve to see if there was a way we could work together as partners to secure the funding, perhaps to submit a joint proposal. I thought that Steve agreed to this. Steve worked on the proposal and subsequently contacted me to invite me to act as a research assistant for him, and to be employed by him using only a small proportion of the funding. I did not see this as a partnership and expressed my dismay to Steve, and did not agree to this arrangement. I ended up not applying for the funding at all, but Steve was successful and went ahead without my involvement.

Stage 1 reflections for Syra

> I asked a couple of research colleagues if they would help me reflect on what this experience meant to me, and what assumptions I thought I was making. They asked questions like: 'What was I assuming about partnerships?'; 'How

did I view competition?'; 'Why did I not go ahead and make an application in my own right and what was my thinking behind this?' These questions made me think about how I viewed partnerships as involving equal partners (and of course I assumed that Steve thought the same, which is why I was affronted at his actions). I realized that I did not enjoy competition, and that I felt resentful towards people who were competitive. This led me to not attempt to apply for the funding myself (which would have meant, in my thinking, that I was being competitive). My reflections on these questions led me to think more about competition, what I did not like about competition, and wonder how I could work effectively when many work situations involved competition, especially for research funding. It also made me realize that not everyone valued partnerships, and that if I was going to seek partnerships, I probably needed to be much clearer with potential partners about what this meant to them, as I could not assume everyone else thought the same as me. I also wondered, from a *critical* reflection point of view, how I viewed power in relation to partnerships. I realized that I was not comfortable with the exercise of power, and often saw 'power' as a threatening thing, which is why the idea of equality appealed to me. I seemed to have belief that 'equality' meant that power would not be exercised between partners. In a way it became clearer to me that my assumptions about, and value on partnership, were also a way of being 'safer' in relation to power, and also in relation to competition.

Stage 2 reflections for Syra

Going into stage 2 reflections, I was able to be clearer with myself that the main issue for me was how to work with competition, and power, in a way which felt safer for me. I realized I could not avoid power or competition, as these were part of the workplace which I did not feel I could change. So I needed to change my thinking about power and competition (and how I could change what I did about competition). I thought more about power and competition in relation to research. I wondered which bits I was scared of, and which bits were OK. I think that perhaps I was scared of failing at competition, and also of other people (and myself) being treated unfairly. Yet in saying this I had to recognize that there might be ways of conducting competition fairly. I started to realize that perhaps not all power (or even competition) were bad things. For instance, competition in relation to Steve might not have been a bad thing. He had already shown that he was competitive, so it might have been a bad thing (from his point of view) for me to compete against him. Therefore there was no good reason for me *not* to submit my own application. Also competition might have been a good thing if it gave the funding body some choice about the type of research which they were going to fund. Perhaps I had a problem with exercising my *own* power, and this was perhaps something I needed to reflect more on. So at the end of my stage 2 reflections

I labelled my new understanding or approach as something to do with 'being comfortable with using power and competition in good ways'. This effectively gave me a new principle to guide my further thinking and actions in relation to partnerships in research.

This example illustrates how critical reflection, using questions and an atmosphere aimed at unearthing and examining deep assumptions in a non-judgemental way, can lead to a different approach with new possibilities for action. You can also see from this example how the new principle that Syra devised need not be confined to research practice, but might transfer further to other aspects of professional practice and the way she lives her life. In this sense, Syra has successfully made new meaning from her experience and remade new guidelines for practice.

Activity

Now take an incident from your own practice (preferably one which involves research practice).

Make your initial stage 1 reflection (to unearth underlying assumptions) and then move on to stage 2 reflection (to make new meaning of the experience).

REFLECTION AND PRACTICE-BASED RESEARCH

Why is reflection important to practice-based research? I have often argued that we need more research which focuses directly on practice and/or which emanates directly from the concerns of practice (Fook, 2004). A major problem with researching practice is that the concerns of practice exist in a very different social world than that of research, so it is often problematic to conceive of practice in such a way that makes it readily researchable (in researcher terms). Indeed it was Schön who talked about the 'messy lowlands' of practice (1983), whereas it was Einstein who pithily observed that much research is like 'looking for the thinnest part of the board and drilling as many holes as possible in it' (Einstein in Frank, 1949). I believe a helpful way to address this problem is to conceptualise practice as similar to experience, that is as holistic, encapsulating emotions, ideas, materiality and actions, and making an integrated meaning of these. Conceptualising experience in this way ensures that we do not fragment the practice experience – for instance, just focusing on actions would be only one aspect of practice and might not be meaningful without an understanding of the thinking or emotions involved. Often I suspect we can unwittingly distort our understanding of practice by focusing on specific aspects perhaps taken out of context. Experience is initially sensed, and includes actions as well as feelings, which are interpreted or made meaning of through the use of social or cultural ways of thinking. So while it might be initially sensed on a personal or individual basis, it is interpreted with recourse to social contexts. It is both personal and social.

If, therefore, we understand reflection to be 'learning from experience', then it can also be a form of learning from practice. And, of course, if we understand learning to be similar to research, in that it involves the making of new knowledge, then reflection can also be a form of researching practice.

On another level, drawing similarities between practice and experience also draws attention to the subjective element of both, and the capacity for the meaning of both to be constantly remade in different contexts (historical, social and cultural). Reflection, as we have discussed, is a process which can help articulate and enhance this meaning-making aspect of practice. I would argue that it is the meaning-making aspect of practice which in some ways integrates our understanding of practice by including all the elements of practice – the emotional and intellectual sides, the action aspects – into a holistic composite. This perhaps best captures the complexity of the practice experience. If you refer back to Syra's example, you can see how critical reflection on her critical incident helped illuminate the reasons behind her approach to Steve, and also the emotional aspects of her reasoning in not pursuing her own funding application. Combining an understanding of these different elements helped Syra see how she might be able to find a new way of working with competition. She was able to acknowledge possible contradictions and also find a way of working with them. Using a form of critical reflection in research can then be a useful way of recognising the contradictions and complexities of practice.

If we conceptualise reflection as a form of practice-based research then the sorts of research questions which would be addressed would focus on issues like the following: *What constitutes professional practice (in this field)? How is professional knowledge developed through practice? What professional knowledge is developed through practice? How do different elements of experience (emotions, past experience, values, interpretations) work together to form professional practice?* While these may appear overly broad and too difficult to research, I would argue that these in some ways are the very issues which often go begging in research, because they are seen as just that. Consequently we know too little about the complexities of practice, and how different influences work together, and tend to confine our study of practice in ways which fragment it.

DIFFERENT WAYS IN WHICH REFLECTION CAN BE USED IN RESEARCH

There are four main ways in which reflection can contribute to research.

- Reflection as an approach to research.
- Reflection as an aspect of research.

- Reflection as research design.
- Reflection as research method.

REFLECTION AS AN APPROACH TO RESEARCH

What a reflective approach is and how it influences the way research is undertaken. I would argue that a reflective approach should always underpin any research, no matter what final design or approach is decided upon. For example, even if a randomised control trial is proposed, researchers should still reflect beforehand on why such a design has been chosen. A reflective approach, therefore, does not mean that the design of the research needs to be reflective. Based on our previous discussion, a reflective approach to research might involve ensuring that the research project is planned and conceptualised in a reflective way. This would mean that the reasons for the research, the topic and problem focus, the terminologies, design and methods used, are reflected upon beforehand with awareness of different possible perspectives (and the reasons for the choices made about these); an awareness of contextual and subjective factors which might influence the choices; and an appropriate justification of the choices made. Examples of reflective questions which might help in this approach are: *Whose interests are being served by conceptualising the topic in this way? What are possible other terms which could be used and why have I chosen the ones I have? What personal experiences do I bring to this research and how have I used these in my approach and design? How might the method of data collection I have chosen influence the type of data I will be able to collect?*

REFLECTION AS AN ASPECT OF RESEARCH

How reflection can be incorporated as a stage in the research process, or an aspect which augments the research in some way. This focus might be taken if you decide that your research should be undertaken in a particular way which is not necessarily reflective, but which might benefit from an additional reflective dimension. For example, action research designs can incorporate a reflective stage which can contribute to the design of subsequent stages of the research (Burns, 2007). An example of this might be with participatory action research, where a reflective focus group is held with all researchers and participants involved during the project, and it is decided to change direction in the project.

Another example might be to build in a reflexive element, by using researchers who deliberately analyse research findings from different perspectives, in order to ensure that a range of viewpoints has been incorporated. An example of this might be to ensure that research assistants are employed who come from a variety of backgrounds, or that the research team incorporates people who are known to take different perspectives. Keeping a diary of course is a common device used, so that there is a record of the thinking and experiences which influenced the researcher's decisions during the course of the research project. This sort of diary record can prove invaluable in providing an overview of the process of research and the influence of the 'human element'. Entries from a diary might also be used as another form of data: that which records the 'back story' of the research. In this way a diary might provide further contextual information which can illuminate the researcher's interpretations.

REFLECTION AS RESEARCH DESIGN

How reflection can influence the entire design of a research project, from choice of topic to overall design, data collection and analysis of results and dissemination. In this approach, the underlying principle is to show how a reflective process influences each aspect of decision making about the research project. This in particular would make clear how the research question is best addressed through the use of a reflective approach. An example of this might be a heuristic approach (Moustakas, 1990) in which the research topic and question themselves emanate from the researcher's personal experience, and in turn this experience is used to elicit research data and also to interpret it. Using personal experience as a prism through which to understand other people's experience is a well-known approach in anthropological circles, and can be a valuable way of avoiding making ethno- or egocentric judgements about other peoples' experiences, cultures or actions.

REFLECTION AS RESEARCH METHOD

Elsewhere I have written about how the use of the critical reflection process I outlined earlier might be used as a method of data collection (Fook, 2011). The data collected would consist of the knowledge or assumptions underpinning practice and the changes made to this knowledge through the critical reflection process. There are quite a few other research methods which are similar to a critical reflection process and which are theorised from slightly different angles. These include: some autobiographical methods (e.g. auto ethnography (Davis and Ellis, 2008)); collective biographical methods (Davies and Gannon, 2006); memory work (Haug et al., 1987); and discourse analysis (Alvesson and Skoldberg, 2009). There are clear advantages in using reflection as a method of data collection which I will discuss in the following section.

ISSUES FOR FURTHER DISCUSSION
IS REFLECTION A METHOD ITSELF OR JUST AN 'ADD-ON'?

This question has partly been answered in the foregoing section. Reflection can be used as a method or even overall design or as an 'add-on' to provide an extra dimension to the research which might not be strictly necessary in order to answer the overriding research question. The main thing is to be clear about exactly how it is being used and why.

An example, as mentioned earlier, might be when it is used within an action research design, as a stage which ensures that maximum learning is taken from the experience with the research project to date. Sometimes a reflection stage can be included at the end of a research project, as a way of helping to sum up the broader implications of the research, but also as a way of thinking through systematically how the research might have been done differently, or even improved upon. It is especially helpful to include such a stage to identify any unintended consequences of the project and how these might be learnt from or built upon. In this sense reflection might be seen as a stage of *learning from the experience of conducting the research*, and so there is no good reason why it should not be included in the final stages of any research project, no matter the original design. I think this is a particularly helpful strategy when conducting multi- or interdisciplinary research, or even mixed methods research, so that the meta-learning about how to incorporate and integrate different disciplinary perspectives, and the different data resulting from different methods, can be captured.

WHAT IS THE PROBLEM WITH *NOT* USING REFLECTION IN RESEARCH? IS IT OK *NOT* TO USE REFLECTION IN RESEARCH?

Of course there are many methods, designs and approaches which do not build in reflection and therefore are not dependent on its inclusion in order to arrive at robust findings. These might be research projects which are focused on answering very specific questions, particularly where there has been quite a bit of research conducted already. An example might be research designed to map out the scope or incidence of a particular problem, such as investigating whether placements in children's homes is on the increase. When, however, we introduce an element of investigating *why* a problem is increasing, or wish to understand differing perspectives in some depth and how they interplay, then it is likely that some reflection will assist in getting to the issues in more sophisticated ways.

However, I do think it is imperative that all researchers, no matter what their research topic or approach, are clear and convincing about the nature of what they are researching, their research questions and how their approach, design and methods allow them to answer their research questions adequately, and in a way which is appropriate to the nature of the research topic. I find too often that this is not always the case, because researchers often assume what is known already, or what other researchers will take for granted. I do think that some very focused critical reflection would often make these issues more obvious before commencing the project. There is no substitute for careful and thoughtful planning, and reflection should be built in as an integral part of the planning process. Constantly asking

- what the research is,
- why it is important,

- why it is important to me as a researcher,
- what I bring to it, and
- what I hope to contribute

are reflective questions in the sense that they help us to focus on the bigger (and also the underlying) picture about our research. We should never assume that our research is important just because I or other people think it is. Being able to answer why, and for many different reasons and from many different perspectives, will help keep the research focused on what is important, and how this can be communicated to different audiences with different interests. It will also ensure that the research includes different perspectives and help us to keep factoring in the influence of different contexts.

There are in fact several key ways in which using reflection can help address some of the limitations of conventional research. As Denzin and Lincoln (1994: 2) observe, '*objective reality can never be captured*' – any research can only ever capture a partial view. It is limited usually because of the dominance of one perspective and contentions as to validity and/or relevance (Fook, 2011). Using reflection can address some of these issues by making the research process more dialogic (created in interaction between different viewpoints); more 'valid' by integrating (not fragmenting) experience; and more relevant by focusing on relevant experience and the potential for remaking meaning.

CRITERIA FOR MAKING DECISIONS ABOUT HOW TO USE REFLECTION IN RESEARCH

I have argued that some form of critical reflection is important for all forms of research, as part of the planning phase, and also as part of the concluding phase. However, what other criteria help guide us in making decisions about whether to use specifically reflective methods or design? Below are some questions which will help in thinking these issues through:

- How important are my own experience and perspective in this research? How might they affect the way I interpret the findings and their implications?
- Can I bring something unique, new or original to the research, which is potentially significant in this topic area because of my own experience, or who I am?
- Can using reflective methods or an approach elicit findings about people's experiences which might not be brought out in any other way?
- Is it likely that there might be severe 'blind spots' in my approach to the key points of the research? Might I have unconscious biases because of who I am,

which I either need to safeguard against, or can use to advantage in doing the research?

- Is there a danger that so much research has been done in the area that we have a taken-for-granted orthodoxy in relation to the topic area, the conception of the research problem, the appropriate design/methodology or theoretical framework? Do we need a completely fresh approach which turns others on their heads?
- Is there a fashion or trend, or a 'flavour of the month' approach which needs to be questioned?
- Is it possible that using some reflective methods might add significantly different perspectives from what I might expect to obtain, or from what I imagine my findings might be? Am I going to move into some relatively unknown territory which I need to understand in new and unforeseen ways?
- How important is the complex and holistic understanding of participants' experiences?

Key Points

- Reflection and reflexivity are integral to research.
- Refection on our own experience is a form of learning from experience in order to formulate new principles.
- Reflexivity involves a reflection on ourselves and our experience in order to articulate and understand how we influence the knowledge we create.
- An integrated definition is: initiated by a process of unearthing and examining deeply held assumptions embedded in experience, in order to redevelop the meaning of this experience and reformulate new guiding principles (more congruent with fundamental values) for practice. This in turn should enable a more ethical and compassionate engagement with the social world.
- There are four main ways in which reflection can be used in research: reflection as an approach to research; reflection as an aspect of research; reflection as research design; and reflection as research method.

ANNOTATED BIBLIOGRAPHY

Fook, J. (2011). Developing critical reflection as a research method. In J. Higgs, A. Titchen, D. Horsfall & D. Bridges (eds) *Creative Spaces for Qualitative Researching* (pp. 55–64). Rotterdam: Sense Publishers.

A helpful overview of critical reflection and argument for its use as a research method (data collection tool). It makes an argument for how a critically reflective research tool might overcome some of the limitations of other methods.

Fook, J., Collington, V., Ross, F., Ruch, G., & West, L. (eds) (2016). *Researching Critical Reflection: Multidisciplinary Perspectives*. London: Routledge.

This book is an edited volume which attempts to provide a framework for researching critical reflection. This includes an overview of different perspectives, some of the issues involved in researching it, and what is needed as a way forward.

Morley, C. (2014). *Practising Critical Reflection to Develop Emancipatory Change*. Farnham: Ashgate.

This book details a research study using a critically reflective method. It is extremely useful for illustrating how critical reflection can be used to conduct research, but also how it also functions to allow transformative change.

REFERENCES

Agger, B. (1998). *Critical Social Theories*. Oxford: Westview Press.

Alvesson, M., & Skoldberg, K. (2009). *Reflexive Methodology*. London: Sage.

Boud, D., Keogh, R., & Walker, D. (1985). *Reflection: Turning Experience into Learning*. London: Kogan Page.

Brookfield, S. (1995). *Becoming a Critically Reflective Teacher*. San Francisco: Jossey-Bass.

Brookfield, S. (2005). *The Power of Critical Theory*. San Francisco: Jossey-Bass.

Burns, D. (2007). *Systematic Action Research*. Bristol: Policy Press.

Collington, V., & Ross, F. (2016). Researching critical reflection in health care: current issues and new directions. In J. Fook, V. Collington, F. Ross, G. Ruch & L. West (eds) *Researching Critical Reflection: Multidisciplinary Perspectives* (pp. 158–70). London: Routledge.

Davies, B., & Gannon, S. (eds) (2006). *Doing Collective Biography*. Maidenhead: Open University Press.

Davis, C. S., & Ellis, C. (2008). Emergent methods in auto ethnographic research. In S. Nagy Hesse-Biber & P. Leavy (eds) *Handbook of Emergent Methods* (pp. 283–302). New York: Guilford Press.

Day, S. (2012). A reflexive lens: exploring dilemmas of qualitative methodology through the concept of reflexivity. *Qualitative Sociology Review*, VIII(1), 62–85.

Denzin, N. K., & Lincoln, Y. S (eds) (1994). *Handbook of Qualitative Research*. London: Sage.

Dewey, J. (1933). *How We Think A Restatement of the Relation of Reflective Thinking to the Educative Process*. Boston, MA: D.C. Heath & Co Publishers.

Einstein, A. quoted in Frank, P (1949). Einstein's Philosophy of Science. *Reviews of Modern Physics*, 21(3).

Fook, J. (1999) Reflexivity as Method. *Annual Review of Health Social Sciences*, (9)1, pp. 11–20.

Fook, J. (2002). *Social Work: Critical Theory and Practice*. London: Sage.

Fook, J. (2004). What professionals need from research. In D. Smith (ed.) *Evidence-based Practice* (pp. 29–46). London: Jessica Kingsley.

Fook, J. (2011). Developing critical reflection as a research method. In J. Higgs, A. Titchen, D. Horsfall & D. Bridges (eds) *Creative Spaces for Qualitative Researching* (pp. 55–64). Rotterdam: Sense Publishers.

Fook, J. (2016). *Social Work: A Critical Approach to Practice*, 3rd edn. London: Sage.

Fook, J. (2017). Finding fundamental meaning through critical reflection. In L. Beres (ed.) *Practising Spirituality* (pp. 17–28). Basingstoke: Palgrave.

Fook, J., & Gardner, F. (2007). *Practising Critical Reflection: A Resource Handbook*. Maidenhead: Open University Press.

Fook, J., & Gardner, F. (eds) (2013). *Critical Reflection in Context: Applications in Health and Social Care*. Oxford: Routledge.

Fook, J., White, S., & Gardner, F. (2006). Critical reflection: a review of current understandings and literature. In S. White, J. Fook & F. Gardner (eds) *Critical Reflection in Health and Care* (pp. 3–20). Maidenhead: Open University Press.

Fook, J., Collington, V., Ross, F., Ruch, G., & West, L. (eds) (2016). *Researching Critical Reflection: Multidisciplinary Perspectives*. London: Routledge.

Foucault, M. (1972). *The Archaeology of Knowledge*. London: Tavistock.

Gardner, F. (2011). *Critical Spirituality*. Farnham: Ashgate.

Ghaye, T. (2010). In what ways can reflective practices enhance human flourishing? *Reflective Practice, 11*(1), 1–7.

Hart, M. U. (1990). Liberation through consciousness-raising. In J. Mezirow et al. (eds) *Fostering Critical Reflection through Adulthood* (pp. 47–73). San Francisco: Jossey-Bass.

Haug, F., Andresen, S., Bünz-Elfferding, A., Hauser, K., Lang, U., Laudan, M., Thomas, C. (1987). *Female Sexualization: A Collective Work of Memory*. (E. Carter, Trans.). London:Verso.

Hunt, C. (2016). Spiritual creatures? Exploring an interface between critical reflective practice and spirituality. In J. Fook, V. Collington, F. Ross, G. Ruch & L. West (eds) *Researching Critical Reflection: Multidisciplinary Perspectives* (pp. 34–47). London: Routledge.

Mezirow, J. (2000). *Learning as Transformation: Critical Perspectives on a Theory in Progress*. San Francisco: Jossey Bass.

Moon, J. (1999). *Reflection in Learning and Professional Development*. Abingdon: Routledge/ Falmer.

Moon, J. (2004). *A Handbook of Reflective and Experiential Learning*. Abingdon: Routledge/ Falmer.

Morley, C. (2014). *Practising Critical Reflection to Develop Emancipatory Change*. Farnham: Ashgate.

Moustakas, C. (1990). *Heuristic Research Design, Methodology and Applications*. Newbury Park, CA: Sage.

Newton, B. J., Rothlingova, Z., Gutteridge, R., LeMarch, K., & Raphael, J. H. (2011). No room for reflexivity? Critical reflections following a systematic review of qualitative research. *Journal of Health Psychology, 17*(6). DOI: 10.1177/1359105311427615.

Nussbaum, M. (1997). *Cultivating Humanity: A Classic Defense of Reform in Liberal Education*. Cambridge, MA: Harvard University Press.

Pellicer, L. O. (2008). *Caring Enough to Lead: How Reflective Practice Leads to Moral Leadership*. Thousand Oaks, CA: Corwin Press.

Purvis, D., & Hunt, A. (1993). Discourse, ideology, discourse, ideology, discourse, ideology.... *British Journal of Sociology, 44*(3), 473–99.

Schön, D. (1983). *The Reflective Practitioner*. London: Temple Smith.

Shaw, R. L. (2010). Embedding reflexivity within experiential qualitative psychology. *Qualitative Research in Psychology, 7*(3), 233–43.

Steier, F. (1991). *Research and Reflexivity*. London: Sage.

5

ETHICS

John Fulton and Carol Costley

INTRODUCTION

In any research study ethics is an important consideration, not only in terms of study design, but as an area that should be considered throughout the study. Ethics is not an exact science; rather, it is a conscious mindset as opposed to a strict procedure that one follows legalistically. Additionally, in practitioner research, there are very specific issues that can arise when carrying out research in the context of the workplace. This chapter aims to explore ethical issues in research by examining the general procedural principles, and then considering the challenges of micro ethics in these contexts.

Ethics committees have a responsibility to ensure that research undertaken is methodologically robust and due attention has been paid to potential ethical issues that may arise during the course of its execution. The committees also ensure that those undertaking research are suitably qualified, credible and skilled in the data collection approaches they undertake. The Economic and

Social Research Council (ESRC, 2018) outlines some of the key principles of research ethics, details of which are included in the box below. When planning research, detailed consideration should be paid to these issues, and it is imperative that the research project receives the necessary approval from the relevant ethics committee.

Economic and Social Research Council

- Research should aim to maximise the benefit for individuals and society and minimise risk and harm.
- The rights and dignity of individuals and groups should be respected at all times.
- Wherever possible, participation should be voluntary, consensual, and appropriately informed.
- Research should be conducted with integrity and transparency.
- Lines of responsibility and accountability should be clearly defined.

The independence of research should be maintained and where evident conflicts of interest cannot be changed they should be made explicit.

A BRIEF HISTORY OF ETHICS AND PHILOSOPHICAL PRINCIPLES

The traditional starting point for consideration of the issues concerning research governance occurred after the Second World War. People were justifiably appalled by the unethical practices that took place in concentration camps under the guise of medical research. The Nuremberg Trials gave rise to the Nuremberg Code, which outlines the principles on which research should be based. This was the starting point for the key discussions that led to the Helsinki Declaration, which governs research ethics. In the 1960s, in social sciences, a number of studies took place that raised specific ethical issues. This brought about an even greater degree of awareness of ethical issues: attention was focused on the subject of the research and, to a large degree, many of the principles of bioethics were carried over into other fields of research investigation.

Currently, most, if not all, institutions and organisations involved in research have formal ethics committees and/or have general ethical principles in place that govern and make institutions accountable for their research activities. Additionally, many professional bodies have clear guidelines for research, especially that which is most relevant to their particular professional field. BERA (British Educational Research Association) and BPS (British Psychological Association), for example, have precise guidelines. When planning research, it is useful to access relevant guidelines. Most countries have organisations that produce similar guidelines. A compelling issue is the difference between procedural and micro ethics. This division is considered by Guillemin and Gillam (2004), where they outline the differences between ethics as a procedure in which certain requirements must be met, as well as ethical sensitivity, which should be considered throughout research studies. In Kate Maguire's following chapter this is expressed as personal and professional integrity whereby for professional doctorates, in particular where the researcher is closely connected with the context of the research, there is an imperative of trust for the researcher to act continually with integrity for the duration of the research that may be in a familiar context. Many of the ideas and underlying philosophies in research ethics arise from the discipline of medicine and the exploration of medical ethics, where the key principles are noted as: beneficence, respect for autonomy, justice, and non-maleficence.

Through the principle of beneficence, we have an obligation to do good, and our actions ought to be reflective of this. Our actions should also be concerned with the good of other people. In research terms, this means that the underlying reason for doing research is essentially altruistic, and that in some way all research undertaken should benefit other people, regardless of study type or size. An additional factor is that researchers should take proactive and positive steps to prevent causing harm to others during the research process.

The second principle, the respect for autonomy, means that we should respect the rights of other people and their right to make autonomous and informed decisions. In other words, we should respect the dignity of others. The British Medical Association (BMA, 2016) states that it is the right of people to make informed choices about their own care. In research terms, this means in practice that people can have the right to refuse. It also means that, in practice, when asking people to participate in research, it must be ensured that they have sufficient information according to which they can make an informed choice about their participation or the continuation of it. An important issue here is that we should not be overtly coercive, either by putting moral pressure on people, or by providing excessive rewards for their participation.

It also raises issues for vulnerable groups of people and their right to have information provided to them in a form that is readily accessible; for example, when researching children, information must be presented in a form that a child can understand, thus enabling them to make an informed choice. It also raises issues about groups of people or people in institutions, and about making collective decisions.

The principle of justice means we should always treat people fairly and impartially, and this also applies to those which can be defined as 'vulnerable groups', for whom making an informed decision may pose a challenge. An example of this is people with any degree of cognitive impairment, such as those living with acute psychosis. It is easy to identify target populations about whom one can undertake research (e.g. people in prison), and we must respect their rights. It also means that, for example, if one is undertaking research in another country or a poor area, the research should be of benefit to that specific population of people. This can be observed in medical research, where clinical trials might be carried out in one country and, when the drug becomes available, it cannot be afforded by the people of that country.

The principle of non-maleficence means we should do no harm to others, and avoid the risk of harm to those participating in research. This means that we should avoid physical harm to others, but also emotional or financial harm to those participating in a research study. While this may seem obvious, maleficence can often be much subtler, largely undetectable and in some instances a degree of harm cannot be avoided. For example, some medical research treatments, while beneficial, can also have side effects; in such cases, the benefits must outweigh the risks, and participants should be informed of this in advance of the study. Additionally, when researching emotionally sensitive issues, those being interviewed may find talking about and revisiting their experiences emotionally draining and upsetting. The participants should be aware of this before they consent to participate, and sources of additional support should be identified in particularly sensitive situations. In such research, the benefits should always outweigh the potential risks.

In practice, the ethical issues are not always obvious, and there are many subtleties involved. It is important to remember that ethics is not an exact science. There are many ambiguous areas, which is why we need ethics committees, where the research can be reviewed by an independent group of people and informed decisions can be made about the potential ethical impact of the research. There are also certain procedures that researchers are expected to follow when designing a research study. It is easy to view these measures as unnecessarily complex, but as Guillemin and Gillam (2004) point out, any research study is permeated with ethical dilemmas, and it is important to follow ethical principles throughout the study, and not to assume that once the requirements of the ethics committee have been met, the researcher is free to move forward without further consideration of ethical issues. The ethics committee can help set up a structure for the research, which will provide, throughout the study, a framework that will facilitate ongoing respect for participants, and ensure that ethical principles permeate the entirety of the research.

We have considered the underlying principles on which research can be based, and this can be translated into key and practical issues.

Activity

Take the four principles and state how, in designing your research study, these can be addressed:

- Principle of beneficence
- Principle of respect for autonomy
- Principle of justice
- Principle of non-maleficence.

Compare your answers to the table below.

Principle of beneficence	The basic reason for the research is for the good of other people
	The research study should also be well designed
	The researchers should be competent to carry out the study
Principle of respect for autonomy	Participation should be voluntary, and no coercive practices should be involved for convincing people to participate in the study
	People should be allowed the right not to participate in the study and the right to withdraw at any time
Principle of justice	Care should be taken in the case of vulnerable groups and where there is a gatekeeper or guardian, permission should also be obtained from this individual
	People should be sufficiently informed about the purpose of the research, and what the research will actually involve
Principle of non-maleficence	The risk of harm should be avoided or minimised
	Additionally, research data should be anonymised and participant confidentiality should be always maintained on the part of the researcher

TRANSLATING THE PRINCIPLES INTO THE RESEARCH DESIGN

The research approaches generally applied in practice-based research include questionnaires, interviews, focus groups, case studies, observational studies and ethnographic studies. Much of the information below is concerned with these methods. Ethical approval is essential, and the researcher must prepare an application to the relevant ethics committee. Often, if the research does not concern a sensitive issue or involve vulnerable groups, the process of approval can be expedited or, in some instances, approved by the researcher's supervisor. This must be discussed with the relevant supervisor, and the researcher will need to ensure that approval is not required from a relevant committee or agency external to the university.

These are methodological issues that researchers must consider regarding the research design and when applying for ethical approval. It is useful to review both the relevant professional body and its ethical guidelines. Universities have ethics committees, and prior to commencing the research, it is important that the researcher gains the necessary approval. It is also important that the researcher has ample time available, as this process can often take longer than anticipated. Depending on the groups being examined, ethical approval may be required from another organisation. For example, in England, when collecting data from National Health Service participants, the researcher will need approval from the NHS ethics committee. The researcher may also be governed by other legislation; for example, in the United Kingdom, adherence is required to the General Data

Protection Regulation (GDPR), or, if the research involves human tissue, adherence to the Human Tissue Act 2004. Other examples are that there are also likely to be protocols around research with children under a certain age and research with animals.

The research must be correctly designed and the information gathered should be for a specific and clearly identifiable purpose. If it involves the collection of sensitive information, this should be done for a specified reason, and should ultimately serve the greater good. It is also important that the person collecting the data should be competent at doing so, particularly when collecting data of a sensitive nature. For example, when exploring the experiences of racism among British Asian individuals, the topic served as an unpleasant memory that people may not have wished to revisit, but the process of doing so was aimed at gaining a greater understanding of the phenomenon, to indicate that it was an issue, and that it was something that most of the participants had experienced. Thus, the resultant benefits to the participants outweighed any potential disadvantages.

Participation should always be voluntary, and people should be sufficiently informed of the purpose of the research. This involves preparing an information sheet that clearly spells out exactly what the researcher will be doing, and the reasons why they are undertaking the research. Additionally, what is expected from the participants in terms of time commitment for participation should be stated. It is important that people feel free to decline participation at any stage of the research process. Often when carrying out research which involves colleagues, many might not want to say no, because of the existing relationship, so it is advisable to get someone else to make the request. Participants must sign a consent form, although in the case of a questionnaire, either paper based or online, the act of completing the questionnaire is taken to be consent. It should also be made clear that people can withdraw from the study at any time: that is, before, during and after the data collection processes. There will be a point, however, after the study has been completed and the data analysed or published, where it will no longer be possible to withdraw, and this should be made clear to the participants at the outset.

When considering vulnerable groups, which will include people with learning disabilities, elderly people in care situations, people who are ill, and children (below the age of 16), permission should be gained from a parent or guardian. It is also important to gain the consent of the individual who is taking part in the research, which requires putting the information in an accessible form.

An example of putting the information in an accessible form for a vulnerable group is from Anna's research study. Anna explored the experience of street children in Africa. She believed it was essential to gain an awareness of their experience, or, in other words, to tell their stories. Many of the children had poor literacy skills and, although she explained her research, she wanted to give them time to think about it. As such, she presented the research information on an information sheet in the form of a comic sheet. The children liked this very much, but, more importantly, fully understood their commitment to the research and its requirements.

Anonymity and confidentiality are central issues when conducting research. People often share information that they have not even shared with friends or family. At a more practical level, they may be sharing views about the workplace and do not want their family and friends to know this information. The researcher thus needs to ensure that participants cannot be identified. This requires some thought, and much depends on the data the researcher is collecting. If it is an interview or observation, the researcher will need to assign participants an identifier, but one that will ensure no one can work out who they are, thus retaining their anonymity. In questionnaires, participants are generally anonymous; however, biographic information can sometimes indicate who the respondent is if the researcher is not careful. If, for example, the researcher asks the participant to identify their ethnicity, and there are one or two Chinese people in the sample, they can potentially be identified. This highlights the need for always being aware of ethical issues.

In the United Kingdom, the Data Protection Act 2018 must be adhered to. Storage of data is important: data stored on a computer should be encrypted. Thus, should the laptop be lost, no one will be able to access the information. If the data is paper based, the information should be stored in a locked filing cabinet. The time the data will be stored for should also be stated and, once this period is complete, the data should be securely destroyed. While no one other than those involved in the research should have access to the data, the university may wish to audit the research process. All this information should be included on an information sheet sent to the participants and, where appropriate, also on the consent form.

Deceptive practices that contravene ethical principles nonetheless do occur in research studies.

Activity

Can you think of any situations where this might occur?

In psychological research, where, for example, an emotive subject such as prejudice is studied, if the researcher were to indicate the real purpose of the research, participants might deliberately skew their answers. Additionally, when examining large groups in a public setting, it will be difficult to gain permission from everyone. When carrying out a boxing study that involved attendance at more than 100 boxing matches, people were not informed of the presence of a researcher on any of these occasions. The organisers knew of the researcher's purpose, but it would have been impossible to gain permission from everyone involved. Care was taken to record general observations or comments, but when recording a specific situation, individual permissions were gained to include this information. Research conducted with particular groups, for example drug dealers, where the researcher might have been at significant personal risk if their identity were to be revealed, is another type of deceptive practice. However, the latter example is unlikely in practice-based research.

PRACTICE-BASED RESEARCH

When the researcher's self is part of the other's narrative, the narrative of the researcher and the researched become intertwined. The researcher is forced to look both outwards and inwards, to be reflective and self-conscious in terms of positioning (Taylor, 2011: 5).

The central issue is that the researcher is generally an insider in practice-based research, researching on their own, or working in collaboration with others to investigate and develop practice. In situations where individuals work as consultants to develop an organisation, a network of relationships is created, and the situation is no longer that of the outsider coming in to investigate. It is worth exploring exactly what this means. In the next chapter, Kate Maguire points out the value of consistently maintaining a strong ethical stance throughout the research process. The researcher should be aware of the often small and non-dramatic ethical issues that are present throughout the research process. Much of the literature relating to practice research considering ethics is taken from an action research perspective, or ethnographic studies. In this section (while drawing from these traditions), the general principles applicable to practice-based research will be reviewed.

An issue that requires some detailed consideration for practice-based researchers is that they should attempt to be consciously aware of their positional stance within the research process. Whereas there is no set position that should be taken, at times practice-based researchers may be entirely focused on their own practice, while, at others, the researcher is brought in as an expert in a particular situation, and often the research takes place somewhere between these two positions. This has been conceptualised as insider versus outsider research. When considering the researcher as a participant, much of the literature stems from an ethnographic, rather than a practice-based, position. This provides many useful and interesting insights. The key differences between insider and outsider research have been highlighted. Labaree (2002) provides a useful summary in which he states the advantages of being an insider as follows: shared experiences, greater access, the ease of interpretation of a particular culture, and the researcher having a deeper understanding of what is happening in practice. The disadvantages are described as greater possibilities for insider bias and not being able to maintain objectivity, whereas an outside researcher is more likely to question aspects of practice that may otherwise be taken for granted. The outsider–insider debate is not a binary outcome measure, but rather a continuum along which researchers can relatively position themselves. De Andrade (2000) points out that doing so requires continual reflection and negotiation.

A useful framework is that of Banks (1998), who provides a typology and the following model, in which he considers African Americans as a discrete group. This model can be applied to both practice-based research and the specific position in which researchers may find themselves.

Indigenous insider	An individual who works in the organisation and ascribes to its values, and is fully socialised within these values and practices
Indigenous outsider	Someone who works in the organisation but has been exposed to other influences and more diverse experiences, and can question what is happening and adopt a wider perspective. They can question the customs and practices that many take for granted
External insider	This category refers to people carrying out research who may not belong to the organisation in question, but nonetheless ascribe to the values of the organisation. They can identify with the people within the organisation and ascribe to the values and goals of the organisation
External outsider	This category refers to someone who is a true outsider and who only partially understands the organisation. During the course of the study, they have to learn a great deal about the organisation and much, if not all, of this information will be peculiar. The first task of the researcher will be to gain an understanding of the context of the organisation and make sense against this context

Researchers need to reflect continually on their position and, while researching, can change their position. Chavez (2008), using Banks' typology, presents it as researchers determining their position on an axis. Banks illustrates how researchers' positions can iteratively change during the study. For example, they might start the study as indigenous insiders and, as the study develops, begin to question the ethos of the organisation and become intentionally disengaged from its customs and practices. Alternatively, researchers might commence practice-based research as external outsiders and move to becoming external insiders. During the research study, they might move along the axis, from outsiders to insiders, as they gain deeper insights, or, as they gain deeper insight, they may find themselves becoming outsiders.

Practice-based research includes specific ethical issues, as the nature of the research and the position of the researcher may give rise to several multidimensional issues connected to the researcher's own practice and the researcher's position within that practice. As stated above, many of the procedures and processes in place for managing ethics arise from a biomedical perspective and, by implication, are focused on research doing something to, or considering, others (Taylor, 2011). Practice-based research has a strong focus on insider research and the active participation of others in the research process. Guillemin and Gillam (2004) differentiate between procedural and micro ethics. Procedural ethics is focused on what is required to receive ethical approval, whereas micro ethics constitutes the ethical stance or an awareness and consideration of ethical issues throughout the research process.

An underlying premise is not so much the individual working from within an objective framework, but rather ethical decision making as an iterative and continual process of reflection and consideration. In practice research, this often involves others. Chavez refers to this as knowing your own head. Earlier in this chapter, we considered the ethical principles that can guide us in our decision-making processes. Angrosino and Mays de Perez (2000), discussing observational research, suggest the following principles:

- That we know proper relations exist between a specific value and other elements of an act through experience.
- That we know proper relations exist through our own institutions, and that some acts are inherently disproportionate.
- That we intrinsically know through processes of trial and error (although this is not always acceptable).

These principles reflect the disposition of the individual and their professional practice. At this point, it is important to emphasise that many professions have a code of practice, and that this is something which should shape and guide our actions.

Gibbs et al. (2007) and Carr (1995) discuss Aristotle's ideas of *phronesis* and take this to mean working ethically and using ethical knowledge to shape and guide practice. 'Wilfred Carr describes phronesis as a comprehensive moral capacity which combines practical knowledge of the good with sound judgement about what, in a particular situation, would constitute an appropriate expression of this' (McLaughlin, 2017: 358).

Ethical decisions are made during the process of research, but often from the standpoint of an individual researcher's disposition. *Phronesis* can be defined as having a moral understanding from which we work, and the ability not only to make moral decisions, but to enact them. In research terms, this means to put into practice our ethical decisions and to do what we consider to be right. This is similar to the principles outlined by Angrosino and Mays de Perez (2000), particularly in the trial and error dictum. Here, the message does not mean that researchers should blindly attempt things, but rather to learn from and use learning experiences to shape the iterative ethical development of the research.

We tend to refer to people who are part of the research study as 'participants', whether they are working in a collaborative way with the researcher in, for example, an action research project, or when providing information in an interview. This word is used in a conscious and explicit manner, and means that others are involved not as those on whom the research is enacted, but as people who have made a conscious decision to assist the researcher, at whatever level. In other words, they collaborate in the research, and, in terms of ethics, a collaborative approach can therefore be taken. Ethical issues, while they need to be thought through before a study commences, can be discussed with the participants of the study and collective decisions can be reached. For example, Zeni (1998), considering ethical issues in action research, argues that action research is a collaborative action and as such ethical decisions should be made collaboratively. Mockler (2014) argues that, in action research, the ethics of practice and research work together in a synergistic manner.

ISSUES TO CONSIDER IN PRACTICE-BASED RESEARCH

In practice-based research, whether an insider or outsider researcher, there are nuances or ethical issues that, although not dissimilar to issues occurring in other types of research involving people, nonetheless require special consideration, due to the nature of the relationship of the research with participants. The ethical principles discussed thus far will provide guidance for managing the ethical problems that may arise, and which will require consideration. The researcher's ethical stance and the principles of beneficence, respect for autonomy, justice and ensuring non-maleficence can provide a framework within which the researcher can make decisions. The balance between subjectivity and objectivity needs to be considered. No one can ever be entirely objective, and although prior knowledge can enhance research, it can also give rise to ethical issues and dilemmas.

The power balance within an organisation is important within the context of the organisation. Researchers can assume powerful positions and may often find themselves mediating between management and employees. The research study may be a management initiative, and this raises issues such as workers being required to collect data as well as doing their day-to-day jobs with no extra payment.

Relationships need to be managed, and the researcher–participant relationship can be difficult to negotiate when pre-existing relationships had been in place. In practice research, particularly when the setting is the individual's day-to-day work space, the participants may be close colleagues or close friends of the researcher, which can present the researcher with challenges of relationality. The researcher will know if participants exaggerate or undersell themselves – and how to present this in a final report can present difficulties to be overcome.

Additionally, feminist researchers have discussed power relations when those in more dominant positions use their authority or use intimidation when interviewing respondents. Reflecting on ethical issues as a researcher should also consider the rise of intersectionality (the intersections and power relations of identity categories like gender and class, or race and gender) and researcher positionality (Winker and Degele, 2011). Positional power can also be an issue if the researcher is a senior member of the organisation, who asks others to contribute to the research; in this situation, the latter may wonder whether saying 'no' is an option, even if assurances are given that they have no obligation to do so. Conversely, if the researcher is junior, and wishes to involve senior individuals, this can present a range of different challenges.

Standpoint theory (Hekman, 1997), a feminist theory originated by Harding (1987), has wider implications for insider researchers. It is useful in the current context and can help determine the researcher's positionality and what this can mean regarding ethical implications in the research process. These issues raised by feminist thinkers have salience for practitioner–researchers who are insiders in regard to their positionality within their work situation. Standpoint theory involves considering one's position in the organisation, especially in relation to power dynamics which may include one's gender, ethnicity, sexual orientation and social class, all of which situate the researcher within a particular context, in accordance with the relevant discourses. This provides the researcher with a particular characteristic perspective on the world.

As well as colleagues, many practice-based contexts involve users of that service, and it is important to receive the views of users. This is often relatively straightforward; however, when dealing with vulnerable people or children, this can present challenges in terms of approval, as there may be additional bodies or gatekeepers who will need to give permission. The consent of participants must be gained and information may need to be made accessible, thereby ensuring that participants can provide informed consent. This is paramount and should never be viewed as an extra step to be taken, but as an integral part of the research process. To return to an earlier point, rather than considering the management of ethical issues throughout the research study, ethical considerations should guide the actions of the researcher.

Ethics committees may decide that a particular study is not a process they would classify as research, but rather as an integral process of ongoing service improvement. This means they perceive it as an issue that people could (or should) be doing as part of day-to-day work, concerns improving a specific service, and therefore does not necessitate ethical approval. This does not mean there are no ethical issues involved, and detailed consideration still needs to be given to the study, particularly in relation to micro ethics. When exploring practice, suboptimal practice may be uncovered and the researcher has a duty to address this.

Confidentiality in research is a general principle that should be followed, but it can present difficulties when it is a clearly defined group with whom the researcher is working. Participants may provide views that they genuinely do not wish to be shared, and the researcher must be aware of this and respect the rights of the individuals involved.

Confidentiality versus accuracy can be a challenge, as the researcher will wish to protect the participants. However, this is often difficult within an organisational context, where people may potentially be identifiable. To illustrate this point, Alice Goffman (2015), an American sociologist, carried out an innovative and illuminating study that, although not practice based, does have some parallels. Goffman examined a community in Philadelphia, focusing on the arrest rates among young black men, and considered the strategies people use to prevent arrest and the way women help them avoid arrest. Goffman's work was published to great acclaim; however, some of her details were challenged, and it was found that they did not match police reports or public records. An argument was that her research was complicated and lengthy and there was a need to protect confidentiality. This is the balance which should be achieved: confidentiality should always be maintained, while still striving for accuracy.

If the research work is to be published, the identity of the company or organisation may need to be protected, which can sometimes be a difficult balance. In practice-based research, publication often occurs in professional publications and other media as well as peer-reviewed journals. So, for example, when publishing in the popular press, the control that is in place for peer-reviewed journals is not usually a procedural norm. While most journalists behave responsibly, part of their job is to sell papers; as such, findings may be overdramatised, and this is a factor that must be considered.

Activity

Consider the scenarios below and decide what action you would take.

Scenario 1

In undertaking a study, Paul received ethical permission to conduct one-to-one interviews with a particular group; an organisation arranged these interviews, and Paul subsequently discovered it had instead organised a focus group

Scenario 2

Helen is a GP in an inner city practice. She wanted to interview some of her patients. Were they really free to say no? How should she deal with this situation?

Scenario 3

Anne carried out a study in a particular organisation and wanted to highlight an employee with strong views. To do so would render him identifiable; what should she do?

Scenario 4

Azid worked with a community-based organisation. In the process of the research he identified a clear tension between the mangers of the organisation and the workers. The conflict was interesting, and the way in which it was resolved also delivered important messages. Azid was unsure about how to present this conflict; he did not want to offend management or workers nor did he wish to distort data

Scenario 5

Natalie interviewed employees about a new work-related system. One employee broke down and said that the system was causing unimaginable stress

Key Points

- Ethics is a key consideration in any research study and requires detailed deliberation.
- Various bodies external to universities may be required to provide permission for conducting research. All universities have ethics committees that formally approve

(Continued)

(Continued)

research; depending on the nature of the research, the researcher may be required to gain additional external approval from other regulatory or formal ethical bodies.

- Key ethical principles are: beneficence, respect for autonomy, justice and non-maleficence.
- The above principles can be translated into the following areas for practical consideration. The research should be conducted for a purpose, the consent of participants should be gained, data must be stored safely and securely, deceptive practices must be avoided, and participants' anonymity and confidentiality must be ensured.
- The differences between ethics as a procedure in which certain requirements must be met and ethical sensitivity – which runs throughout the research study – are significant; in reality, however, this separation can be artificial, and micro-ethical principles should guide the study throughout its course.
- Practice-based research can have specific ethical issues that require detailed consideration. For example:

  o Issues associated with being an insider or somewhere on the continuum between being an insider and outsider.
  o The researcher needs to be aware of their position in the research context.
  o In practice-based research, ethical issues can be multi-factorial. The researcher needs to adopt a basic moral stance and consider their own values, which can be encapsulated in Aristotle's concept of practical wisdom.
  o In collaborative research, ethics should be a correspondingly collaborative process.

ANNOTATED BIBLIOGRAPHY

Carr, W. (1986). Theories of theory and practice. *Journal of Philosophy of Education*, 20(2), 177–86.

This is an excellent paper that considers ways of knowing, and explicitly addresses a moral–ethical approach or way of knowing in practice. The author considers a variety of knowledge in relation to practice and, as such, considers *phronesis* in some detail.

Guillemin, M., & Gillam, L. (2004). Ethics, reflexivity, and 'ethically important moments' in research. *Qualitative Inquiry, 10*(2), 261–80.

This is an excellent article that considers ethical issues in research. It discusses the distinction between procedural and micro ethics, and emphasises the need for an ongoing conscious awareness of the potential ethical issues throughout the research study process.

Labaree, R. V. (2002). The risk of 'going observationist': negotiating the hidden dilemmas of being an insider participant observer. *Qualitative Research*, 2(1), 97–122.

This article does not explicitly address ethical issues, but considers the inside position, particularly when researching within one's own organisation. It discusses aspects pertaining to insider–outsider research particularly well.

REFERENCES

Angrosino, M. V., & Mays de Perez, K. A. (2000). Rethinking observation from method to context. In N. K. Denzin & Y. S. Lincoln (eds) *Handbook of Qualitative Research* (2nd edn) (pp. 673–702). Thousand Oaks, CA: Sage.

Banks, J. A. (1998). The lives and values of researchers: implications for educating citizens in a multicultural society. *Educational Researcher*, 27(7), 4–17.

BMA (2016). Autonomy or self determination. *British Medical Association*, www.bma. org.uk/advice/employment/ethics/medical-students-ethics-toolkit/2-autonomy-or-self-determination. Accessed 18 February 2018.

Carr, W. (1995). *For Education: Towards Critical Educational Inquiry*. Buckingham: Open University Press.

Chavez, C. (2008). Conceptualizing from the inside: advantages, complications, and demands on insider positionality. *The Qualitative Report*, 13(3), 474–94.

De Andrade, L. L. (2000). Negotiating from the inside: constructing racial and ethnic identity in qualitative research. *Journal of Contemporary Ethnography*, 29(3), 268–90.

ESRC (2018). Research ethics: our core principles. *Economic and Social Research Council*, https://esrc.ukri.org/funding/guidance-for-applicants/research-ethics/our-core-principles/. Accessed 20 April 2018.

Gibbs, P., Costley, C., Armsby, P., & Trakakis, A. (2007). Developing the ethics of worker-researchers through phronesis. *Teaching in Higher Education*, 12(3), 365–75.

Goffman, A. (2015). *On the Run*. London: Picador.

Guillemin, M., & Gillam, L. (2004). Ethics, reflexivity, and 'ethically important moments' in research. *Qualitative Inquiry*, 10(2), 261–80.

Harding, S. (1987). *Feminism and Methodology: Social Science Issues*. Bloomington: Indiana University Press.

Hekman, S. (1997). Truth and method: feminist standpoint theory revisited. *Signs*, 22(2), 341–65.

Labaree, R. V. (2002). The risk of 'going observationist': negotiating the hidden dilemmas of being an insider participant observer. *Qualitative Research*, 2(1), 97–122.

McLaughlin, T. H. (2017). *Liberalism, Education and Schooling: Essays by TH McLaughlin* (Vol. 9). Luton: Andrews.

Mockler, N. (2014). When 'research ethics' become 'everyday ethics': the intersection of inquiry and practice in practitioner research. *Educational Action Research*, 22(2), 146–58.

Taylor, J. (2011). The intimate insider: negotiating the ethics of friendship when doing insider research. *Qualitative Research*, 11(1), 3–22.

Winker, G., & Degele, N. (2011). Intersectionality as multi-level analysis: dealing with social inequality. *European Journal of Women's Studies*, 18(1), 51–66.

Zeni, J. (1998). A guide to ethical issues and action research. *Educational Action Research*, 6(1), 9–19.

PART II
Methodological Frameworks

METHODOLOGY AS PERSONAL AND PROFESSIONAL INTEGRITY: RESEARCH DESIGNING FOR PRACTITIONER DOCTORATES

Kate Maguire

INTRODUCTION

This chapter explores the dilemmas facing new researchers from professional fields of practice relating to choices in methodologies and methods. It positions reflection on such choices, the making of them, how they are carried out and how the data is analysed and applied, firmly in the context of personal and professional integrity as this constitutes the coherence and the internal consistency of any piece of research. The nomenclature of *research* is used throughout and not *inquiry* or *enquiry* as *re-search* holds within it the notion of looking again, and again, and each time finding layers of that which increases the reliability of whatever is produced. It looks at methods in particular, criteria of reliability and appropriateness to context.

This chapter supports a shift in thinking and nomenclature to complement or replace standard practices which have emerged out of the philosophical and traditional divides regarding what constitutes knowledge and reliability. Rather than repeat details and applications of particular methodologies and methods which can be found in numerous publications, it offers the lens of personal and professional integrity to professional practitioners undertaking doctoral-level research through which to view their choice and develop, through reasoned argument, a justification for the choice and its criteria of reliability; in other words, their methodology. It supports a shift away from the dominance of binary language in doctoral research to one of complementarity by positioning methodology and methods in *research design*. I draw on the world of professional doctorates, particularly the doctor of professional studies. Tasking itself with bringing professional practice and academic theoretical knowledge into a closer and more equitable relationship, and affirmed by government policies (United Kingdom) as supporting knowledge for the future, it has taken the opportunity to face up to a number of the challenges this coming together poses, such as traditional expectations of reliability; concepts of knowledge and how it is attained; and prescriptive guidelines on how things should be done and written about. Its final shift away from traditional form is not to reference each idea within the text, but to provide a list of readings at the end which relate in various ways to what is being written about. The language of the academic world contributes to misunderstandings and misapplications of concepts, methodologies and methods. As a supervisor of professional doctorates, I find myself in the role of distilling or translating academic language to ease access for senior professionals into discourses which could enhance their research. I draw on my experiences and those of staff and candidates in our transdisciplinary programmes in a large university and on those of other universities where I have had the privilege to be an external examiner.

THE CONTEXT

Methodologies and methods need to be in a constant state of development as academia responds to the requirements of the fluid world outside academia which has to navigate complexity, whereas most public institutions are content with attempting to manage it. Some disciplines have expectations of what particular methodology/methods are to be used as this, it is claimed, can offer some guarantee of the reliability of the research, the trustworthiness of the evidence that is produced and of the agent who has produced it. In scientific terms, the proofs have to be accessible to scrutiny or one cannot have faith in the findings.

A common misunderstanding for university students, and for senior professionals entering higher education after years of experiential learning and sector-related training, and a misunderstanding which is often shared by their employers, is the conflation of these terms of methodology and methods. In general they tend to extract a hybrid understanding or misunderstanding from their reading: that there are broadly two methodologies, positivist and phenomenological (post-positivist/social constructivist), and two sets of method types, quantitative and qualitative. The sciences 'do' the former and therefore produce measurable and thereby more reliable findings; the humanities and the rest of the non-sciences and the arts 'do' the latter, producing interesting but subjective findings more akin to good storytelling. This binary notion is as out of date and simplistic in the twenty-first century as is the binary of 'good and evil' or of 'us and them'. As human beings, we may be driven to reduce everything to binaries as a way of managing complexity, denying the grey areas for their inconvenience and messiness, but if we are to walk into the future with eyes wide open we cannot go around managing complexity; we need to navigate it, engage with it and contribute to its seemingly endless capacity for dynamism and evolution.

In this chapter, I propose, firstly, the placing of personal and professional integrity at the centre of any research undertaking and as a key assessment criterion for doctoralness; and, secondly, the imperative for facilitators of doctoral research, variously known as supervisors, advisers and coaches, to be open to and encourage innovative research approaches appropriate to complexity and to be competent disentanglers of academic language and concepts which can be unnecessary obstacles to knowledge for new researchers working in particular contexts where they speak a different language. Assumptions that this difference in language equates to unfamiliarity with the concepts need challenging.

PERSONAL AND PROFESSIONAL INTEGRITY

In 2012 the *Concordat to Support Research Integrity* was published. It was an agreement by leading universities endorsed by a range of influential bodies including the HEFCE, the Higher Education Funding Council for England, on the desirability of each higher education institute to establish a research integrity environment. Its focus was mainly, but not exclusively, on the environments of the STEM (Science, Technology, Engineering, Mathematics) subjects. In his foreword, the then Minister for Universities and Science, the Right Honourable David Willetts MP, stated:

If we are to maintain our position at the very forefront of research and scholarship, then we must be sure that the work of our research community is
underpinned by common values of rigour, respect, and responsibility.
Excellence and integrity are inextricably linked. I do not doubt that our
researchers understand their responsibilities and take them seriously.

Professional practitioners coming into higher education institutes for the first time,
or re-entering for further study, bring with them several years of working within
professional codes of conduct and practices within their organisations or communities of practice. Professional bodies encode values and expectations in prescribed
procedures and attainments to ensure a standard of ethical and professional practice across their members regardless of where their practices are situated. These
have held the frame for behaviours, attitudes and expectations of individuals and
teams. Research also has ethical codes of conduct (procedural) and codes of practice enshrined in quality assurance mechanisms which the researcher and the
supervisor have to uphold. Just as it is not too challenging to distinguish between
being a professional and *being professional* as being one of attitude, what research
into practice requires is an attitude towards the research undertaking that becomes
a way of being as well as a way of doing.

As will be discussed further on, this approach is the guiding principle of what we
choose to explore, how we do that and the responsibility embedded in producing
evidence on which decisions will be made and others impacted. This way of being
is fundamentally achieved by exploring and making explicit personal and professional integrity. For this reason critical reflection on self, reflexivity in relation to
the local context and wider contexts (the micro, meso and macro) in addition to
notions of trust, truth and knowledge are the defining features of practitioner
research. In other words, reliability, accountability, validity, credibility and responsibility in qualitative research are predicated on the ability of the researcher to
research themselves as part of the contexts in which the research is located.

DISENTANGLING PARADIGMS, METHODOLOGIES, APPROACHES AND METHODS

There are numerous publications, some excellent ones, on research methodologies
and methods and the preferred choices of a range of disciplines for a particular
research apparatus exerting influence on the researcher to meet those expectations.
In the case of science, it could be argued that while this may increase trust in the
reliability of the findings as 'proven' methods are used, thereby increasing internal
and external reliability, it can also repress, marginalise or indeed erase other possibilities for discovery. In the case of humanities, the choice of research apparatus
could lead to a lack of reliability and rigour and decisions being made based on

social constructive views on the value of subjectivity, making it difficult to justify the findings as useful contributions to knowledge in the sector or discipline itself and across sectors and disciplines; that is, at the meso and macro levels.

The relationship between methodologies and methods in particular disciplines, for example quantitative methods in a positivistic paradigm, can be like some long-term partnerships. They suit each other as the ground rules have been established over time with regards to behaviours and routines. While there are consistency and reliability, there can be a lack of checking assumptions and a tempering of expectations. Behaviour outside the norm is treated with a certain amount of suspicion. Long-term partnerships can develop an island mentality, a sense of exclusiveness even when what the island has established as a norm may no longer be the norm in all circumstances and for all purposes. This type of relationship not only boundaries expectations and criteria of reliability, but can, in some cases, inhibit innovation, distinctiveness or originality as these are in the context of each island's views on how hypotheses are developed and tested and how knowledge is created. As previously stated, this can produce a certain consistency in standard, and assessment of success is contextualised in any new research's position in the existing knowledge accumulated and tested over time by such preferential methods.

However, assumptions made on the basis of familiarity and not checked against shifting contextual factors can have wider implications. For example, on science islands some medical research findings have generated treatments which have been discredited even a few years later, having been introduced to the world as based on reliable research. Acceptance of the reliability, without questioning its basic assumptions and the motivations of sponsors of the research, has held back certain branches of medical research as well as resulting in serious consequences for patients. Pioneers, who step out of the mainstream, are often considered maverick or outsiders. Returning to the metaphor of long-term relationships, this stepping out of line can be perceived as a partner betraying the sanctity of the traditional relationship accompanied by similar responses of anger, accusations and rejection towards the maverick individual concerned.

On humanities islands, traditional expectations and proven methods of reliability also face challenges. For example, many pieces of research are only relevant for a limited period and for a limited segment of society, becoming historical archives before they have reached maturity. Reliability and contributions to knowledge often depend on a meta-analysis of several such case studies to mine enough commonalities to impact changes in practices and policies. Those case studies in themselves have to be reliable and this is dependent on the researcher having a demonstrated sense of self and other awareness and to have made ethical choices, which is not always the case. Yet, for both islands, as Koestler so eloquently stated in 1959 in his aptly titled *The Sleepwalkers*:

> The act of wrenching away an object or concept from its habitual associative context and seeing it in a new context is … an essential part of the creative process. It is an act of both destruction and creation, for it demands

the breaking up of a mental habit, the melting down, with the blow-lamp of Cartesian doubt, of the frozen structure of accepted theory, to enable a new fusion to take place. This perhaps explains the strange combination of scepticism and credulity in the creative genius. Every creative act – in science, art and religion – involves a regression to a more primitive level, a new innocence of perception liberated from the cataract of accepted beliefs. It is a process of *reculer pour mieux sauter*,[1] of disintegration preceding a new synthesis. (1959: 489)

KNOWLEDGE

The *knowledge context* of the sciences sits within the *scientific paradigm*, also known as the *positivist paradigm*, which does not concern itself with human perspectives. The sciences' response to, and management of, the natural world through humans as probes requires the researcher not to have a personal perspective. The integrity of the researcher in this sector is therefore defined by an assiduous following of the rules of objectivity. Human data is in the service of the probe in so far as its contribution is to the betterment of the tool. For example, algorithms are developed scientifically but their success is based on a constant feed of codified human behaviour which in this form can disregard what the system sees as anomalies. These are variables which cannot be standardised as they are in a constant state of flux influenced by immeasurable pressures which change over time depending on the context. These contexts range from the psychological and social to the economic and political.

The *knowledge context* of the humanities sits within the *social constructivist* or *post-positivist paradigm* and actively concerns itself with individual and group agency and the contributions to practice and knowledge that an exploration and analysis of these human perspectives can make. So we can say of a paradigm that it is *a set of assumptions, concepts, values, and practices that constitutes a way of viewing reality* (McGregor and Murnane, 2010). Positivism and constructivism are two different paradigms. It is not surprising then that these *paradigms* have traditionally used different *methods* to gather data and use different criteria of reliability.

Methodology is not a method or group of methods. *Methodology* is that which encompasses the *rationale* for the choice of methods, which includes which paradigm, which conceptual or theoretical basis being drawn upon and how the methods relate to the conceptual, theoretical, paradigmatic choice and how the methods relate to each other to achieve the evidence and reliability required to make a contribution to existing knowledge. *Methodology* is the coherent link between all aspects of the research. The *method*s are the data-gathering tools and the type of analysis employed. There are *quantitative methods* which are employed when the data being gathered is statistically measurable and *qualitative methods*

---

[1]To draw back in order to make a better leap.

employed when the data being gathered is that of experiences and perspectives. Both types of data produced will require different methods of analysis. For decades, research has trodden separate paradigm paths and suspicion has been expressed of each other's methodologies and methods, particularly in relation to reliability.

The *paradigm* then is how we view reality, the *methodology* is how we view knowledge that will influence the methods and the sources of data we choose and *methods* are data-gathering and analysis tools. An example might be that you believe reality is socially constructed, therefore you will want your methodology to acknowledge and contribute to that so you will select methods which will include social and subjective elements of experiences of reality. Another example might be you are a programmer and you view reality as scientifically constructed and ruled by certain laws. You believe that only the scientific method can contribute to scientific knowledge and only methods which lend themselves to being objectively measured and replicable are reliable. However, reality itself is complex and humans are clearly enmeshed in and contribute to that complexity. There is always a human element involved in research no matter how 'scientifically' one views the world. It is humans who witness the natural world and engage it in relationship; science is only one of the many forms of relationship we are capable of having with our world. Acknowledging the complexity, the algorithms programmer has to include high-quality human data (experiential) or the algorithm will not work. The qualitative researcher may still need a statistical benchmarking survey to check the landscape as part of the contextualisation of the research.

Influences external to the university, such as increased interconnectivity between sectors, disciplines, cultures and peoples, have challenged the value of the traditional binary split. Both have value in our understanding of and contribution to knowledge, both have theoretical underpinnings and both can be applied. Both can be used successfully in the same piece of research and both can be used in different pieces of research but can also be directly or indirectly complementary, creating connective bridges to knowledge. For example, a *theoretical piece* of research on international relations theory finds that existing theory is not able to account for or predict the behaviour of non-state actors, so a new theory is proposed. This is complemented in the same piece of work with a *qualitative* piece of research with a non-state actor group as a case study to support the new theory. An example of indirect complementary research would be a *qualitative* piece of research exploring how dancers experience the physicality of particular movements in order to convey to the audience a metaphor of anguish (field of performing arts). The purpose is not to contribute to knowledge on what physicality does to the muscles in the body but the findings might collaterally reveal that some dancers report stresses to the muscles. This then highlights the need for medical research on the extent of harmful impact of certain dance movements across a wider sample (*quantitative data*). The two studies together then have a better chance of changing physicality in performance, minimising stress to muscles, leading to innovation in creative expression.

THE SIMPLICITY OF AN APPROACH

The term *paradigm* is used rarely now in practitioner doctorates. It has been replaced by the more sensible term of *approach*, reflecting the complexity of the world and the multiple sectors in which the workworld functions. In such a world people are exposed to and can hold many different perspectives at the same time. Practitioners are required to respond to regular changes or modifications in goals and how to reach them, stimulated by internal and external influences. Choices made are often pragmatic which, if deconstructed, reveal that practitioners can have admirable agility in juggling. If contradictions arise it is often between the values of the organisation and those of the individual, but rarely on the basis of philosophical concerns about paradigms and methodologies. What can be a concern is in the area of persuasiveness to a certain course of action to bring about change. Organisations are looking for hard facts, solid evidence to justify a particular course of action. For the pragmatist it can be the bottom line, the market forces, and what practical things need to be done to survive and thrive, which could include such actions as downsizing. However, when it comes to competitive edge, which may mean risking cultural shifts as nothing else seems to be working, the evidence for a particular course of action or new strategy has to be convincing to those who deal with the finances. In such cases, the researcher, in a sense, serves two authorities, the university and the organisation, and the criteria for reliable evidence can be different. In order to capture this multidimensionality of the workworld collaborating with academia, borrowing from different paradigms is sensible and is explained through the researcher's *approach* to the research.

Whether positioning oneself in a positivist or post-positivist paradigm or in a non-binary approach, the personal and professional integrity of the researcher sits at the centre of every action and every choice, replacing the security and criteria of reliability which, adhering solely to one paradigm and its prescribed methods, would have afforded it in the less complex past. Now, the trustworthiness of the research is dependent on the trustworthiness of the researcher and their ability to articulate and account for their choices. Practice theory and research pedagogy in professional doctorates are committed to how that trustworthiness can be developed, articulated and demonstrated. The bridge across binaries, the facilitator of understanding across difference, is then the researcher themselves. It is the quality of the researcher which defines the quality of the work and that quality can be revealed and developed through critical reflection and undertaking the requirements of the researcher to check what knowledge already exists in the area and challenging it; articulating their practice and their role within the practice, as the researcher is always part of the context whether they think they are or not; awareness of the power dynamics at play when the researcher is a member of the culture being researched; selecting methods that not only have the best chance of producing reliable data but recognise the integrity of the participants; and the responsibility of the researcher to pay attention to the impact on participants of the method itself as well as the potential impact of the findings on them and their environments.

At the end of the day it is about using *reliable* methods, *reliable* as in trustworthiness of all aspects of the research including the researcher, to gather the data that will make the evidence of most value to the intention of, and to the stakeholders in, the research; and the quality of data is strengthened by cross-referencing the results from each of the different data sources. This is commonly referred to in the social sciences as triangulation. However, there are two common misperceptions of triangulation. Firstly, that it is to do with a triangle and therefore the number 3. In fact, the term comes from the mathematics of mapping through the use of *more than two points* to determine the position of a single point. Secondly, that it is restricted to establishing that data sources somehow confirm the findings of each other. Triangulation, in fact, has more than one function. It is the examination of two or more sets of data to enrich the findings by including different perspectives; to offer a more balanced perspective of that which is being researched; to seek commonalities but not manipulate them; and to increase the reliability of the findings if commonalities emerge.

BEGINNING RESEARCH DESIGNING: CONCEPTUALISING 'YOUR PRACTICE' IN ORDER TO CONCEPTUALISE AND THEORISE 'PRACTICE'

The concept of research designing I am proposing is an *approach*. Following the notion that methodology is positioned in personal and professional integrity, then all choices from the outset of the research undertaking – research preparation, execution and analyses – are viewed through and informed by this lens, therefore everything the researcher undertakes is a vital component of this *methodology of integrity*. This is also a *methodology of integration*. It achieves the establishment of coherence and internal consistency through personal and professional integrity. Therefore research designing becomes the creative product of engagement with personal and professional integrity whether one is in the role of the scientist following an established script or in the role of the practitioner capturing experiential learning with multiple variables.

There are preparatory steps to research designing for a professional/practitioner doctorate. The first is to conceptualise individual practice and the researcher's contributions to the interactions within and beliefs about this context. This contextualisation of practice may start out as a description but becomes a deepening recognition and refined articulation of the complexities of environments in which practices sit and to which practices have to respond, usually through rapid adaptation. That context includes the existing knowledge environment which is traditionally referred to as the literature review. *Conceptualising* practice develops an articulation of what is tacit knowledge and anticipates field conditions, resistances to and facilitators of change and the implications of any change, which is an ethical dimension of the research. *Theorising* practice is predicated on the ability to conceptualise it. In professional doctorates, we tend to use the word 'positioning' to help practitioners who wish to research their own practice, sector, organisation or community of practice to position themselves within the layered contexts in which their practices operate and their beliefs about those layers. This is also referred to as the *situatedness* of practice. However, the term *positioning* implies the possibility of shifting and holding concurrently different perspectives in fluid contexts. Contexts are both informed by and inform perspectives and help to illuminate the tensions and contradictions which arise in complexity. For example, when the values of the person and the values of the organisation collide; when the goals of the individual are in tension with the goals of the group; when the capacity of the organisation or the individual to change is diminished by internal or external factors; when the conditions for change seem hostile; when people say one thing and think another; when beliefs and assumptions held by an individual are never challenged by the individual.

FORMS OF CONCEPTUALISATION

How we conceptualise our practice or even aspects of our practice depends very much on learning style, formative educational influences and our own personal dispositions. Visual conceptualisation can take the form of mapping, graphics, doodles, illustrations both simple and complex. There are many examples available on the Internet or in art galleries, advertising boards, scenes from well-known films to depict a particular situation or scenario. Often practitioners enjoy creating their own images. There are ladders to depict hierarchy; snakes and ladders to depict the unpredictable nature of a workworld; the image of a court room to conceptualise the atmosphere in an organisation and to locate an individual in that room. Images of seas, mountains, bridges and rivers are all metaphors which assist in articulating the complexity and interplay of a workworld and provide vehicles for articulation in text. Textual conceptualisation can be extracts from all kinds of literature, from plays and poetry or from models and theoretical concepts from other disciplines. We regularly borrow from biology and science to conceptualise how organisations work: from biology we can conceptualise an organisation as an ecology and from anthropology as a cultural ecology, and develop the image for our own particular situation. From a combination of biology and technology we can conceptualise practices as linked parts of a superorganism such as the brain or the internal board of a computer; or from geography as islands in an archipelago with some connections having more fluid and speedy exchanges than others and some islands being cut off altogether. One conceptualisation which seems to resonate with a number of professional practitioners is transdisciplinarity. This speaks to the nature of current work practices in which the individual has to develop knowledge of a number of tangential sectors in order to be successful in their job. For example, the engineer is no longer solely an engineer if they have to run the company. This concept expands to enable theorising of practice in general to enable informed actions, for example when an organisation has a critical problem and requires all parts of the organisation to put aside their differences and work together to resolve the problem. It extends further into the sticky problems on national and global scales of climate change, diminishing resources, the end of species where solutions lie in divesting stakeholders of their assumptions and traditional methods and coming to the table ready to be open to creative solutions based on what matters *in practice*, in real life. An aspect of transdisciplinarity which particularly resonates is the value of social responsibility. It is very rare in our experience for a senior professional to undertake research who is not motivated to change something for the benefit of others, to contribute in some way towards making situations better in their specific contexts and more generally to make a difference to how things are done and to change how people think. This requires the researcher to start with self.

Activity

Conceptualising our practice

In the previous section there was discussion on conceptualising practice. Taking a large sheet of paper, think about your practice area and begin the process of looking at it and the knowledge which is valued in that practice. What would you like to change and what are the facts which will help and those which will hinder that change?

You might want to write this as bullet points or a spider diagram or use a more visual form. When you progress through the chapter you will find this very helpful.

TRANSPARENCY

Individuals, coming from professional practice into academic environments to design a piece of research that has practice and organisational implications, soon discover that when they try to explain what they do, why they do it and how (their theories in use) so much of what they know is tacit, so much of what they base decisions on is implicit. They may believe they are transparent but in the process of conceptualising and articulating their practice they see that they may not be as transparent as they think, to themselves as well as to others. This does not mean they have not had integrity but that assumptions have been made and accepted. A conceptualisation of one's own practice and of the nature of practice and its relationship to knowledge in general, therefore, is also about moving from description and explanation of 'doing' to a narrative of knowing and being. A post-positivist paradigm cannot meet the same criteria for reliability as a scientific experiment, nor should it. What it must do is improve reliability through the transparency of the researcher and their ability to research themselves thereby revealing their positionality. This is usually achieved through articulated critical reflection.

The second step in research designing is exploring the influences that need to be considered when designing any piece of research. Some of these will surface through conceptualising practice and positioning oneself within context.

RESEARCH DESIGNING: INFLUENCES TO CONSIDER

Perhaps the questions that need to be asked next of the new researcher at this stage are: Is what you want to research worth it to yourself and to others? Have others, even from other fields, got something useful to offer? Is there validity in your research target, its purpose and aims? The answers to these questions lie in carrying out a knowledge review. A rationale for the choices is necessary. However, the scope in practitioner doctorates is not limited to peer-reviewed journals and seminal texts. Cases can be made to access additional materials such as professional journals; policy documents and other kinds of reports; live literature in the form of substantiated conference talks; and social media to track and source trends, for example. The key word here is substantiated. The integrity of the researcher informs what is needed to meet the criteria of validity as validity is part of reliability of evidence and of interpretation of data. People who will make decisions based on our research findings attribute to us a trustworthiness which has to be proved worthy through the research write-up we produce. It is an ethical issue of some magnitude that decisions which impact people's lives/livelihoods are based on trustworthiness. A methodology of integrity provides the proofs of that trustworthiness. A knowledge review is also the opportunity to reflect on how others have carried out research and to declare our acknowledgement for the research work that has gone before us because we also learn from the positions with which we do not agree.

The next question then is how you will carry out the research ethically to get the evidence you need, and from whom, to achieve the aims of the research unencumbered by prescribed approaches. This frequently reveals a spectrum of strategies from the genuinely innovative to the unethical, from an Alice in Wonderland lens to a Pollyanna naivety, from basic lacks and gaps to unrealistic fantasies. But it does reveal and that is the point of the question. Lacks and gaps revealed in this process of thinking through how the researcher might design a piece of research unencumbered by prescribed approaches include gaps or lacks in knowledge, in self-awareness, in other awareness, in anticipatory skills, in appreciation of complexity, in criticality, validity and reliability, in ethics, in challenging assumptions and in understanding the nuances of power dynamics. Fantasies include being able to change embedded practices quickly, having the right answer, being able to make people do better, not recognising resistance, self-perception as rescuer or hero and seeing oneself as the next and better CEO. Insights include seeking relevance, recognising the impact of the research process as well as findings on participants, appropriate samples, attention to accessibility and feasibility, calculated risks, harnessing imagination appropriately, courage, being informed, being professional as a researcher as well as a practitioner.

Considering these influences when formulating a design helps the developing practitioner–researcher to achieve the core criteria of sound research in any paradigm: reliability, validity, credibility, feasibility, criticality, ethics, professionalism and, for the post-positivist approaches, add transparency and reflexivity.

Table 6.1 offers a summary of influences to consider when imagining a research design. It is not designed to be exhaustive but to act as an illuminator of factors which are often hidden or parked, a necessary 'stratagem', when faced with fast-moving environments.

Table 6.1   Influences to consider when imagining a research design

	Researcher awareness	Research integrity
1	Level of self awareness	Reliability
2	Capacity to challenge your own assumptions	Reliability and criticality
3	Awareness of motivations and what sustains them	Reliability
4	Positioning in your own practice	Transparency and validity
5	Comprehensive conceptualisation of your practice and practice environment	Reflexivity
6	Positioning yourself and your practice in knowledge	Validity
	Capacity to dialogue with existing knowledge	Criticality
	Beliefs about self and others	Transparency
7	Parameters of research activity imposed by location of research activity	Feasibility
8	Potential impact on others by engaging others in change through the research activities themselves	Ethical sensitivity
9	Insider–outsider perspectives and impact of your role in influencing responses and levels of engagement	Ethical sensitivity
10	Professional and research ethics awareness	Professionalism
11	Researcher-intended impact and context appropriate impact	Professionalism
12	Piloting opportunities	Validity
13	Opportunities for collaboration	Validity and reflexivity
14	Availability of and accessibility to participants	Feasibility
15	Availability of and accessibility to materials and resources	Feasibility
16	The kind of evidence needed to bring about valid, reliable and context appropriate change	Reliability
17	Managing data	Feasibility
18	Field conditions for change	Reliability and feasibility
19	Realistic targets	Professionalism
20	Ownership	Ethics and reflexivity
21	Commissioned or non-commissioned research	Ethics and transparency

Table 6.2 offers suggestions for the types of questions we might ask at each stage of the research process. These too are not exhaustive but can stimulate other questions, the answers to which begin to offer some coherence to the assembly of the parts. You can also use this as an exercise and add to the questions.

Table 6.2   Questions to ask at different stages of the research process

Engaging the reader	Navigation, signposting Short summary/ abstract Introduction	What is the main impact which you want to bring about?
		How would you go about making this happen?
		What are your main research questions?
		What convinces you that your research interest is worthwhile?
		What do you want to achieve?
Your work and your position in that context and the internal and external influences on that context	Context	What is the context of your research?
		What limitations does the context impose and what opportunities does it offer?
		Who cares?
		Is it needed or is it just you who thinks it is needed?
		What do you intend to do about what you have identified?
		Are you part of the context or do you feel apart from the context?
Conceptualising your existing practice and the practices of your sector	Conceptualising your practice Reflexivity, i.e. your impact on your environment and its impact on you	What is your practice?
		How can you explain it to someone else?
		Do your values conflict or resonate with your workplace/ organisation?
		How can you explore your own position in and your impact on your environment?
		What might be the inhibitors or facilitators of the change you want to bring about?
		Which one are you?
		How can mapping out the complexity of your practice help you?
		How can you prepare the ground for change to be received?
		Are you a maverick?
		Are you a collaborator?
		What's going to work best?
Choice of area to research	Rationale for focus	On what evidence do you base the need for change?
		What is the driver?
		What needs attention?
		What is not happening that you think should be happening?
		Are you being realistic?
		Is this all your idea or have you been commissioned or tasked with the delivery of something that has already been formulated?

Checking what knowledge is already out there in this area or related area	Rationale for choice of literature Exploring the knowledge landscape that is relevant Validity Reliability	On what basis are you going to choose the kind of literature to look at as you cannot look at everything? Has someone already tackled similar issues elsewhere? Can you find some insights from fields/sectors other than your own? Do you want to be a replicator or a generator/innovator?
Using your existing knowledge and the knowledge of others to dialogue with what you find	Criticality	How do you evaluate existing knowledge? What lens are you using? Do you agree with what is being written? What informs your judgement on this? Do you accept as truth what is published because they must be the experts? Do you rate academic literature as more reliable than professional literature? Does what you read resonate with complex practice, with your own experience? If not why not?
Clarifying what you want to find out, from whom and why	Feasibility, evidence needed Reliability	Do you know the difference between purpose, aim/s and objectives? Who are your intended audience/s? What will convince them? What would convince you if you were them? How do you go about identifying who or what has the knowledge you think will be helpful to you? Do you know the difference between methodology and methods? How can you ensure your research is reliable? Are there limitations on your access to the sources which you believe have the information you seek? What is evidence? Is evidence different for different audiences? Can you mix and match ways of getting information?
Influences on a research design	Rationale for methodology and methods	If you did not have to use a particular methodology/ methods, what design would you come up with, taking into consideration all the above issues? What would you have to think about? Your world view? What constitutes evidence? What are the criteria for reliability? Can you get access? Is your position in the context going to inhibit honest responses? Have you thought about the ethics?

(Continued)

Table 6.2 (Continued)

Research ethics	Ethical considerations	What about the ethics of impact?
		How might your research impact those involved?
		Is just asking a question of a participant going to have an impact on that person?
		Is your research ethical?
		How can you ensure it is?
		Are there political issues?
		Are there personal issues?
		Are there any conflicts of interest?
		Have you thought about the ethics of reliability – about people making serious decisions based on your research?
		How can you mitigate possible harm?
		Have you gone through a risk assessment?
		Have you checked you have ethical clearance for everything?
		Does your organisation, professional body have a code of ethics?
		Have you compared this to research ethics?
		How will you ensure that the conclusions are reasonable and justifiable?
		Who owns the research?
		Who owns it if you have used someone to help you?
		Can participants own it?
Details of what, when, where, how and with whom, and how many, data storage	Realistic purpose, aims and objectives	Do you know the implications of scope?
		Do you know the difference between depth and breadth?
		Between a bounded piece of research and one that is generalisable?
		What is benchmarking and what is it for?
		How many people would you have to target with a survey to get a response rate that could be deemed reliable?
		How much data is generated by a 45-minute interview?
		What is triangulation?
How you analyse your data and arrive at your findings	Method of analysis Triangulation Interpretative frames	What method/s of analysis will you use?
		What is the difference between software and researcher immersion in raw data?
		What is an interpretative frame?
		What is the link between literature and findings?
		What constitutes findings?
		What is the difference between results, findings and conclusion?
		Have you answered the issues/questions you started out with?

Impact Inhibitors of impact Facilitators/ facilitating factors of impact Recommendations	Impact based on findings and impact based on fantasy	Who are your audiences?
		Does this influence how you write about your research and how you report it?
		What is the purpose of recommendations?
		What is the value of sharing your work as you go along?
		Who is going to listen to you?
		What is your answer to the *So what?* question?

Activity

The stages of research are outlined in this section. With your proposed project in mind, take one of the areas and answer the questions on it and choose whatever one you are most comfortable with at this stage in your research.

Reflect on the implications that the answers may have on the development of your research.

Did this challenge any of the ideas you previously held? Did it reinforce any of them?

YOUR DESIGN

There is probably an existing design that comes close to what you would design after considering all the influences in Table 6.1 and all the questions in Table 6.2. That would be something you and your supervisor could explore once you have proposed your own research design. I would state clearly here that many practitioner–researchers do not use one paradigm or methodology as it was originally designed but tend to take a utilitarian view and choose perspectives which are multiple and methods on the basis of 'what works' in a particular context. This constitutes the *approach* coherently integrated by *integrity*. However, the advantage of seeing a piece of research through using the methods expected of a particular paradigm offers an internal consistency with less justification required on the part of the researcher. Integrity in such a context is judged then by whether the steps laid down by the paradigm have been scrupulously followed. The researcher is informed by the arguments of the paradigm. For those who choose an *approach*, that is a range of methods borrowed from different discourses, paradigms and methodologies, a clear rationale for the choices and how each method chosen relates to the other methods chosen has to be ensured. Here the integrity is in the quality of the explanation.

Returning to the notion of a research approach reflecting your way of seeing, doing and being in the world, there are introductions below to two areas of discourse which may help you to think more deeply about what you do, what matters to you and what difference you want to make, and very importantly to conceptualise these at a more critical level which is an ethical responsibility of any researcher, that is to do justice to knowledge and to the participants.

HELP WITH CLARIFYING AN ATTITUDE TO THE WORKWORLD TO ACHIEVE WHAT MATTERS

TRANSDISCIPLINARITY (TD)

TD, like anthropology, is an attitude to the world. Examples of transdisciplinarity as a research approach have been on the whole confined so far to large sticky problems like climate change, conflict resolution, international strategies in various sectors. The archive is not yet substantial at the meso level, but at the macro level large-scale initiatives have been accumulating rapidly. Basically TD proposes a group approach to a problem which impacts cross-sections of the population and the solution is likely to be found if a cross-section of voices is consulted. In terms of climate change on littoral communities, for example, this could include climatologists, seismologists, oceanographers, architects, sociologists, engineers, fishing communities, local health practitioners, and so on. Each of those participants would come to the table informed by their different knowledges and traditional/discipline ways of doing things. They would set them aside and listen to each of the perspectives before making a contribution. Such collaboration has resulted in proceeding with a course of action that does not necessarily follow any one way but arrives at something that is more than the sum of the parts. The coherence of the group is provided by a shared value that the solution needs to be of benefit to the widest number of stakeholders in the particular context being examined and no group will be unduly harmed or disadvantaged by the solution.

For practitioners, TD presents a way of bringing about solutions through not only engaging difference but embracing it. This holds some appeal for organisations which are already in processes of exchange with organisations and individuals with whom they would like to engage more deeply. China for example offers significant opportunities for companies from other parts of the world to develop new markets. However, the nature of business is competitive. Bringing together different knowledges and different cultures to resolve a complex problem that benefits all the participants promotes trust and reciprocity. China now agreeing to a ban on the marketing of ivory is an outcome of transdisciplinary-type thinking and action. On a smaller scale this could be resolving differences in workworld cultures for employees from a host culture in an organisation whose work practices and expectations are those of the culture which owns the organisation.

EMBRACING COMPLEXITY

Like TD, complexity is also an attitude to the world which informs our behaviour as researchers. It conceptualises the world as a vast interconnected and interdependent set of entities that are held together by various rituals and practices which have emerged and been reiterated over time through a process of adaptive responses. Through this process of evolution many entities are shed and new ones spring up.

These always have a human cost. Technology has accelerated the interconnection of things. In order to carry out research in such an environment there has to be the recognition of what complexity is and how it can be approached. Attempting to manage it through a series of control mechanisms runs the risk of stagnating the entities. Embracing complexity as proposed by Boulton et al. can run the risk of getting entangled in it: *The future is a dance between patterns and events* (2015: 29). Like TD, it seeks collaborative solutions across sectors, disciplines and voices and focuses on the common good. Methods are not prescribed but focus is given to what needs to be achieved from methods including those that can trace the development of situations over time, multiple perspectives, critical subjectivity, emergent phenomena. A comprehensive guide is given by Boulton et al. (113) for practitioner–researchers who enjoy situating themselves along the interconnecting lines of an archipelago rather than on one or two relatively safe islands.

All approaches throw up ethical considerations from making the choice of what to research and why; the methods to use and with whom; the intended impact and mitigating unintended consequences. Trust in the choices and in us as researchers making those choices is the most convincing thread of coherence if it is made on the basis of personal and professional integrity demonstrated by reasoned argument, attention to detail and authenticity and rigour in every thought, word and action underpinned by self- and other awareness and respect. This lens of personal and professional integrity is a methodology of integrity and integration that supports confidence to explore other exciting and relevant methods to use, to take risks to search for what lies beneath, to be illuminated by the unexpected. Fundamentally the learning of each practitioner–researcher can be seen in description being transformed into a knowledge narrative that has some usefulness in the world whether that be at the individual, local or global level. Why else do it? Being guided by integrity and integration will help you shift from Koestler's Sleepwalkers to the creative researcher with a chance of revealing something which is hidden which may not at first be what was wanted but is likely to turn out to be what is needed. When you start to use a personal and professional integrity compass you will know when you are going wrong – it just won't feel right.

Key Points

- Traditionally in research, paradigms are discussed which determine the research method and methodology. In practice-based research the world is considerably more complex and the approach taken to deal with issues is a better way of looking at things.
- An important step in designing research is conceptualisation of practice.
- Reliability of the data is important and collection of multiple types of data is a way of ensuring this. The process is often referred to as triangulation.

(Continued)

(Continued)

- Trustworthiness that comes from the reliability of the researcher and their stance and their ethical stance is essential.
- A key principle is transparency where people can follow and see the logic of the decision-making process of the research.

ANNOTATED BIBLIOGRAPHY

Boulton, J., Allen, P., & Bowman, C. (2015). *Embracing Complexity: Strategic Perspectives for an Age of Turbulence*. Oxford: Oxford University Press.

This book is a welcome addition to conceptualising not only the workworld but life. It takes complexity as an opportunity to advance our thinking and actions towards social justice and what is good for the many, not just the few. But this is also an intellectual adventure seeing the world made up of not silos but as interconnected hubs in a state of constant change and the challenges not only to understanding it but researching it.

Gibbs, P. (ed.) (2015). *Transdisciplinary Professional Learning and Practice*. Berlin: Springer.

Gibbs, P. (ed.) (2017). *Transdisciplinary Higher Education: A Theoretical Basis Revealed in Practice*. Berlin: Springer.

Professor Paul Gibbs and his contributors have been adding to the growing literature on transdisciplinary thinking and practice. Their chapters propose TD's relevance for future directions in not only closing the gap between academic knowledge and professional knowledge, but exploring the possibilities when we take a knowledge exchange view. Working together can help both to go beyond mere potential by focusing on what kind of change really matters and the transformation in thinking and practice which needs to happen to bring this about.

Kincheloe, J., & Berry, K. (2004). *Rigour and Complexity in Educational Research: Conceptualizing the Bricolage*. Maidenhead: Open University Press.

Kincheloe is a well-known name in the understanding and use of 'bricolage', first coined by the anthropologist Lévi-Strauss. In this work Kincheloe and Berry give articulation to what anthropologists and researchers generally struggle with when researching in and on living practices that shift and shape often at a rapid pace. They demonstrate the challenges of such research and how choices can be explained and reliability ensured through conceptual and methodological rigour and articulation.

Koestler, A. (1959). *The Sleepwalkers: A History of Man's Changing Vision of the Universe*. Harmondsworth: Penguin Books.

Koestler was a commentator on philosophy, science, literature and the human condition. As the title suggests, he challenges how we have revered scientific knowledge at the cost of creative vision and action. A good read for the scientist.

McGregor, S. L., & Murnane, J. A. (2010). Paradigm, methodology and method: intellectual integrity in consumer scholarship. *International Journal of Consumer Studies*, *34*(4), 419–27.

An example of how academic and professional knowledge from different sectors can inform each other raising the question for the reader of what is 'academic' knowledge and what is the application of academic knowledge.

Nicolini, D. (2013). *Practice Theory, Work, and Organization: An Introduction*. Oxford: Oxford University Press,

In his introduction Nicolini has a comprehensive list of reasons why 'a practice based view of social and human phenomena is distinctive' (6–7). He reviews the history of knowledge and practice and uses examples from the field of health to illustrate his case. His contribution to practice theory is a welcome addition to a sparse field.

Robinson, D., & Garratt, C. (2003). *Introducing Ethics*. London: Icon Publishing.

When it first came out this was an international bestseller. It takes a humorous but penetrating look at what we mean by ethics, its history, its applications and its contradictions. In its own way it supports the notion of integrity and moral awareness over the contentious field of ethics.

REFERENCES

Boulton, J., Allen. P., & Bowman, C. (2015). *Embracing Complexity: Strategic Perspectives for an Age of Turbulence*. Oxford: Oxford University Press.

Koestler, A. (1959). *The Sleepwalkers: A History of Man's Changing Vision of the Universe*. Harmondsworth: Penguin Books.

McGregor, S. L., & Murnane, J. A. (2010). Paradigm, methodology and method: intellectual integrity in consumer scholarship. *International Journal of Consumer Studies, 34*(4), 419–27.

UK Universities (2012). The concordat to support research integrity. www.universitiesuk. ac.uk/policy-and-analysis/reports/Documents/2012/the-concordat-to-support-research-integrity.pdf. Accessed 20 June 2018.

ALTERNATIVE DISSERTATION MODELS: THE DEVELOPMENT OF MODERN CAPSTONE DESIGN

Valerie A. Storey

KEY TERMS

Capstone: a capstone is the final (often decorative) brick put on a building. It is used to refer to the final product of a period of study or a research study which can be presented in ways which best showcase the work rather than the traditional report or essay.

Modernist: stems from the Enlightenment and the establishment of scientific disciplines and the scientific approach.

Postmodernist: developed in the mid-to-late 20th century, often associated with schools of thought such as deconstruction and post-structuralism.

INTRODUCTION

This chapter examines the history and evolution of the dissertation. We learn that classifying twentieth-century dissertations and theses in a 'traditional' way is both inappropriate and incorrect for professional doctorates (PDs). Moreover, we should return to the original intent of the dissertation, which was to encourage critical thinking and debate, as this better characterises twenty-first-century models. In PD programmes with the focus on practice-based research and the generation of more practice-based knowledge, the traditional thesis is often not the best way to describe or think about PDs or other more practice-based doctorates. A research capstone produced as an individual or group project with associated written and oral presentation is what is called the capstone approach and can be used to showcase PD work.

In this context it is the final product of the doctorate and the culminating experience in most students' doctoral work; the capstone product is an essential component of any programme (Dawson and Kumar, 2016). In most institutions of higher education, PDs have been introduced according to regulations, systems and mindsets established for PhD programmes (Costley, 2013). However, PD candidates tend to study on a part-time basis, with the expectation that they will also be working in the industry or in a professional organisation, while PhD candidates are more likely to be full-time students (Bourner et al., 2001).

Irrespective of the doctoral programme, the twenty-first-century capstone product is in the process of transition, having received attention in the literature from both researchers and practitioners (Archbald, 2008; Shulman et al., 2006; Wergin, 2011). Specifically, PD capstone design is more likely to be an instrument for transformative development rather than a route followed to achieve an individual's personal and professional goals. Graduates of PD programmes are required to promote change and generate knowledge that positively address a complex problem of practice from their professional domain (Storey and Maughan, 2014).

Additionally, from the institution's perspective the programme's capstone should provide for an authentic assessment of doctoral candidates' learning and their ability to perform successfully in the workplace (Willis et al., 2010). Rule (2006) conducted a literature review on authentic assessment in higher education and determined that there were four common characteristics of authentic assessment: namely that they (a) involve real-world problems; (b) include open-ended inquiry, thinking skills and metacognition; (c) engage students in discourse and social learning; and (d) empower students through choice to direct their own learning. These characteristics should ground PD capstones, which should require students to conduct open-ended inquiry, improve their thinking skills, be involved in social environments, and direct their own learning to solve a problem of practice in the workplace (Biddle, 2015).

Activity

List what you consider to be the key components of a dissertation. Add or subtract from your list as you read through this chapter.

When you have finished the chapter, compare your list with one you started with.

Have your ideas changed?

Are they still the same?

SETTING THE STAGE
NOMENCLATURE

Due to the variety of PDs available and the various subject areas covered by PDs, issues of nomenclature are complex (Mellors-Bourne et al., 2016). A review of the literature suggests confusion between the terms 'thesis' and 'dissertation'. According to the *Oxford English Dictionary*, a thesis is

1. a proposal laid down or stated, especially one maintained or put forward as a premise in an argument; or
2. a dissertation to maintain and prove a thesis, especially one submitted by a candidate as the sole or principal requirement for a university degree.

Whereas a dissertation is

1. a discussion, debate;
2. a spoken or written discourse on a subject in which it is treated at length; or
3. an extended scholarly essay submitted for a degree or other academic qualification.

In summary, a dissertation expounds a theory. For the most part, this chapter refers to a dissertation as a programme's capstone or crowning achievement.

CONVENTIONAL DISSERTATIONS: THE MODERNIST MODEL

The invention and adoption of print directly impacted academia, causing the collapse of the medieval oral system of learning. Cheap and reliable printing made it easier to claim authorship and thus ownership of knowledge. Ironically, the ability to communicate with a wider audience transitioned the doctoral learning process from a collective pursuit to an individual one.

By the eighteenth century, some universities began requiring the publication of research findings as a prerequisite to become a professor (McClelland, 1980). German scholars became more concerned with producing new empirical knowledge rather than engaging in the dialectical argumentation that was so central to the medieval university. In the Germans' view, a dissertation ought to conform to a model based on controlled experimentation and empirical deduction, and should constitute what might be called an extensive laboratory report, as evidenced in the dissertation chapters of today (i.e. methodology, results/findings, analysis and interpretation).

Towards the end of the eighteenth century, students were required to produce written dissertations (Malone, 1981). This model was adopted in American institutions resulting in an immediate proliferation of academic journals (e.g. American Chemical Society, Modern Language Association, *Journal of Mathematics* [Johns Hopkins University]) (Rudolph, 1962). While the disputation had given way to a different form of argumentation, rhetoric and logic retained their importance, particularly as a thesis still had to be presented and defended orally (Willis et al., 2010).

ALTERNATIVE DISSERTATIONS: THE POSTMODERNIST MODEL

In the late 1970s, the structuralist approach to knowledge came under attack by post-structuralist thinkers, who challenged many of the underlying assertions of scientific reasoning and even notions of authorship, originality and the neutrality of so-called objective knowledge. They highlighted the need to enact alternatives to conventional assumptions and practices, and criticised the measuring of prominence in terms of seminal works and the frequency with which these works are cited in other works of scholarship.

Post-structuralist thinkers advocate for the termination of the dissertation as a single-authored piece of original scholarship. Four major concerns validate their position:

1. new developments in science make the current form of the dissertation untenable as individuals undertake few major scientific projects;
2. to succeed as a scientist, a student must learn to collaborate successfully and not work as an individual;
3. the ability of an individual student to produce a book-length treatment is less important to contemporary scientific practice than is the ability to collaborate; and
4. the conception of scholarship as the mass production of commodities in the forms of scholarly books and articles is both historical and detrimental to the future of the scholarly enterprise.

TRANSNATIONAL NETWORK MODEL

Today, we have transitioned to a digital world in which new technology tools appear almost daily. Doctoral candidates are challenging academia to utilise technology tools that are foundational to their professional practice and to commit to new paradigms of scholarship that reflect our digital world. Such paradigms might have more in common with professional learning communities, communities of practice, learning networks, or wikis, rather than the conventional, individual, five-chapter manuscript (Barton, 2005), the goal being not merely to argue and propose changes, but to defend those changes well enough to have them accepted by academia, the profession and the field of practice.

When Shulman et al. (2006) argue for a doctoral programme capstone that requires programme graduates to learn how to conduct applied research and critically read research reports, and have serious grounding in scholarship, using their workplace as a clinical setting or experimental laboratory for local research and evaluations to guide practice (29–30), they are being purer in their view of the purpose of the dissertation than the conventional five-chapter dissertation with which we are so familiar.

WHAT CHARACTERISES A PD DISSERTATION?

Numerous national and international bodies govern qualifications and specifications for what doctoral-level work should look like (e.g. European University Association; Council of Deans and Directors of Graduate Studies (Australia); UK Council for Graduate Education; Council of Graduate Schools (United States); Quality Assurance Agency (United Kingdom)). Common to all is the emphasis on critical assessment of the originality of findings presented in the dissertation in the context of the literature and the research.

In the United Kingdom, the final assessment of a PD candidate is through submission of independent research and an individual viva voce (Park, 2007). Written research tends to range from 13,000 to 80,000 words. Alternatives to a thesis are required in some practitioner doctorates, particularly within creative and performing arts and design (Mellors-Bourne et al., 2016). In the United States, PD candidates complete a research capstone (either as an individual project or as part of a team effort) and associated written and oral presentation products culminating in a defence before the dissertation committee.

KEY CHARACTERISTICS

Scholars in both the United States and the United Kingdom have identified some key characteristics common to many PD capstones or Dissertations in Practice (DiPs). For example, Fulton et al. identified three such characteristics:

1. Ability to design research objectively and logically.
2. Ability to critically review and evaluate findings.
3. Demonstration of knowledge production that makes a significant contribution to the profession. (2013)

Further descriptions of PD dissertations have highlighted similar characteristics, particularly in relation to a DiP being rooted in the professional practice of the candidate, addressing a complex problem of practice from the field, and producing knowledge that impacts both the profession and practice. O'Mullane lists nine essentials of a professional practice dissertation:

1. Create new knowledge;
2. Make a significant contribution to your profession;
3. Explicit conceptual framework;
4. Literature review should provide the context to the research question, and should demonstrate that the question is worth asking;
5. Demonstrable evidence of how ideas have been synthesized in the light of experience and in the context of academic literature, and how this has created new knowledge;

6. Demonstration that findings have been reflected on, logically planned, and progressed through the research;
7. Independently construct arguments for and against the findings and use evidence to support your interpretation;
8. A distinctive voice should be clearly heard although what is said should be supported by evidence; and
9. Use the university's designated reference style consistently. (2005: 149–50)

O'Mullane also identified six outputs currently used by universities to demonstrate a significant contribution to the profession:

1. Thesis or dissertation alone;
2. Portfolio and/or professional practice and analysis;
3. A reflection and analysis of a significant contribution to knowledge over time or from one major work;
4. Published scholarly works recognized as a significant and original contribution to knowledge;
5. Portfolio and presentation (performance in music, visual arts, drama); and
6. Professional practice and internship with mentors. (2005: 13–14)

EXTENDING THE DISSERTATION SPECTRUM

Integral to a PD programme is the capstone, which in recent decades has changed both in purpose and in form (Golde, 2011), leading to calls in the United States for expanded definitions of dissertations. In 1960, Berelson called for a new dissertation format that was easily publishable for a wider audience. He advocated for article-length dissertations in order to increase publication rates and provide greater dissemination to a wider audience. Duke and Beck (1999) also focused on the relationship between dissertation format and effective dissemination to a wide audience.

In the twenty-first century, voices on this topic have become both louder and more prolific (Archbald, 2008; Grogan and Andrews, 2002; Guthrie, 2009; Levine, 2005; Malen and Prestine, 2005; Murphy and Vriesenga, 2005; Shulman et al., 2006; Wergin 2011). Archbald (2008) suggests that the PD dissertation should have a distinctive format that demonstrates 'developmental efficacy' and 'community benefit', as well as the preservation of 'intellectual stewardship' by demonstrating intellectual and methodological rigour. A recent report published by the Modern Language Association (2014) recommends that institutions of higher education 'reimagine the dissertation', suggesting that 'departments should extend the spectrum of forms the dissertation may take' (2). However, only 20 per cent of graduate schools have official policies that allow for alternative dissertation formats (Duke and Beck, 1999).

In the United Kingdom, the sciences have accepted alternative dissertations longer than other disciplines; these alternatives generally take the form of multiple manuscripts that have been submitted or accepted for publication. Examples of such practices may be found at Oxford University (Biology Department) and the Universities of Birmingham and Ulster. More commonly permitted is a compilation thesis consisting of submitted, accepted or published papers. Examples are found at Kings College, Oxford University (Geography Department), the London School of Economics, Durham University, the University of Lancaster, and many international institutions – from Australia to Denmark and Sweden – where this practice is industry standard.

Taking a holistic view of dissertation models and design, the UK Council for Graduate Education (UKCGE, 2011) – an independent, representative body for postgraduate education – stated that many European countries, and Australia, have introduced an alternative dissertation model or integrated format for a PhD dissertation, sometimes known as the 'continental model', which allows for the submission of previously published papers and other artefacts as evidence that research has been conducted soundly, securely, ethically and with a robust methodology.

THE CHALLENGE: ALTERNATIVE DISSERTATION FORMATS

As awareness increases as to available PD dissertation options, the conventional model consisting of five chapters – introduction, literature review, research methodology, results, conclusions/recommendations – is giving way to new media, coupled with new technologies to offer candidates more opportunities to provide evidence that they are ready to make the transition from doctoral student to scholarly practitioner (Imig, 2011). The challenge to faculty members is determining what should constitute the culminating project. To date, research suggests that the capstone must be scaffolded by functions of the doctorate: developmental efficacy, community benefit, and stewardship of doctoral values (Crow et al., 2016). Such a PD dissertation then becomes a 'dynamic instrument for transformative development and development of an identity change and commitment to making a difference or effecting change' (Kochhar-Bryant, 2016: 37).

The common factor across the varying PD dissertation models is not one of structure, then, but one of the impacts of the scholarly practitioner in a specific professional domain resulting in change in practice. Fulton et al. (2013) suggest that the capstone includes reviewing the literature, summarising the overall methodological approach, outlining the aims of the work and the questions it addresses, summarising and contextualising the results, and making a case for its contribution to knowledge and practice (101).

Kochhar-Bryant identifies six characteristics of the PD dissertation process:

1. Provides a challenging opportunity to express one's values and talents and thus to actualise one's identity as a skilled professional.
2. Offers an opportunity to define and reflect on personal and professional transformations that contribute to one's identity as a change agent and commitment to a larger community project.
3. Provides an opportunity to construct a theory that is grounded in the understanding of the history of previous interventions into the problem.
4. Offers the opportunity to develop a sense of mastering a challenging situation and, through this, to feel a sense of responsibility for future outcomes.
5. Provides a deep sense of commitment to a research problem that is compelling for the individual and the community or organisation in which it occurs.
6. Provides an opportunity to envision solutions to problems within organisations and the community as they identify significant problems in the field. (2016: 7–8)

This PD dissertation process enables the candidate to embrace the scholar–change agent's doctrine: impact the world and be in the community. This interactive relationship is immediately evident in the growing number of programmes that are adopting non-traditional dissertation models to demonstrate understanding of core professional knowledge and the application of this knowledge to complex problems of practice (Perry and Imig, 2008) with a resulting change within the workplace (Maxwell, 2003).

THE CARNEGIE PROJECT ON THE EDUCATION DOCTORATE

In 2012, the Carnegie Project on the Education Doctorate (CPED) consortium developed performance indicators for assessing DiPs submitted for its annual award:

1. Demonstrates an understanding of, and possible solution to, the problem of practice. (Indicators: Demonstrates an ability to address and/or resolve a problem of practice and/or generate new practices.)
2. Demonstrates the scholarly practitioner's ability to act ethically and with integrity. (Indicators: Findings, conclusions, and recommendations align with the data.)
3. Demonstrates the scholarly practitioner's ability to communicate effectively in writing to an appropriate audience in a way that addresses scholarly practice. (Indicators: Style is appropriate for the intended audience.)
4. Integrates both theory and practice to advance practical knowledge. (Indicators: Integrates practical and research-based knowledge to contribute to practical

knowledge base; frames the study in existing research on both theory and practice.)

5. Provides evidence of the potential for impact on practice, policy, and/or future research in the field. (Indicators: Dissertation indicates how its findings are expected to impact professional field or problem.)

6. Uses methods of inquiry that are appropriate to the problem of practice. (Indicators: Identifies rationale for method of inquiry that is appropriate to the dissertation in practice; effectively uses method of inquiry to address problem of practice.) (2015)

In an action research study (Storey et al., 2015), members of the CPED Dissertation in Practice Awards Committee, examined the format and design of 25 submitted DiPs through surveys, interviews and analysis to determine if the dissertation had changed as a result of the project and redesign by participating programmes. They found that the format of 25 DiPs was the traditional (five-chapter) dissertation, with one non-traditional chapter, and all had single authors. Two submissions implemented results of their study and showed immediate impact. The average page length of the 25 DiPs was 212, with a range of 85–377 pages; 4 studies used quantitative methods, 17 used qualitative methods and 4 used mixed methods. The methodologies used in 10 of the studies were action research, case study, grounded theory and phenomenology.

A characteristic of all submitted DiPs was addressing immediate needs in practice. Some were assessments of existing programmes; others delved into theoretical constructs and enquired about their applicability to educational issues within the local, regional or national context (Storey et al., 2015).

ALTERNATIVE MODELS: ACTIVE INGREDIENTS

All models situate the DiP as a dynamic artefact guiding change to help resolve a complex problem of practice.

APPLIED DISSERTATION

The applied dissertation at Johns Hopkins University is embedded within its EdD programme's coursework. Candidates identify their problem of practice as well as its underlying causes and associated factors during their first year in the programme. During the second year, a potential solution is crafted, such as an intervention or policy change, and a plan to study the implementation and predicted outcomes. In the third year, the effectiveness of this solution is then evaluated as their applied dissertation. The DiP is then presented at a final oral defence before the student's dissertation advisory committee.

Johns Hopkins identifies three characteristics of the applied dissertation that make it unique:

1. Written assignments focus on the student's problem of practice.
2. Coursework leads students to consider solutions that hold the potential for significant change or impact within their organisation and/or have implications for policy.
3. DiP components are embedded within coursework and distributed across the three years of the programme.

CLIENT-FOCUSED

One type of capstone suited to a professional doctorate is a client-based DiP. In this type of capstone, students, either individually or as a team, address a problem of practice faced by an institution or programme (the client) in the candidate's area of professional practice. Client-based problems of practice have the advantage of being authentic problems whose solution can have a positive impact on the client and those served by the client. Client-focused studies enable PD candidates to apply analytical capacities, professional knowledge, contextual understandings and team-work skills acquired and accumulated throughout the PD programme to a focused project undertaken for a real-world client (Smrekar and McGraner, 2009). Virginia Commonwealth University identifies four steps in client-focused DiPs:

1. Clients prepare a request for assistance description of a project. This request includes a context statement, the problem to be addressed, the expectation of the client, the data sources that will be made available and/or the agreements for data to be collected, the expectations regarding communication and reports, and the expectations for the final report.
2. Students 'bid' on the project they wish to work on. Once a student team has selected a project, the team presents a scope-of-work memo to the client, and the scope of the project is agreed.
3. The final project is a written and oral report of the analysis undertaken, including a description of the literature that informed the topic, a description of the data used, and the policy and practice recommendations.
4. The final project is reported to both faculty reviewers and client reviewers. (Source: http://cpedinitiative.site-ym.com/page/virginiacomm)

For students, the scope of work to be done for the client includes assessing current practice, conducting a review of the literature to identify best practices, gathering stakeholder perspectives, developing a strategic plan with proposed solutions or interventions, piloting elements of the proposed solution, and maintaining communication with the client. The final product can vary depending on the needs of the client.

Consulting Reports

This model provides the pivot to advance students along the pathway from doctoral training to high-performance management, leadership and professional practice

(Smrekar and McGraner, 2009). At Vanderbilt University's Peabody College, potential clients for the capstone are cultivated though professional contacts and previous work associations, faculty suggestions and independent development activities undertaken by the capstone director. Clients are selected annually according to scope, rigour, faculty expertise and programme priorities. The clients then present their proposals to doctoral candidates prior to their final year. Candidates are assigned to teams in line with their proposal preferences. To support this collaborative capstone, students develop a document that outlines the scope of responsibilities for each member of the team. The contract between student and faculty informs individual evaluation at the end of the capstone experience. Although capstone projects vary by focus, geographical location, institution and scope (case study, systemic review, programme evaluation, environmental scan), Smrekar and McGraner have identified a set of common characteristics that all capstones share to facilitate rigorous analysis in an authentic operational setting:

- Derived from client interests and intended to address operational issues.
- Present-day, problem-centred orientation analysis linked to the relevant literature.
- Are both capstone adviser and client approved?
- Management consultant report format.
- Practically oriented and client centred.
- Analytically rigorous.
- Intended as a component of a professional portfolio and helpful to career advancement. (2009: 49)

Client-Oriented Group Dissertation

EdD candidates at the University of Colorado Denver's School of Education and Development have the choice of three project options: a project selected from and guided by shared research options associated with the university's Center for Practice Engaged Education Research (C-PEER); a thematic or group DiP; and a more individualised DiP that can be done as a small group or as an individual. There are also four format options: a C-PEER research report appropriate to the C-PEER client partner; an individually or collectively produced capstone monograph to be presented to members of the learning organisation and supported by detailed appendices; an individual or collective conventional five-chapter dissertation; or a fourth option designed with the candidate's adviser and committee.

C-PEER maintains ongoing relationships with districts, schools, community organisations and other institutions of higher education in order to maintain an ongoing research agenda that is based on the priority improvement needs of the partners and co-designed with field practitioner partners to help ensure that the results of the inquiry project will make a contribution to improving support for student learning and growth. C-PEER projects focus on the school building as the unit of change, but include community, district and state projects if these provide usable knowledge for improvement at the classroom and/or building level, or if they provide unique opportunities to learn across different local sites to better under-stand the contexts of supporting students' success.

GROUP DISSERTATION

Working as an investigative/consulting team, and in most cases in parallel, students address a common problem of practice in multiple contexts. At Virginia Commonwealth University, students work in groups on problems of practice articulated by field organisations. This is a collaborative endeavour that requires students to understand the problem as posed, analyse the issue from a number of perspectives, and respond with policy and practice. The model used is a consultancy project. One variation of the group dissertation is the closed cohort delivery model (Guo and Rose, 2015). Students in the EdD programme at Lynn University collec-tively produced an Apple iBook and multimedia artefacts, and published papers as part of their ensemble.

DISQUISITION

An innovative model at West Carolina University is the 'disquisition', a practice-driven model where doctoral candidates engage in 'moving the needle' on problems of practice (Crow et al., 2016). The disquisition is a capstone exercise designed to address a practical problem situated within a candidate's organisational context. Early in the programme, candidates build self-efficacy by leading a team including stakeholders and constituents within their organisations most affected by the iden-tified issue to name and frame the problem and to identify its potential solutions. Ultimately, students develop a perspective on the problem and lead the team to frame the problem in a way that facilitates organisational intervention. Inclusion of 'improvement science' as a primary methodology grounds the research curriculum: 'This inquiry course develops candidates' ability to incrementally formulate and test interventions aimed at improvement, and to document and assess impact to stakeholders and constituents' (211). Methods in improvement science are then utilised in disquisition projects and include the use of 'driver diagrams, Plan-Do-Study-Act and 90-day improvement cycles, charters, PICO evidence-based frameworks, gap analyses, and logic models' (211). These methods allow for diag-nosis, remediation and evaluation of problem-focused efforts and underpin the utilisation of these improvement science approaches. Capstone artefacts are varied depending on context.

MONOGRAPH MODEL

The monograph model is similar to that required for a traditional five-chapter dis-sertation, but the format of the resulting document differs. The key difference is that instead of five chapters that cover the problem and conceptual framework, litera-ture review, methods, findings and conclusions, a much more succinct and clear monograph, or research report, of approximately 30 pages is produced for the community partner or organisation. The monograph focuses on implications for practice and is supported by appendices that cover the problem addressed, a review of the literature, methods and a detailed presentation of the analysis employed in the study. The University of Colorado Denver identifies the following components of the monograph model:

- Abstract of the inquiry project (one page)
- Synopsis of the study (like an executive summary) (three to five pages)
- Statement of problem and framework (ten pages)
- Situating the problem in the research literature and local context as well as the theoretical and/or conceptual frameworks
- Brief description of methods of data collection and analysis (three to five pages)
- Empirically grounded findings of the study (three to five pages)
- Implications and recommendations (five to ten pages)
- Appendix A: Detailed methodology revised from proposal/prospectus (fifteen to twenty pages)
- Appendix B: Sample of analytic work that supports key findings (up to ten pages)
- Appendix C: Prospectus/proposal (problem statement and review of the literature, twenty-five to thirty pages) (University of Colorado Denver, 2015: 21)

ARTICLE (TAD)/MULTIPLE PAPER FORMAT/MANUSCRIPTS FOR PUBLICATION

Perhaps the longest accepted model of alternative dissertations is the three-article dissertation, known as TAD/multiple paper format/manuscripts for publication. In 1978, this was described as an innovation (Reid, 1978). Today, it is used in biological and natural sciences, social sciences and, of course, education (see e.g. Harvard Graduate School of Arts and Sciences, Stanford University and Rutgers University). Typically, three to five manuscripts support a singular theme. These manuscripts might have been published already, might be in the publication pipeline or might be a draft still in preparation (Golde, 2011). Additionally, manuscripts may have multiple authors. These dissertations typically include an introductory chapter that explains the overall research programme and the relationship among the manuscripts, as well as a conclusion that ties the papers together and proposes both general implications and future scholarship that follows from the work completed (Willis et al., 2010).

PROGRAMME EVALUATION DISSERTATION

This model provides practitioners with research skills that are rigorous and also relevant for those who plan to address problems in the field while they serve as practitioners (Stewart, 2016). While this model still follows a written five-chapter format, there are unique chapter differences that deviate from the conventional dissertation. Faculty and students at the University of Rochester and Alabama State University have found the evaluation dissertation to be a rigorous research process adding value to the developing knowledge and skills of the scholar–practitioner. In this model, chapter 1 serves as the introduction to the topic being studied but also includes the research questions. Chapter 2 consists of the theoretical framework, a description of the organisation or programme under study written as an in-depth case study, and the logic model. Chapter 3 is the methods chapter. Chapter 4 presents the findings that correspond with the areas of the logic model that were researched. The contents of chapter 5 are consistent with a conventional dissertation (i.e. key findings, conclusions, discussion, recommendations).

PORTFOLIO

This is a flexible model and varies among programmes. In the context of the PD, a portfolio is defined as 'a selection of products of research, which best establish the candidate's claim to have carried out research to a doctoral standard' (Walker, 1998: 94). A portfolio embraces the ideas in the mode 2 conceptualisation of knowledge production, with overlap among the disciplinary context, the profession and the workplace or laboratory of practice. Commonly, the portfolio is grounded on reflection, evidence and collaboration, and contains a mixture of past work and studies generated within the context of the PD (Fulton et al., 2013; Maxwell and Kupczyk-Romanczuk, 2009; Zubizaretta, 2009), although this can vary depending on the institution. It should be highly organised, well structured, and serve both a formative and summative purpose. Fulton et al. suggest that the following could be included in a portfolio:

- strategic organizational reports
- reports of projects that have been carried out as part of the work programme
- published conference or journal papers
- work of publishable quality
- strategic policy documents
- evaluation reports
- CD-ROM, DVD, and web work
- reflections on professional practice
- reflective diary extracts
- letters of validation
- objective evidence of the impact of the students' work
- personal development plan
- monitoring reports. (2013: 104)

At the University of Colorado Denver, students complete a report or written paper discussing the portfolio artefacts demonstrating that their work is of a doctoral standard and has made a professional impact. The portfolio contents are assessed against a set of outcomes. Fulton et al. identify the elements that should be contained in the report and map them to portfolio artefacts:

- A review of the relevant literature in which the investigation is fully and rigorously explored.
- The methodological approach, which has shaped and focused the study.
- The aims of the work and the research questions to be addressed.
- The results, including a contextualization and discussion of the results in which the literature is explored.
- A demonstration of the contribution to the knowledge and to professional practice. (2013: 101)

THEMATIC MODEL

The University of Southern California's Rossier School of Education has a thematic group option for its EdD programme's DiP. The thematic group consists of eight to ten students with a DiP chair. Students work on a common problem or around a common theme. Each student has a different research question or focus within the theme or problem area. Thematic groups may use common research questions and/or common methodologies. Alternatively, some groups may pursue a common theme, though students pursue their own questions and use their own methodology. Students may produce individually authored DiPs (the most common approach) or they may collaborate and co-author some of the chapters while still producing their own final product, which could be a conventional five-chapter study, a three-article design, a policy brief or analysis, an evaluation, or some other approved project or product.

EdD students at the University of Colorado Denver also complete thematic DiPs, which are organised around a broad, complex, field-based issue or problem. Each student on the team is required to pose and explore a line of inquiry while maintaining an overall connection to the group.

Activity

Select the approach which you think might be useful for the presentation of your project, and give reasons why.

Check your university's guidelines and ensure the approach is in keeping with the regulations.

CONCLUSION AND RECOMMENDATIONS

The analysis of DiPs and the narrative presented indicates both the challenges that institutions face and the pervasiveness of those challenges, as faculty wrestle with the design of a PD programme capstone. Is there one medium that best showcases candidates' mastery, or should the capstone artefact be tailored to context while maintaining a commitment to high and rigorous standards? At the core of PD programmes is the creation of generative knowledge that forms a substantive epistemology to guide the construction of meaning and build confidence in decision makers.

Transitioning from the written word to demonstrate mastery of varied media and technology tools such as film and gaming requires international dialogue focused on rigour. As alternative models of choice become the 'conventional' model, a collective understanding of effective outcomes will emerge leading to programme rigour and consistency at both a national and an international level.

Key Points

- This chapter explored the approaches to the development of the final dissertation in the professional doctorate.
- The traditional PhD thesis might not always be the appropriate way to develop the final product.
- There are key principles which guide the development of the professional doctorate and it is very important that these are followed regardless of the particular approach which is being taken.
- It is also very important that you ensure that the approach you have chosen meets your particular university's guidelines.

ANNOTATED BIBLIOGRAPHY

Costley, C., & Pizzolato, N. (2018). Transdisciplinary qualities in practice doctorates. *Studies in Continuing Education*, *40*(1), 30–45. DOI: 10.1080/0158037X.2017.1394287.

This excellent article extends the body of work on dissertation design by examining pedagogies and curriculum innovations that better facilitate the development needs of knowledge production in practice situations. Programmes endeavouring to situate candidate research at the interface between academia and their professional work via alternative dissertation models will see a natural extension in transdisciplinary research.

Murphy, J., & Vriesenga, M. (2005). Developing professionally anchored dissertation. *School Leadership Review*, *1*(1), 33–57.

This two-part article consists of an excellent literature review examining the impact of the arts and science dissertation model, and current efforts to transform or replace a PhD-focused model. The research section of the article examines the number of EdD programmes actually requiring an alternative-style dissertation and explores the gap between rhetoric and reality.

Storey, V. A., & Maughan, B. D. (2014). Beyond a definition: designing and specifying *Dissertation in Practice (DiP) models*. The Carnegie Project on the Education Doctorate.

This CPED-commissioned report describes alternative capstone designs, analyses dissertation content and gives examples of institutions utilising the various designs. It is an excellent overview of EdD dissertation models in the United States, Canada and New Zealand.

REFERENCES

Archbald, D. (2008). Research versus problem solving for the education leadership doctoral thesis: implications for form and function. *Educational Administration Quarterly, 44*(5), 704–39.

Barton, M. D. (2005). Dissertations: past, present, and future. Doctoral dissertation. *University of South Florida.* http://scholarcommons.usf.edu/etd/2777. Accessed 21 June 2018.

Berelson, B. (1960). *Graduate Education in the United States.* New York: McGraw-Hill.

Biddle, J. C. (2015). Dissertation requirements in professional practice education doctoral programs to facilitate K-12 school improvement in the United States. *Work Based Learning e-journal International, 5*(1), 55–85.

Bourner, T., Bowden, R., & Laing, S. (2001). Professional doctorates in England. *Studies in Higher Education, 26*(1), 65–83.

Carnegie Project on the Education Doctorate (2015). Examining EdD Dissertations in Practice: The Carnegie Project on the Education Doctorate. www.hetl.org/examining-edd-dissertations-in-practice-the-carnegie-project-on-the-education-doctorate. Accessed 21 August 2018.

Costley, C. (2013). Evaluation of the current status and knowledge contributions of professional doctorates. *Quality in Higher Education, 19*(1), 7–27.

Crow, R., Lomotey, K., & Topolka-Jorissen, K. (2016). An adaptive model for a rigorous professional practice doctorate: the disquisition. In V. A. Storey and K. A. Hesbol (eds) *Contemporary Approaches to Dissertation Development and Research Methods* (pp. 43–53). Hershey, PA: IGI Global.

Dawson, K., & Kumar, S. (2014). An analysis of professional practice Ed.D. Dissertations in Educational Technology. *TechTrends, 58*(4), 62–72.

Duke, N. K., & Beck, S. W. (1999). Education should consider alternative formats for the dissertation. *Educational Researcher, 28*(3), 31–6.

Fulton, J., Kuit, J., Sanders, G., & Smith, P. (2013). *The Professional Doctorate: A Practical Guide.* New York: Palgrave Macmillan.

Golde, C.M. (2011). Thoughts on the research doctorate dissertation. *UCEA Review, 52*(3): 10–12.

Grogan, M., & Andrews, R. (2002). Defining preparation and professional development for the future. *Educational Administration Quarterly, 38*(2), 233–56.

Guo, X. E., & and Rose, S. (2015). Ensemble work as a 21st century model for the Doctorate in Education nontraditional Dissertation in Practice (DiP) at Lynn University. *International Journal of Educational Policy Research, 2*(2), 25–31.

Guthrie, J. W. (2009). The case for a modern doctor of education degree (Ed.D.): multiple education doctorates no longer appropriate. *Peabody Journal of Education, 84*(1), 3–8.

Imig, D. (2011). Dissertations or capstones: the conundrum facing EdD programs. *University Council for Educational Administration (UCEA) Review*, Fall, 12–13.

Kochhar-Bryant, C. A. (2016). Difficult passage: culture change and the emergence of the Professional Practice Doctorate. *CPED White Paper Project 1*(1). https://cdn.ymaws.com/

cpedinitiative.site-ym.com/resource/resmgr/docs/CPED_data/white_papers/Difficult_Passages_Kochhar-B.pdf. Accessed 21 June 2018.

Levine, A. (2005). *Educating School Leaders*. Teachers' College, Columbia University. New York: Education Schools Project. www.edschools.org/reports_leaders.htm. Accessed 21 June 2018.

Malen, B., & Prestine, N. (2005). The case for revitalizing the dissertation. *UCEA Review*, 46(2), 7–9.

Malone, T. L. (1981). A history of the Doctor of Philosophy dissertation in the United States 1861–1930. Doctoral dissertation, Wayne State University.

Maxwell, T., & Kupczyk-Romanczuk, G. (2009). Producing the professional doctorate: the portfolio as a legitimate alternative to the dissertation. *Innovations in Education and Teaching International*, 46(2), 1–11.

Maxwell, T. W. (2003). From first to second generation PD. *Studies in Higher Education*, 28(3), 279–91.

McClelland, C. E. (1980). *State, Society, and University in Germany, 1700–1914*. Cambridge: Cambridge University Press.

Mellors-Bourne, R., Robinson, C., & Metcalfe, J. (2016). *Provision of Professional Doctorates in English HE Institutions*. Report for HEFCE by the Careers Research and Advisory Centre (CRAC), Higher Education Funding Council for England.

Modern Language Association (2014). Report of the MLA Task Force on Doctoral Study on Modern Language and Literature. www.mla.org/pdf/taskforcedocstudy2014.pdf. Accessed 21 June 2018.

Murphy, J., & Vriesenga, M. (2005). Developing professionally anchored dissertation. *School Leadership Review*, 1(1), 33–57.

O'Mullane, M. (2005). Demonstrating significance of contribution to professional knowledge and practice in Australian PD programs: impacts in the workplace and professions. In T. W. Maxwell, C. Hickey & T. Evans (eds) *Working Doctorates: The Impact of PDs in the Workplace and Professions* (pp. 8–23). Geelong: Deakin University.

Park, C. (2007). *Redefining the Doctorate*. York: The Higher Education Academy.

Perry, J.A., & Imig, D.G. (2008). A stewardship of practice in education. *Change Magazine*, November/December.

Reid, W.J. (1978). Some reflections on the practice doctorate. *Social Service Review*, 52(3), 449–55.

Rudolph, F. (1962). *The American College and University: A History*. Athens: Georgia University Press.

Rule, A.C. (2006). The Components of Authentic Learning 1 Editorial: The Components of Authentic Learning. *Journal of Authentic Learning*, 3(1), 1–10.

Shulman, L. S., Golde, C. M., Bueschel, A. C., & Garabedian, K. J. (2006). Reclaiming education's doctorates: a critique and a proposal. *Educational Researcher*, 35(3), 25–32.

Smrekar, C., & McGraner, K. (2009). From curricular alignment to the culminating project: The Peabody College EdD capstone. *Peabody Journal of Education*, 84(1), 48–60.

Stewart, T. J. (2016). Educational leaders and the program evaluation dissertation with logic model. In V. A. Storey and K. A. Hesbol (eds) *Contemporary Approaches to Dissertation Development and Research Methods* (pp. 43–53). Hershey, PA: IGI Global.

Storey, V. A., & Maughan, B. D. (2014). Beyond a definition: designing and specifying Dissertation in Practice (DiP) models. The Carnegie Project on the Education Doctorate.

Storey, V. A., Caskey, M. M., Hesbol, K. A., Marshall, J. E., Maughan, B., & Dolan, A. W. (2015). Examining EdD dissertations in practice: The Carnegie Project on the Education Doctorate. *International Higher Education Teaching & Learning Review*, February. www.hetl.org/examining-edd-dissertations-in-practice-the-carnegie-project-on-the-education-doctorate/. Accessed 21 June 2018.

UKCGE (2011). *Professional Doctorates in the UK*. Lichfield: UK Council for Graduate Education.

University of Colorado Denver (2015) Doctorate of Education (EdD) Leadership for Educational Equity Student Handbook Cohort #6, Summer 2015 Start. www.ucdenver. edu/academics/colleges/SchoolOfEducation/CurrentStudents/Resources/program_docs/ Cohort%206%20EdD%20Handbook.pdf. Accessed 21 August 2018.

Walker, R. (1998). Writing down and writing up in the professional doctorate journals and folios. In T. W. Maxwell & P. J. Shanahan (eds) *Professional Doctorates: Innovations in Teaching and Research*. Proceedings of 2nd National Conference on Professional Doctorates, Coffs Harbour, 8–10 July. Armidale: Faculty of Education, Health, and Professional Studies.

Wergin. J. (2011). Rebooting the EdD. *Harvard Educational Review*, 81(1), 119–40.

Willis, J. W., Inman, D., & Valenti, R. (2010). *Completing a Professional Practice Dissertation: A Guide for Doctoral Students and Faculty*. Charlotte, NC: Information Age Publishing.

Zubizarreta, J. (2009). *The Learning Portfolio: Reflective Practice for Improving Student Learning*. John Wiley & Sons.

AUTO-ETHNOGRAPHY

Kath Woodward

INTRODUCTION

This chapter engages with one of the big issues of research practice, which highlights the role of the researcher and, in particular, the relationship between the researcher, their subjects and the field of research, in the production of knowledge. Debates about this relationship have often been located within discussion about objectivity and the more subjective ways in which the researcher is implicated in the outcomes of a research project. What difference does the researcher and their own position make to what happens when they carry out a study of a particular social world? If you are a participant in the field of research, to what extent do you influence and shape the findings? Research can never be entirely objective, but what happens when researchers put themselves and their subjectivity at the centre of the process and how can you do this? What is involved? Questions of particular relevance to this volume concern the implications for professional practice of researching the depth and detail of people's experiences in a social world which ethnography offers and the enhanced understanding which reflection upon the researcher's own experience affords.

There are many qualitative research practices, especially those that involve participant observation in its many forms, or ethnography, where the situation and subjective position of the researcher has to be addressed directly. Researchers are an embodied presence in the field, which auto-ethnography recognises as linking the researcher to the field of research and the subjects of research inextricably. Researchers create knowledge about other people's lives as well as discovering the truth about different social worlds, by being involved in the field and by explicitly recognising their involvement. This chapter focuses upon auto-ethnography as a particular approach, which takes these issues on board and connects the researcher and the field of research through specific practices and strategies. Ethnography can reach the parts other more 'objective' approaches fail to access and auto-ethnography offers additional material, which is enhanced by explicitly locating the researcher in the research process.

RANGE AND SCOPE OF AUTO-ETHNOGRAPHY

Auto-ethnography provides a way of making sense of what sociologist Charles Wright Mills called the 'sociological imagination'. This is the ability to translate the routine and often personal activities of everyday life and how people think and feel into an understanding of the wider society and the point at which private troubles become social issues (Wright Mills, 1959). For example, going through a divorce is a private, personal trouble, which is also a social issue in societies, especially where this is a recurrent, wide-scale phenomenon; and exploration of the personal experience, which always take place within a specific society and culture and at a particular time, can generate greater understanding of social phenomena which have practical, policy implications.

By immersing oneself in the field of research and reflecting upon the experience and one's situation as a researcher, it becomes possible to make connections between the private troubles which beset individuals within the world with which they are most closely associated and the social issues which 'transcend these local environments of the individual .... An issue, in fact, often involves a crisis in institutional arrangements' (Wright Mills, 1959: 8). Mills expresses it as a 'conjunction of institutional and psychological forces' (1956: 292). More recent research has developed these connections within different frameworks, such as those explored in psychosocial studies (see e.g. Woodward, 2015), but the important point for the purposes of this chapter is the development of methods and practices for exploring social worlds which can accommodate the perceptions of all participants, including those carrying out the research.

Auto-ethnography goes further than participant observation. The researcher is still a participant in the process and offers a methodology and a practice, which enables the researcher to make connections and understand the point at which private troubles become social issues and the links between individuals and their inner worlds and social, cultural and political forces.

This chapter outlines the main features of auto-ethnography as a research practice or, more specifically, a set of practices, within qualitative methodologies, many of which have been adopted and developed by researchers across a wide range of disciplines and interdisciplinary fields, such as feminist and gender studies and those engaging with other forms of social exclusion such as racialisation and ethnicisation or marginalisation of grounds of disability.

In the chapter, I use examples from my own work on sport, particularly boxing, to illustrate and explore what is distinctive about an auto-ethnographic approach and what it can contribute to a deeper understanding of how research is undertaken and the knowledge that social scientists produce and publish.

AN OUTLINE OF AUTO-ETHNOGRAPHY

Auto-ethnography is a qualitative methodology which provides a way of not only acknowledging the role of the researcher, but also of reflecting upon that role and providing explanations of the connections between different elements which make up the practice of research. Most importantly, auto-ethnography provides a way of investigating and understanding personal and social worlds through a process which explicitly includes the researcher. As Tami Spry argues, 'Autoethnography is … a self narrative that critiques the situatedness of self and others in social context' (2001: 701). Storytelling is an important component of auto-ethnography. As Carolyn Ellis argues, it includes 'research, writing, story and method that connect the autobiographical and personal to the cultural, social and political' (2004: xix). Auto-biography is not the same as autobiography, though, because it embraces personal experience in order to make sense of social worlds, rather than providing a biographical account without analysis (Maréchal, 2010).

As Norman Denzin demonstrated, it is also possible to understand other people's experience, which may be very different from your own, especially in terms of privilege and social inclusion, through locating yourself and reflecting upon how marginalisation and social exclusion work. For example, in his own experience of researching Native American people, in Yellowstone Park, Denzin uses two cultural worlds, separated by time in which Native American people are represented. (It is worth noting that the term 'Native American' has become contentious, partly because the category is not homogeneous and does not specify the particular ethnicities which it encompasses. The rich data derived from auto-ethnographical studies can make manifest the details which a more generic term fails to show.) The one cultural world is Iowa in the 1940s and 1950s, where Denzin watched Cowboys and Indians films and television programmes such as *Red Rider and Little Beaver* and *The Lone Ranger and Tonto*, *Shane*, *Stagecoach* and *Broken Arrow*, in which particular narratives shaped his understanding of Native Americans in a white imaginary (Denzin, 2016). The other is Yellowstone Park in the 1870s.

Denzin uses his own cultural experience as a child in the United States in the 1950s to present different voices in order to write his way out of his own white narrative, which positions the Native Americans as the bad guys and the white American cowboys as brave heroic figures, by acknowledging how cultural and cinematic histories shaped his perception as a researcher.

Those who study social worlds are part of the contemporary culture and have their own legacies and acquired values and understanding of social relations. This is why film and other cultural texts often form part of auto-ethnographic accounts. Auto-ethnography can cut across the grain too, where the researcher is 'outside' as well as 'inside' the field of research.

This approach, which is growing in popularity, has been developed by anthropologists, sociologists and feminists who seek to foreground personal experience and reject the idea that research must, or could, be objective and neutral. In sport research auto-ethnography has been used to accommodate the idea of the embodied participation of the researcher. For example, building upon ethnographies of boxing (Wacquant, 2004), mixed martial arts (Spencer, 2009), work on capoeira (Downey, 2005), running (Allen-Collinson and Hockey, 2001; Nettleton, 2013) and dance (Potter et al., 2008) provides just some examples of textured, complex auto-ethnographic research that embraces the sensory experiential specificities of physical practices and diverse cultures. Such auto-ethnographers have challenged accepted views about silent authorship, where the researcher's voice is not included in the presentation of findings, by writing themselves into their own work as major characters (Holt, 2003: 2).

The writer's personal experience has been particularly influential:

> I start with my personal life. I pay attention to my physical feelings, thoughts, and emotions. I use what I call systematic, sociological introspection and emotional recall to try to understand an experience I've lived through. Then I write my experience as a story. By exploring a particular life, I hope to understand a way of life. (Ellis and Bochner, 2000: 737)

In emphasising the centrality of the personal, this account necessarily embraces the social or cultural world in which the writing occurs and makes it possible to read the social and cultural through the personal, which has long been an aspect of feminist methodologies.

For example, Patti Lather revisits the storyline of publications which marked her journey as a feminist methodologist, suggesting what she calls an 'Interlude' between each of the texts in her 2007 book. In folding her new and old writings both forward and back, she attempts to achieve a *polytemporality* by situating feminist research both inside and counter to and outside traditional approaches to social science, so that, as she has argued earlier, it 'makes it possible to probe how feminist research re-inscribes that which it is resisting as well as how it resists that re-inscription' (Lather, 1991: 27).

Laurel Richardson posits two questions which are particularly relevant to the auto-ethnographic project: 'How do the specific circumstances in which we write affect what we write? How does what we write affect who we become?' (1997: 1). Richardson cites the example of the co-authored ethnographic drama *The Sea Monster* that is illustrative of the 'writing-story' genre and offers some explanation of the story of how a text is constructed. She goes on to argue that the process of co-authorship permits her to write *her* story, 'not allowing another voice to penetrate the text' (74). By rereading and revisiting existing pieces of writing, it becomes increasingly evocative, 'illuminat(ing) a different facet of the complexity of a writing-life' as 'Forewords' or 'Afterwords' (5).

In such an account, writing is seen as a method of inquiry (Richardson and St Pierre, 2005) so that it articulates 'the common elements of these alternative approaches to research so that each individual and each research project is not an isolated effort to break through the unsayable to new knowledge' (Somerville, 2007: 225). The attraction of the unsayable has enormous resonance for auto-ethnographic accounts, because it suggests some ways of saying what cannot otherwise be said, for example in existing representational systems. Somerville has gone further than deconstruction so that her new theory of representation is cyclic and focuses upon 'creation of meaning from the relationship between the parts ... creation from working the space in between' (239). These different parts become something greater than the sum of each element.

These examples demonstrate what matters about auto-ethnography in different ways. Firstly, there are deconstructive notions of diverse writings from different times, published in a single volume (Lather, 2007). Secondly, writing is itself a method of inquiry (Richardson and St Pierre, 2005) and lastly, the 'auto', that is the self, of auto-ethnography is never complete; it is a 'becoming self' and 'becoming-other' (Somerville, 2007) as a vulnerable observer (Behar, 1996). Auto-ethnographic selves are not fixed and unified but fluid and changing, and the process of research changes the self who undertakes it as well as the field. Some of these fluidities and uncertainties are reflected in the associations between auto-ethnography and challenges to positivism and modernist epistemologies and sources of truth.

Auto-ethnography has many different characteristics but there are distinguishing features:

- It brings together the personal and the social in a way that promotes deeper understanding of the chosen field of research.
- By acknowledging and exploring the role of the researcher auto-ethnography addresses the issue of bias directly and explicitly.
- Affects and emotions can be better understood by adopting an auto-ethnographic approach, because it provides a way of accessing what is unstated.
- It opens up new and creative methodologies.

- Auto-ethnography can permit greater understanding of voices that have been silenced and people who have been marginalised.
- It shows how researchers are part of the process of making knowledge and not just neutral outsiders.

Activity

We have discussed ethnography and auto-ethnography. List the key differences you see between the two approaches.

THEORIES, METHODOLOGIES AND METHODS

Theories and methodologies are closely interconnected and a methodological approach such as auto-ethnography is not only based upon an epistemology, but also part of it and often indistinguishable from it. Auto-ethnography is interpretative and hermeneutic and challenges the claims to objectivity which positivism asserts. Researchers who adopt this approach argue that, far from being the desired goal of the research project, objectivity and neutrality are both unattainable and undesirable. If you pursue objectivity, you miss out on understanding how you are actively involved in producing knowledge. The autobiographer's project uses subjectivity and goes beyond the self and the culture to create new understandings. Thus it is broadly social constructionist in that knowledge is produced collaboratively rather than revealed as authentic truth, but auto-ethnography goes further in its direct use of the researcher's own feelings, emotions and self-knowledge of being part of a particular time, place, culture and set of social relations, including social class and ethnicity. The researcher is also gendered, has a sexual identity and makes and remakes those identities in a social world in which meanings about sex and sexuality are also made and remade and manifest tensions between nature and culture and certainty and uncertainty.

In short, researchers have their own personal and social identities, which they bring to the production of knowledge; the situated researcher is a protagonist in the process which links theoretical frameworks and epistemologies to evidence and findings. As Judith Okely, who writes about traveller and gypsy culture, notes of the work of the pioneering anthropologist Malinowski, 'theory creates fact' (1996: 38).

There are differences among auto-ethnographers. These range from the more analytic approaches through autobiographical narratives (Ellis, 2004; Ellis & Rawicki, 2013) to the performative (Denzin, 2013; 2016). Others work collaboratively (Allen-Collinson and Hockey, 2005) and deploy a huge variety of texts and experiences, including films and film-making, those of popular culture with which researchers are in conversation, diaries, journals as well as individuals' accounts of particular experiences, but, unlike documentaries, auto-ethnographies do not lay claim to particular authenticity or incontrovertible truth.

Methods include the more specific strategies and practices which researchers adopt in order to access the field and their subjects and incorporate a whole range of material, including texts and films as well as encounters, exchanges and observation. Methods include specific techniques such as quantitative or qualitative approaches and, within the latter, types of interview.

Reflexivity is a key component of auto-ethnography. This involves an ongoing process of reflection upon the process of conducting research, which is never a completed activity but always one of becoming and of interactivity. Focusing upon reflexivity involves the researcher being aware of their own affects and impact upon the process of producing knowledge as well as allowing the possibility of revisiting and reinterpreting empirical evidence, which in this case incorporates reflection, which can include a research journal or diary. It means acknowledging that research is relational and interactive and is a dynamic two-way process in which it is necessary to be attentive to the effect of the situated researcher at every stage in the process.

Reflexivity involves an ongoing process of reflection upon the process of conducting research, which is never a completed activity but always one of becoming and of interactivity.

Activity

The case study below is from my own research and takes the form of reflections upon the experience of undertaking research, which could broadly be called auto-ethnographic, in a boxing gym. The main concern of the data is to provide an opportunity to reflect upon a particular research project, which highlights the role of the researcher in relation to the field of research and raises questions about how researchers can engage with their own impact upon the field of research and the relationality of the research process. The first set of field notes was produced after revisiting the gym, where I had previously conducted research, to make a film about boxing and art for the Irish Television Company RTÉ in 2010. These field notes were made after a preliminary visit to the gym.

As you read through these two pieces, think about these questions:

- In this example how are the findings of the research influenced by the situation of the researcher?
- What does the researcher as an observer rather than a participant deliver about interpersonal relations and the culture of boxing?
- What do these notes indicate about how insiders and outsiders are connected?
- How does the idea of the situated researcher contribute to the idea that the research process is one of producing knowledge rather than uncovering realities?
- What might it mean to suggest that the qualitative or ethnographic researcher is always embodied?
- Does the personal account tell you anything a more objective analysis might not?

A BOXING EXAMPLE

FIELDWORK NOTES

The data derive from, firstly, a research diary recording my experience of returning to the field of earlier research, which has been published in a variety of sources including Woodward (2004; 2007; 2008), and, secondly, a summary of the related, relevant highlights of viewing the film on which I was the academic consultant and in which I participated in 2010. The aims of the research were initially to explore the social world of boxing and its embodied culture and subsequently to develop an understanding of the role of the researcher and in particular the notion of the situated researcher as a mechanism for addressing some of the issues arising from debates about the tensions between insiders and outsiders in the research process. Ethnographies of boxing have often been undertaken by researchers who participate actively in the field. They spar and even compete competitively (Wacquant, 2004). I wanted to know what happens when you do not join in.

Going Back: Diary Entry

I've just been back to the gym. It's still St Thomas's Boys' Club, which remains etched in the stone above the door. Wincobank hasn't changed much. Brendan still lives across the road. This place is special because this is where my boxing research, although not, of course, my interest in and connection to the sport, started. I've been back since of course, interviewing and hanging about if not hanging out, but as I parked outside and approached the gym, the first time came back to me: the transition between being outside and being inside and getting back into the field. As I approached the closed door I felt nervous as well as a bit nostalgic, remembering my first visit to this gym, in 1996, just before making the Open University BBC television programme *Whose Body?* there. All those details matter, because, at the time, it was my BBC connections which got me in. I recall being particularly anxious on my first visit to set up details of the filming and what we hoped to achieve in the programme. Women weren't allowed in then, apart from mothers who might be delivering small boys for the Saturday morning sessions and Brendan's family. Everyone thought I was a journalist or worked for the BBC so they were keen to talk to me. All these memories came back to me as I paused at the door to the gym, before I went in. It all looked much the same. The broken mirror had been replaced and there were some new bags with a logo on each one. There were still some torn old photos on the wall but there were some new additions. What was markedly different from every other visit I had ever made to this gym was the music. We had chosen a quiet time for the meeting and the gym was empty apart from the trainer and the film producer and director. There was no pounding beat, no thunderous bag work, and no voices. It was a strange experience, which made me feel even more distanced than I had on my very first visit, although as I walked through the gym its battered equipment and familiar photos and press cuttings randomly stuck around the walls seemed very familiar. Most familiar was Brendan, who welcomed me. He certainly seemed to remember me even if he thought I had more charitable intentions in promoting social cohesion and inclusion among local disaffected youth than I had or have as a researcher – not that I was exactly there as a researcher. Maybe having some social conscience is the only motivation to be attributed to someone like me doing research into boxing and the limited publicity an academic like me – like most of us doing research – can offer is nonetheless, in my case anyway, good publicity. I always give them a copy of my books and articles.

Memories of feeling a fraud because I don't box and never have in spite of my loyalty to the sport also re-emerged. I am an unlikely boxing researcher and this is always in my mind. I am not inside its culture and practice as some male researchers are who engage in boxing's body practices, but I follow it, and although my attitude to its violence is ambivalent, I am inside the culture of the everyday practices of the sport and, as an older woman, am used to being invisible, but for some reason boxing gyms make me feel at home in ways which working in other sports, which I have played as well as followed, if long ago, like cricket, do not. This is about the specificity of the connections between space, cultural connections and traditions and practices: boxing gyms can be family. Having researched boxing for some time and published quite extensively on boxing culture (and more importantly followed the sport all my life) were what got me into this position and led to the invitation to participate in making the film, but my research activities were tangential to this visit or at least not central. Perhaps they were, though? As a sociologist I don't think I'm ever off duty. I knew the film would deliver material that could be really important to my research, my methodologies and to my understanding of why boxing endures.

Ethnographic and indeed all qualitative researchers have to be opportunist, ethical, respectful and honest, but nevertheless you have to seize what chances you get, especially to get inside your cultural and social field.

After a while I felt at home and much more comfortable in a routine conversation with Brendan about boxing and what's been going on at the gym since I was last there three years ago.

The discussion, which included the director, wasn't quite so straightforward because I felt a tension between endorsing my links with the everyday of boxing in the gym and the easy chat with Brendan and establishing my intellectual credibility with the director. It wasn't so much theorising boxing culture and the relationship between boxing and art: Brendan is pretty open-minded. It was some of the issues. Why did I feel uncomfortable talking about the homoeroticism of pugilism in the gym?

Being There in the Film

Watching the film *A Bloody Canvas*, to which the interview in the previous section contributed, was a strange experience. The film was the brainchild of Irish abstract artist Sean Scully, who had been a boxer and wanted to explore some of the connections between art and boxing through different expressions, images, representations and artwork ranging from Caravaggio to Robert Mapplethorpe and discussion and comment from boxers and me. For the purposes of my discussion of the data in this book, I want to reflect upon the experience of seeing oneself in the field, not as part of a research project, but almost incidentally, rather like catching a glimpse of yourself in a mirror while you are in the field, which is something that has occasionally happened to me, because boxing gyms often have large mirrors for boxers to check their technique. It wasn't quite the same, but it was nonetheless a surprise and somehow unexpected. I was down on the credits and had been part of the team making the film, but seeing myself 'in the field' and in the culture of boxing seemed disruptive. My approach has been auto-ethnographic, but I had not actually *seen* myself in the field; I had just reflected upon the experience.

Boxing is a particularly enfleshed set of practices and activities. Boxing is all about bodies, their size, weight, power, beauty and pain, so it is not really surprising that in researching boxing I should be concerned with the relationship between the embodied researcher and the field of research. These connections and disconnections were brought home to me most forcibly when watching myself in the film.

I am an insider and part of the process, but what I see is an outsider – a woman who is neither a boxer nor an artist. My visual image, my face on film, shows the signs of the passage of time, unlike ex-boxers like Barry McGuigan, who carry the scars of a career in the ring. Fleetingly I think that I should have worn make-up: we always used to for television. Maybe I would have looked more as if I belonged in this space if I had been dressed up and made up according to gendered conventions in public spaces of visibility? I'm not sure that's quite it, though, and I think that my experience of feeling a fraud and outside whilst inside is also part of doing auto-ethnographic research.

Participant observation, even what Wacquant calls the observing participant (2004), always involves some distance. The researcher is never fully immersed in the field (and always has the possibility of retreating back to the academy or to another social world).

Activity

We have explored auto-ethnography and its meaning in this chapter.

Usually in professional doctorates you are thinking about your own practice.

How can you use these critical reflections above in relation to your own practice?

What implications do these reflections have more widely for professional practice?

COMMENT

These two reflective pieces indicate some of the ways in which objectivity and subjectivity, insider and outsider status, distance and immersion, the researcher and the field of research and the subjects of research are always interrelated, but in different ways and with different weightings. I have offered a particularly self-conscious version of reflexivity which quite explicitly challenges the insider–outsider dichotomy and the argument that total immersion in the field might necessarily afford greater truths about the field of research and the social world being explored.

Thus it would be useful to consider this evidence in the context of other accounts, for example in the field of sport, where researchers have been considered to establish their own credibility by maximum participation in the field.

Sport offers particular opportunities for joining in, in the hope of accessing deeper insights, especially in relation to body practices, but my work suggests that this might not be necessitated by the research process. Reflection, which includes the perspectives of the situated researcher, might deliver more than description of the field and detailed record of the responses of the subjects of research.

The data also suggest where more careful questioning of the researcher's role in the process of producing knowledge might take us in understanding a social world and a set of relationships with which the researcher is not intimately, or even superficially, familiar.

By considering material that is tangential to the direct research process, in this case making the film, it is also possible to embrace some more surprising and unexpected data, which nonetheless casts light on a study. Researchers have to be opportunistic too.

Key Points

- Auto-ethnography offers a new set of practices for conducting research and for making sense of social relations. Most importantly, it provides another way of linking the personal to the political and the individual to the social.
- By challenging the apparent certainties of positivist approaches, auto-ethnography poses new questions about the connections between inner worlds of feelings and emotions and personal experience and biographies, on the one hand, and social and cultural worlds, on the other. The two are inseparable and, as psychosocial theorists and practitioners argue, it is impossible to live outside the social, cultural and political world you inhabit.
- This approach, which recognises affect and subjectivity, lends itself well to creative and imaginative practices that can accommodate fictional, cinematic material and a wide range of sources of evidence.

(Continued)

(Continued)

- Auto-ethnography can also be seen as demonstrating integrity, which positivist methodologies, when they deny the subjectivity that is necessarily part of any research process, fail to acknowledge about how choices are made about methods and findings.
- Nonetheless auto-ethnography is vulnerable to challenges of bias and overt inclusion of the researcher and for the matter of subjectivity might be seen as failing to meet intellectual demands for rigorous scholarship.
- The fast-expanding field of auto-ethnography does, however, insist upon its own standards to ensure the reliability and substance of its findings and imagination and affect are central to social as well as personal worlds.

ANNOTATED BIBLIOGRAPHY

Allen-Collinson, J. (2009). Sporting embodiment: sports studies and the (continuing) promise of phenomenology. *Qualitative Research in Sport and Exercise, 1*(3), 279–96.

For an interesting discussion of phenomenological, embodied autoethnography within the empirical area of sport.

Denzin, N. K., & Lincoln, Y. S. (eds) (2000). *Handbook of Qualitative Research* (2nd edn). Thousand Oaks, CA: Sage.

This provides an edited collection, which is useful for situating auto-ethnography (and ethnography) within the wider terrain of qualitative research.

Holman Jones, S., Adams, T. E., & Ellis, C. (eds) (2013). *Handbook of Autoethnography*. Walnut Creek, CA: Left Coast Press.

This collection provides a comprehensive range of contributions from a wide range of disciplines and from practitioners and scholars who have engaged with different empirical fields, but are each concerned with making sense of lived experience. A really useful reference, it has practical suggestions as well as covering the history and diversity of auto-ethnography.

REFERENCES

Allen-Collinson, J., & Hockey, J. (2001). Runners' tales: autoethnography, injury and narrative. *Auto/biography, IX*(1–2), 95–106.
Allen-Collinson, J., & Hockey, J. (2005). Autoethnography: self-indulgence or rigorous methodology. In M. McNamee (ed.) *Philosophy and the Sciences of Exercise, Health and Sport* (pp. 187–202). London: Routledge.
Behar, R. (1996). *The vulnerable observer*. Beacon Press/Boston.
Denzin, N. (2016). Mystories: connecting the personal and the political. In *Writing Across Boundaries*, Durham University. www.dur.ac.uk/writingacrossboundaries/writingonwriting/normandenzin/. Accessed 8 October 2016.
Denzin, N. K. (2013). *Interpretive Autoethnography* (2nd edn). Los Angeles: Sage.
Downey, G. (2005). *Learning Capoeira: Lessons in cunning from an Afro-Brazilian art*. Oxford: Oxford University Press.

Ellis, C. (2004). *The Autoethnographic I: A Methodological Novel About Autoethnography.* Walnut Creek, CA: AltaMira Press

Ellis, C., & Bochner, A.P. (2000). Autoethnography, personal narrative, reflexivity: researcher as subject'. In N.K. Denzin & Y.S. Lincoln (eds), *Handbook of Qualitative Research* (2nd edn) (pp. 733–68). Thousand Oaks, CA: Sage.

Ellis, C., & Rawicki, J. (2013). Collaborative witnessing of survival during the Holocaust: an exemplar of relational autoethnography. *Qualitative Inquiry, 19*(5), 3.

Holt, N.L. (2003). Representation, legitimation, and autoethnography: an autoethnographic writing story. *International Journal of Qualitative Methods, 2*(1), 18–28.

Lather, P. (1991). *Feminist Research in Education: Within/Against.* Geelong: Deakin University Press.

Lather, P. (2007). *Getting Lost: Feminist Efforts towards a Double(d) Science.* Albany, NY: SUNY Press.

Maréchal, G. (2010). Autoethnography. In A. J. Mills, G. Durepos, & E. Wiebe (eds) *Encyclopedia of Case Study Research: L–Z; Index, Vol. 1.* Sage.

Nettleton, S. (2013). Cementing relations within a sporting field: fell running in the English Lake District and the acquisition of existential capital. *Cultural Sociology, 7*(2), 196–210.

Okley, J. (1996). The self and scientism. In J. Okley (ed.) *Own or Other Culture* (pp. 27–44). London, Routledge.

Potter, K., Kimmerle, M., Grossman, G., Rijven, M., Liederbach, M., & Wilmerding, V. (2008). Screening in a dance wellness program. *A Report of the Education and Research Committees of IADMS.* Available at www.iadms.org.

Richardson, L. (1997). *Fields of Play: Constructing an Academic Life.* New Brunswick, NJ: Rutgers University Press.

Richardson, L., & St Pierre, E. (2005). Writing: a method of inquiry. In N. K. Denzin & Y. S. Lincoln (eds) *The Sage Handbook of Qualitative Research* (pp. 959–78). Thousand Oaks, CA: Sage.

Somerville, M. (2007). Postmodern emergence. *International Journal of Qualitative Studies in Education, 20*(2), 225–43

Spencer, Dale C., (2009). Habit(us), body techniques and body callusing: an ethnography of mixed martial arts. *Body & Society, 15*(4), 199–43.

Spry, T. (2001). Performing autoethnography: an embodied methodological praxis. *Qualitative Inquiry, 7*(6): 706–32.

Wacquant, L. (2004). *Body and Soul: Notes of an Apprentice Boxer.* Oxford: Oxford University Press.

Woodward, K. (2004). Rumbles in the jungle: boxing, racialization and the performance of masculinity. *Leisure Studies, 23*(1), 5–17.

Woodward, K. (2015). *Psychosocial studies: An introduction.* London: Routledge.

Woodward, K. (2007). Real men? Boxing and masculinity. In M. Berkowitz & R. Ungar (eds) *Fighting Book. Jewish and Black Boxers in Britain.* London: UCL Press.

Woodward, K. (2008). Hanging out and hanging about, insider and outsider research in boxing. *Ethnography, 9*(4): 536–60.

Wright Mills, C. (1956). *The Power Elite.* New York: Oxford University Press.

Wright Mills, C. (1959). *The Sociological Imagination.* Oxford: Oxford University Press.

ACTION RESEARCH

Gill Coleman

INTRODUCTION

This chapter considers a particular methodology called *action research*. The term action research covers a number of approaches but what they all have in common is the aim to bring about a change in practice and involve other people in this process. This chapter explores several approaches which may be taken. The need for a continual reflection on the process and the reflective elements which run throughout is emphasised.

> To me, being an action researcher is about approaching life's twists and turns with curiosity, honesty and loads of questions to produce new knowledge and transformation. It is that simple and difficult. (Pascal Tshibanda, Local Council CEO, Sweden. Masters student 2014)

Action research is a form of research that explicitly sets out to make a practical difference to the issue, problem or question being studied, through a robust consideration of the experience of those concerned. It asks fundamental questions about what research is *for*, and what use can be made of the opportunity to conduct research that is really worthwhile for the researcher – to explore topics that are not just academically interesting, but of personal, practical and/or political concern. In so doing, it occupies a place on the boundary between academia and practice, questioning the role of ideas in practice and challenging the ways in which 'the academy' defines and uses knowledge. It invites attention to the political processes through which academic knowledge is created and invested with importance, posing this as a question to be thought about rather than a given.

Reason and Bradbury's description of action research is widely quoted:

a participatory, democratic process concerned with developing practical knowing in the pursuit of worthwhile human purposes .... It seeks to bring together action and reflection, theory and practice, in participation with others, in the pursuit of practical solutions to issues of pressing concern to people, and more generally the flourishing of individual persons and their communities. (2001: 1)

INSIDER RESEARCHERS

For people undertaking masters or doctoral degrees based on their professional practice, action research offers an opportunity to interrogate and question their experience, but also to develop their practice. They can use the research to create something new, connect them to others, build new communities of practice, surface questions that have long bothered them which may sit at the boundaries of what is normally discussed, and find practical ways forward. Action research is often used in situations in which the dynamics of power and oppression are being grappled with – for instance, exploring questions of race, gender, identity and sexuality. It is used in community building and awareness raising, healthcare, education, development work. But it is also used by managers, leaders and other professionals, who want a strong practical orientation to their research. Organisational development professionals will also find strong echoes in action research, since they share some conceptual roots (Weisbord, 2012).

Research conventionally separates the research field from the researcher, carefully trying to avoid affecting the thing that is being studied so as to safeguard objectivity. By contrast, action research is an approach that combines action and systematic reflection. An action researcher holds two aims: to find out more about the issue or question being studied and to be able to positively change or develop it in practice. A good action research project produces both good thinking, grounded in relevant theory, and knowledge which is 'actionable' (Coghlan, 2011; Argyris, 2003) in the sense that it enables those involved to put what they have discovered into practice. For this reason, action research is often used by people who want to affect change in their *own* organisations, and who are therefore 'insider' researchers (Coghlan and Brannick, 2010).

People undertaking professional doctorates are often juggling multiple roles, as practitioners, researchers and human beings with lives outside work. The action research process invites them to bring *all* of these selves into the research process if they wish to, acknowledging their impact on each other – Judi Marshall (1999) calls it 'living life as inquiry'. But at the same time, the edges and potential conflicts between different areas of life are things to be noticed and acknowledged, and the action researcher needs to be able to draw boundaries where they feel it is appropriate to do so – and to explain to those who read their work what choices they have made.

Action research is best thought of not as a single methodology, but as an *approach* that encompasses a range of methods and 'tools' which have some key characteristics. There are a number of positions or camps within the field: they are best thought of as a kind of extended family who do not necessarily agree about everything, but share the principle that the purpose of research is essentially a pragmatic one. Different members have their own name and particular ways of describing themselves (Table 9.1), which can be confusing for those trying to acquaint themselves with the overall field. All are quite eclectic about the actual *methods* of inquiry they use, being driven mainly by what seems an effective, logical and appropriate choice for the situation at hand.

Table 9.1 Members of the action research family

Members of the action research family	There are many members, with significant differences between them but sharing some common principles. Some are more practice oriented, some more research oriented. The following are often found useful for practitioner–researchers:
Co-operative Inquiry	The term was developed by John Heron and Peter Reason, to describe a form of collaborative inquiry in small groups in which every person is both a researcher and a research subject. The research question is devised through dialogue, and members in the group carry out cycles of action (outside the group) and reflection (inside the group)
Action Inquiry	Bill Torbert and colleagues at Boston University evolved an approach that builds on Argyris's Action Science by seeking to open up the possibilities of the present moment through increasing attention and awareness. This involves bringing framing, inquiry and reflection into daily interactions, alongside the more usual advocacy, and in so doing revising assumptions, facilitating significant learning and developing mutual, rather than unilateral, power. Torbert and colleagues link this to a model of leadership/adult development
Appreciative Inquiry	A form of action research that intentionally focuses on what is already successful and working well in a situation, rather than what is deficient. It was first developed by Cooperrider, Srivastva and colleagues at Case Western Reserve University in Cleveland, who explore the 'power of the positive question', and has given rise to a lively community of enquirers, with a virtual 'commons' containing resources and accounts of how the approach is being used at: http://appreciativeinquiry. case.edu/ (Cooperrider and Srivastva, 1987; Ludema et. al., 2001)
Learning history	Involves a retrospective look at an event or process, to pull learning from it. The approach originated in industry, but has developed a more narrative leaning in recent years as it is used to capture social and environmental innovation. Multiple stakeholders involved in the event are interviewed by a researcher, who then compiles a learning history document of their voices together with researcher reflections and comments. It is sometimes called a 'jointly told tale', since it aims to present more than a single view of what has transpired. The document/artefact is a 'transitional object', which is then used as the basis for collective reflection on what has been learned. See Bradbury et al. (2015)

(Continued)

Table 9.1   (Continued)

Participatory action research (PAR)	With its roots in liberatory practices in Latin America and Africa, PAR involves a wide range of techniques and forms, all with the intent of enabling relatively powerless people in articulating their experience and being actively involved in transforming the conditions of their lives. Somewhat contentiously it is now widely used in government and multilateral funded development work as a way to overcome some of the problems engendered by top-down projects, but most practitioners retain a radical political edge. See Chambers (1997) and Swantz (2008)

Since action research contravenes the normal separation between researcher and research subject, and has an orientation towards practical change, it is sometimes thought to be a form of organisational development, consultancy or community development rather than a form of research. There is some overlap in the skills involved in these different activities, but they are not the same. The educationist Laurence Stenhouse defined research as 'systematic and sustained inquiry made public' (1983: 185). Action research constitutes research in that:

- it involves deliberate and careful ways of gathering of information;
- sense is made of information by relating it to bodies of theory (the 'extant literature') and carrying out systematic reflection;
- data is gathered and conclusions are drawn on the basis of evidence, which has been subject to thoughtful scrutiny;
- findings from the process are generally communicated to others outside the research/action group.

It is not concerned simply with problem solving, and like all good research involves questioning assumptions and critiquing 'taken-for-granted' ways of seeing things.

CHARACTERISTICS

In a field with a wide range of positions, the cohering factor is a set of characteristics by which action researchers recognise themselves.

Reason and Bradbury's definition gives rise to five interdependent characteristics of action research, as follows.

1. A PRIMARY CONCERN WITH PRACTICAL ISSUES

Action research (AR) is concerned with the ways that people, as individuals or as groups, communities, organisations and societies, create their world around them through what they do. In an action research project, attention is not given primarily to the theoretical understanding of a situation, but to the ways in which practice in fact does, or more usually, does not conform to the theory. The impetus in conducting action research is to pay good attention to human practice, in all its messiness and complexity, and to 'tell is like it is', not how the researcher thinks it 'should' be. This concern is reflected in the judgements about quality in AR, which is discussed further below.

AR has been called 'science in the realm of practical knowing' (Coghlan, 2011), with its emphasis on making things 'better'. There is a connection here to pragmatist philosophy, which rejects the value of principles and values, except to the extent that they lead to outcomes desired by the communities that hold them. As Rorty says:

> When the question 'useful for what?' is pressed, [pragmatists] have nothing to say except 'useful to create a better future'. When they are asked 'Better by what criterion?' they have no detailed answer .... [They] can only say something as vague as: Better in the sense of containing more of what we consider good and less of what we consider bad. When asked 'And what exactly do you consider good?' pragmatists can only say, with Whitman, 'variety and freedom' or, with Dewey, 'growth'. They are limited to such fuzzy and unhelpful answers because what they hope is not that the future will conform to a plan, will fulfil an immanent teleology ... but rather that the future will astonish and exhilarate. (1999: 27–8)

2. AN INTENTION TO CONTRIBUTE TO 'HUMAN FLOURISHING'

There is an overt positive intent, then, in this approach. AR acknowledges its embedded values, and does not claim objectivity. This connects to the origins of AR, which involves a number of threads, including the organisational problem-solving work of Kurt Lewin and his associates in the United States and United Kingdom in the interwar years, workplace democracy activities in Scandinavia and the consciousness-raising work of Paulo Freire and the Marxist-based liberation movements in the southern hemisphere (Coghlan, 2011). It grew, then, from practices intended to bring about improvement, liberation, greater social and political justice, and so on. Some action researchers still retain that overt commitment to social change, and it is an approach widely used in community development work (Stringer, 2007) and international development (Chambers, 1997; Burns and Wolsely, 2015). The history of participatory AR has had a strong element of social critique, deliberately trying to help otherwise marginalised and silenced groups to find and express their voices (Gaventa and Cornwall, 2015) – to do what the Quakers would call 'speaking truth to power'. But practitioners in other areas that are seemingly less political also use AR in education, in both school and higher education (McNiff and Whitehead, 2009; Zuber-Skerritt, 2002; Carr and Kemmis, 1986; 2005) and in organisation change and management (Coghlan and Brannick, 2010). The push towards social change remains, nevertheless, an important aspect, even though this might appear in subtle ways. Attention is always given, for instance, to power relationships and critical awareness, and to the inclusion of diverse voices and perspectives (see point 4 below.) And a link is increasingly being made not just to human but also to planetary 'flourishing' – encompassing issues of sustainability and corporate social responsibility (Reason and Bradbury, 2008; Zuber-Skerritt, 2012; Marshall et al., 2011).

3. A COMMITMENT TO PARTICIPATION AND DEMOCRACY

In AR participation is held as a strong value that is central to the work: this is a way of doing research *with* people, not *on* them. It is founded on the fundamental belief that people have the right and the capability to make sense of their own lives and situations, and should not have meaning imposed on them by researchers (even well-meaning ones). From this perspective, research is not necessarily an activity conducted by trained people inside the academy, but can also be something done by ordinary people as they consider and shape their lives for themselves, with or without the help of an AR facilitator.

Action researchers who are undertaking their own individual work, for a masters or doctoral degree, consequently need to put effort into engaging the people involved in their research as active participants, not as passive research subjects. Care is taken to avoid the work being conducted as a 'view from the top', by actively seeking out and enabling the perspectives of those whose voices are routinely marginalised or unheard to enter the process.

4. A FORM THAT IS EMERGENT AND DEVELOPMENTAL

If AR projects are conducted in collaboration with the people involved, it follows that how it is actually done is an emergent process rather than fully planned in advance. In practice, there will be a starting intention which is negotiated with those involved, and from there the research proceeds through steps of action and reflection – sometimes referred to as the 'action research spiral' (Figure 9.1) to indicate that learning and change are involved as assumptions are challenged and new thinking is taken into action, rather than a repetitive cycling around the same loop of thinking and understanding.

This emergent quality may be challenging for anyone trying to start an AR project: the initiator may set a process underway, but is not necessarily in control of what transpires, and may need to revise their starting assumptions and even the initial research questions as things develop. Other stakeholders – funders and sponsors of projects, managers and organisational gatekeepers, ethics committees, people who may be thinking of joining in and others affected by the work – may require more certainty than it is possible to give. That is one of the reasons why the principles are important – they provide the framing which enables active curiosity and research sensibility to be brought to the complexity, mess and paradox that constitute real life, to pay good attention to it and to be informed by it.

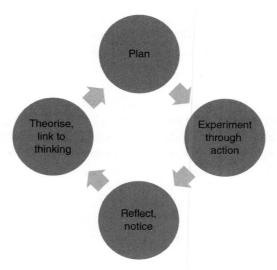

Figure 9.1   The action research cycle

5. A RELIANCE ON KNOWLEDGE-IN-ACTION

The practice orientation of AR lies not only in a desire for practical outcomes, but also in the belief that there is a certain sort of knowing that resides in action, and that is not fully captured in descriptions of action. We know about our world in the process of interacting with it. Theoretical strategies and solutions can be useful – as Kurt Lewin reputedly said, 'there is nothing so practical as a good theory'. But theory and practice are certainly not the same, and the move from thinking and reflection into action generates a different form of knowing, which may in turn speak to theory.

Ison, for instance, argues that 'knowledge arises in social relations such that all knowing is doing'; it is 'both the result of and the process of inquiry where neither theory nor practice takes precedence' (2010: 148).

AN 'EXTENDED' EPISTEMOLOGY

From the discussion above, it will be clear that AR challenges some fundamental tenets of mainstream academic epistemology – the understanding of how valid knowledge is created, and what the purpose of that knowledge is. AR is not alone in this: practice-based researchers inevitably have to grapple with the debates on the merits of quantitative versus qualitative methodologies and their underlying epistemologies that have been taking place for some decades. Denzin and Lincoln describe this discussion as politically charged, robust and ultimately inconclusive (2005: 22). Nevertheless, the default position in academia and beyond remains positivism, the assumption that the world is 'out there', separate from the researcher and waiting to be discovered through objective, value-free, context-free and generalisable research. Those taking positions that differ from this need to be able to articulate their position and explain the choices they have made (Coleman, 2015).

In AR, the epistemological territory embraces a social constructionist perspective (Gergen and Gergen, 2015) and a recognition that not *everything* is socially constructed, that there is a 'real' physical and social/political ecology to be interacted with, and that there is the possibility of a direction of change that is worth doing, which can be positively valued over other directions. Drawing on both systemic thinking (Marshall, 2016; Midgley, 2008; Burns, 2015) and ecological thinking (Capra, 1997) this is often described as a 'participatory worldview' (Reason and Bradbury, 2001: 1) which places humans as active participants in the greater planetary whole.

AR, then, encompasses ways of knowing that are routinely excluded in academia, and so 'extends' the sources of knowing available to the researcher. In addition to formal, rational *propositional* knowing, it draws on the kinds of knowing that are embedded in practice (*practical* knowing) that is understood non-verbally through experience (*experiential* knowing) and that may be contained in expressive representation like dance, drama, song, painting, and so on (*presentational* knowing) (Heron, 1996; Seeley and Reason, 2008).

These wider ways of knowing are in fact widely used in everyday life. For instance, doctors know that they sometimes have 'hunches' about the health of patients that are not being picked up by their measurements or instruments; police detectives know that if they physically follow suspects the person under surveillance is likely to sense their presence and realise they are being watched. The practical ability to ride a bicycle or swim cannot be captured by instructions, it has to be 'felt' in action to be learned. Art, poetry and music convey information about the human condition and move their audiences in a way that is often beyond words, which loses its quality if a verbal translation is attempted. AR deliberately pushes at the boundary that separates propositional thought from this wider territory available to human subjects, and invites these other forms of knowing to be brought into critical scrutiny in a research process so as to enrich awareness of the part played by complex lived experience in how humans make sense of the world.

Activity

We have considered action research and the groups of people one can work with using this approach.

Consider its relevance to your own situation: where might action research fit?

FIRST-, SECOND- AND THIRD-PERSON ACTION RESEARCH

AR is often described in terms of work that is 'for me', 'for us' and 'for them' (Reason and Marshall, 1987). Most AR projects involve a combination of these three levels of focus – they 'represent multiple simultaneous attentions' (Marshall et al., 2011: 245).

FIRST PERSON

The participative worldview of AR implies that the researcher is always *in* the research field – that even if attempts are made to minimise the effect the researcher has on what is being researched, it is logically impossible for their presence to have no significance, since everything is co-creating the present. So in an AR process, it is important for the researcher to develop awareness of themselves, even if the primary purpose of the research is the work of a group, community or organisation. First-person AR involves the individual study of one's own actions and reflections, practices and intentions. It makes the researcher/s themselves the focus of research attention. This involves both a private, reflective process, developing what Marshall (2016) calls 'inner arcs of attention', and a process of actively testing assumptions, experimenting with new actions and their effects, and gathering feedback from others, which Marshall calls 'outer arcs of attention'.

New researchers often find this move to pay attention to the self a difficult step – it challenges the strongly held boundary our culture makes between personal, subjective material and objective 'real' knowledge, and is easily seen as self-indulgent and even dangerous, carrying a fear of unleashing unconscious personal material. But in AR, awareness of self is a foundation for the work. Torbert (2004) calls it 'self-study in action'. This process of including oneself within the field of the research is called reflexivity, which is 'the capacity of the researcher to acknowledge how their own experiences and contexts inform the process and outcome of the inquiry' (Etherington, 2004: 32). It is at the root of all good-quality AR. Reflexivity is not the same as reflection. Reflection is a vital step in the AR cycle – the pause to stop, notice and think that is frequently absent in everyday life. It opens the way to learning. Reflexivity involves turning that reflective gaze on the self, in a way that opens the researcher themselves up to personal learning and change.

The subjective material generated through first-person inquiry is 'raw data', *not* a route to truth. Interpreting lived experience is not a straightforward matter: memories can be misleading, emotions may colour how something is perceived, different things are heard and seen by different people in the same situation. For this reason, the aim in first-person inquiry is to cultivate *critical* subjectivity, rather than a naive belief in the wisdom of one's own position. This requires subjecting the material to scrutiny, seeking ways to substantiate and critique the conclusions that may be drawn from them.

There are a number of ways of carrying out first-person inquiry. Attention to one's own 'inner arc' involves practices that quieten the noise of everyday life, to allow the researcher to pay attention to themselves:

- Journaling is widely used, writing 'into' one's internal chatter, and allowing it to surface on paper.
- 'Free' writing (Turner-Vesselago, 2013) and creative writing help develop the confidence to write outside the confines of the assumed academic voice.
- Using 'two-column' writing (Senge et al., 1994) helps to surface one's own thoughts, and hence assumptions.
- This material can then be analysed using, for instance, the Ladder of Inference (Senge et al., 1994) or the Learning Pathways Grid (Rudolph et al., 2001).
- Torbert and colleagues offer a number of frameworks to help develop awareness of one's own actions, and the gap that often exists between intention and actual action.
- Visual journaling (Gamin and Fox, 1999), painting, collage, 'moodboards', making maps and models are all ways of accessing 'presentational knowing'.

> the notion of first-person research ... might imply a modernist view of a stable and coherent self .... It is important that such ... self-referencing activity ... [be] challenging and developmental rather than self-satisfied. (Marshall, 2004: 306–7)

SECOND PERSON

Second-person inquiry means working collaboratively with others to co-enquire into questions of mutual interest. It lies at the heart of AR practice, given the high value placed on participation and the right for routinely marginalised voices to be heard. It is, nevertheless, not an easy thing to achieve, since it requires the researcher to exercise skills in convening, opening, facilitating and closing some kind of group or meeting, all of which become part of the research experience (McArdle, 2008). The intention in this work is to create what is sometimes called 'communicative space', drawing on Habermas's (1984) notion of arenas in which people can come into a deep enough relationship with each other to enable their beliefs, values and intentions to be spoken, listened to and respectfully interrogated, so that mutuality and understanding can be freely created and collective action taken. Building on these ideas, Kemmis writes:

> The first step in action research turns out to be central: the formation of a communicative space ... and to do so in a way that will permit people to achieve mutual understanding and consensus about what to do, in the knowledge that the legitimacy of any conclusions and decisions reached by participants will be proportional to the degree of authentic engagement of those concerned. (2001: 100)

Co-inquiry can be done in dyads, in interviews/conversations, or it can take place in small, face-to-face groups, which may be clearly led by the researcher, or are wholly collaborative.

Enquiring Conversations

In mainstream qualitative research, interviews are a common way to glean information from people about their life experiences. In AR, interviewing takes on an additional aspect, as a space in which relationship is formed and both parties are changed (in ways that may be imperceptible at the time) by the interaction. This does not involve simply one person asking questions and the other responding – although there may be questions involved which have more meaning to one of the parties than the other. But an action researcher will bring *themselves* to the conversation, willing to share their perspective as well as to listen, and to engage in a shared exploration of the topic which could take a direction they would not have anticipated.

New researchers are sometimes puzzled about whether what they are doing is first-person AR in which they happen to be talking to someone else about their inquiry, or second-person AR in which they are co-enquiring. This boundary is not necessarily a clear one. The second-person place is less a question of quantity, where more than one person is enquiring into a topic, and more one of quality: there is some mutuality – both people are discovering something which they would not articulate in this way on their own. You might say the 'data' has been helped into being by the relationship.

Inquiry Groups

Some action researchers like to convene a group of people specifically to work with them on a topic or question they are pursuing. Typically, this would involve a group which could be as small as 3 people or as large as 20, but would involve agreement on a question to be explored, and a series of cycles of action-and-reflection, with the group members undertaking some agreed action-experiments separately or in subgroups, and then coming together to discuss and make sense of the experience and what they have found. The initiator takes the role of group leader, and would take responsibility for negotiating the practical tasks of meeting and capturing findings. If that person is undertaking the inquiry for an academic degree, they are likely to have an interest in data gathering which may not be fully shared, and will have to work to establish mutuality nevertheless. Wicks and Reason (2009) suggest this gives rise to a number of challenges which anyone convening such a group needs to take into account (see Table 9.2).

Co-operative Inquiry

In this form of group everyone participating is a co-researcher and co-subject. The process of co-operative inquiry is similar to that described above, in that the group

Table 9.2   Paradoxes and contradictions of opening communicative space

1. Contracting: how has the initial setup been done and agreements been reached? Does this enable clarity but also emergence?
2. Boundaries: does the group have enough boundary to give safety to its members? How are these set and upheld? Can people come and go, or is it a 'closed' group?
3. Participation: is everyone expected to participate in the same way? Is that fair? Does it place more demand on some people than on others?
4. Leadership: who is in a leadership position? Is that person exerting undue influence? Could leadership be shared? How does that help or hinder mutuality?
5. Anxiety: how is this being handled? Is there safety that allows anxiety to be expressed?
6. Chaos and order: what is the balance between having and following a plan and allowing things to emerge, encountering the unexpected?
7. Personal development and practicality: how much is the group concerned with the development (and perhaps significant shifts in thinking) of its members, and how much with getting action outcomes?

Based on Wicks and Reason (2009).

meets over an agreed period and undertakes an investigation of a question of mutual interest through cycles of action and reflection. The topic of the research may start with particular individuals, but the inquiry questions, action and reflection cycles and sense-making are all undertaken through collaborative agreement, so everyone is researching and being researched at the same time, with the here-and-now of the group experience explicitly informing the findings (Heron and Reason, 2005). Explicit use is often made of the 'extended epistemology', surfacing intuitive knowing, for instance, and sharing experience through storytelling, poems, drawing, collage, and so on. This form of inquiry has been used to explore questions that require a high level of group trust and mutual support in order for people to feel they are able to bring their experience and find common ground. The process of sharing experience can be powerful and lead to the creation of shared action (see e.g. Yorks et al., 2008). In organisational settings, it can provide a means through which questions that sit on the edge of 'what can be talked about' can be surfaced, validated and tested through action.

THIRD PERSON

Third-person AR involves inquiry with and into large groups or communities, beyond the connection offered by the relational net of small groups. Gustavsen (2003), one of the pioneers of this sort of work, suggests that the action researcher who is seriously interested in growing new practice, of whatever sort, needs to think carefully about their context and

> create many events of low intensity and diffuse boundaries .... Instead of using much resource in a single spot to pursue things in a continuously higher degree of detail in this spot, resources are spread over a much larger terrain to intervene in as many places in the overall movement as possible. (2003: 95)

As systemic and complexity thinking has come to influence contemporary under-standing of processes of organisational change (Senge, 1990; Flood, 1999; Checkland and Poulter, 2006; Midgley, 2008) action researchers have started to think about how small differences brought about by AR projects at local levels may in turn have effects in large organisations, communities, neighbourhoods, villages and beyond. This has led to a wide range of third-person AR strategies, which try either to 'light many fires' through multiple small-scale activities in different places in the 'system', or to engage as many elements of the 'system' as possible in bringing their voices to address the question or problem at hand through large-scale events, or are a combination of the two. These strategies make use of concepts like emer-gence, attractors, tipping points, iteration and amplification (Burns and Worsley, 2015). In practice, such projects often involve the following:

- Mapping some kind of 'system', its interconnections and actors (Ison, 2010) and its boundaries. As Midgley says, 'What we know about any situation has its limits, and it is these limits that we call boundaries. Comprehensive analysis is therefore impossible' (2008: 158).
- Parallel streams of inquiry pursued in small groups that deliberately try to 'infect' those around them, by talking about what they are doing and showing others.
- Holding periodic dialogue conferences (Toulmin and Gustavsen, 1996), Open Space events (Owen, 1997), World Cafés (Brown and Isaacs, 2005), or other activities to bring disparate involved groups together.
- Deliberately pushing information, commentary and tentative findings outwards to wider audiences.

Some third-person AR projects are ambitious, large scale and extend over many years. For instance, in 2002 the Weatherhead School of Management at Case Western Reserve University in Cleveland – at which the theory and practice of Appreciative Inquiry originated – launched a 'world inquiry into business as an agent of world benefit' drawing on Appreciative Inquiry principles. It involved management school faculty and students setting out to discover and publicise examples of profitable business innovation based around environmental sustaina-bility and social entrepreneurship, with the purpose of highlighting, valuing and growing that kind of business practice. They conducted more than 2,000 inter-views, and concluded that they were 'documenting a revolution' in how businesses of the future will operate (https://weatherhead.case.edu/centers/fowler/about/history), which has led to a growing network of business, academics and not-for-profits oriented around the idea of the 'flourishing business'.

At the other end of the socio-economic spectrum, the Community Led Total Sanitation (CLTS) movement involves a process in more than 60 countries in Asia, Africa, Latin America and the Middle East to address the problem of non-existent or inadequate sanitary facilities endured by 3.5 billion people worldwide, which gives rise to disease, polluted water and malnutrition. The initiative is supported by multilateral donors working with local NGOs and development agencies, including the UK Institute of Development Studies, who bring expertise in Participatory Action Research. Through facilitated processes at local level, communities conduct their own appraisal and analysis of their sanitation situation and take improvement action. As well as the impact of the work on the ground, the project has created an interactive website of news, case studies, stories, blogs, downloadable handbooks of methods, and other freely available resources.

The possibilities for third-person inquiry have been significantly shifted by the growth of the online world. As a recent commentator noted, though, 'documentation of the nascent practices of conducting action research virtually is both exciting and limited' (Embury, 2015).

Here is an example of the ways in which the first-, second- and third-person focus in AR can be integrated, within one study:

> Terry is an educator in one of the healthcare professions. He used his professional doctorate as an opportunity to design a new curriculum. He was interested in the ways in which scientific principles could be used in practice and the importance of the students being grounded in these principles. He used action research as a means of shaping and guiding his work. It was important that he brought the other members of his team on board and this was an excellent means of doing so (second-person focus). However, on reflecting on his focus and interest, he realised that the interest in the application of scientific principles was not new but had shaped and focused his professional interests since his initial qualification. While not making it explicit, he realised he had (implicitly) followed the action research model throughout his career (first-person focus). An additional challenge was his interaction with the professional body and its representative, and he needed to ensure that the programme he developed met their requirements (third-person focus).

Activity

We have examined three broad approaches to action research: first-, second- and third-person.

List the key elements of each one.

PUTTING IT INTO PRACTICE

AR offers no simple template for the conduct of a research project – and there is no one right way to do it. The researchers make choices according to what is pragmatic and is likely to be an effective way of getting insight into the issue or problem – guided by the characteristics and values of the approach.

The examples in the tables that follow show ways in which the practices discussed above can be combined to create substantial, systematic and sustained inquiry.

Table 9.3 Example 1

Ghada Howaidy held a leadership post in a university in Cairo when she undertook her professional doctorate. The government of Hosni Mubarak was overthrown around the time she began her doctorate, and the unstable political events in Egypt that followed were a vivid backdrop to her research. She was interested in the role of responsible business in helping build a democratic civil society, and in the leadership she might exercise in her workplace to support that.

Title/question	The role of business in society: creating space to live the question within the paradox of change
Practical concern	To develop an effective way of handling complex change processes in a university business school. To develop an appropriate leadership practice in post-2011 revolution Egypt. To contribute to the creation of a viable civil society
Human/planetary flourishing	To enable the business school in which she worked to develop its understanding of, and response to, responsible business practice and responsible management education. Through that, to help grow a socially and politically responsible role for business that could support democratic transformation in Egypt
First-person method	• Cycles of plan, act, reflect, think • Self-reflection on own leadership practice using 'critical moment' approach, captured in writing • Construction of a narrative of events in post-2011 Egypt through contemporary newspaper clippings • Real-time inquiry into a life-coaching experience with a religious group. Confronting and attempting to bridge different 'worldviews'. Captured in notes. • Series of action-experiments with ways of creating dialogue in the workplace
Second-person method	Facebook conversation in the wake of the mass killings of August 2013 that ended the sit-in of Islamist demonstrators. Presented through excerpts and commentary
Theoretical underpinning	Business stakeholder and shared-value theories, CSR Critical theory Systemic thinking and complexity theory 'Bricolage' and conversation forms of change practice
Findings/insight	'I set out to inquire into "change": personal, organisational and social, and ended up accepting and embracing "becoming". Whereas change implies clear direction and predetermined results, becoming is interactive, relational and emerging. Change privileges ends, becoming respects the journey and the context.'

Table 9.4   Example 2

Pavica Barr completed her professional doctorate while she was an Organisational Development Practitioner within a global team in a European-based multinational company. Recognising her own struggles with a sense of displacement, she enquired into the impact this had on herself, her colleagues and the business, in the midst of normalised expectations for successful executives to be globally mobile.

Title/question	An inquiry into the tension between displacement and belonging as experienced by globally mobile professionals: an emerging practice of shallow-rooted belonging
Practical concern	How to support herself and colleagues better as they experience themselves as uprooted by frequent international relocation and overseas assignments Implications for corporate practices, particularly in HR and OD
Human/planetary flourishing	How globally mobile professionals could create a sufficient sense of belonging in a postmodern world of global mobility that would enable them to flourish and live a healthy, fulfilled life
First-person method	Deep personal inquiry into her experiences of leaving her home country, using journaling, photographs, poetry, conscious time spent 'dwelling' 'I wanted to understand the ongoing tension between the pull towards exploring the wider world and the equally strong pull towards belonging to a community or a place that could be called home.'
Second-person method	• Enquiring conversations with six corporate leaders, their lived experience of belonging while pursuing globally mobile careers • Inquiry group with five organisation development practitioners into experiences of connectivity with self and others and possibilities for creating a greater sense of belonging in global organisations
Theoretical underpinning	Existential philosophy, with a focus on concepts of 'homeworlds', 'alienworlds' and 'liminality' Social psychology, with the focus on belonging as a core social motive and attachment theory Developmental and relational psychology Humanistic and postmodern perspectives of organisation
Findings/insight	The inquiry generated three main insights: (1) globally mobile professionals who participated in this inquiry lived permanently in liminality (2) home seemed to hold a transient quality for these professionals (3) the acceptance that deep-rooted belonging was not theirs to have. This acceptance led global leaders to shape an alternative form of belonging which the author has named 'shallow-rooted belonging' – a form of belonging that nurtures a functional existence in liminal social and psychological space.

Table 9.5   Example 3

Lowcarbonworks was a project funded by the UK Engineering and Physical Science Research Council and the Economic and Social Research Council which was conducted over four years at the University of Bath (Reason et al., 2009). It adopted an action research approach to address complex questions about the adoption of low-carbon technologies.

Title/question	What is it that encourages and inhibits the adoption of low-carbon technologies by businesses and other organisations?
Practical concern	To overcome barriers so that low-carbon technologies can be more readily used To contribute to the efforts by both companies and governments to reduce carbon released into the atmosphere
Human/planetary flourishing	To contribute to the physical sustainability of the planetary environment we all rely on
First-person method	Reflective meetings of the action research team Relational work within the team Individual journaling
Second-person method	Narrative approaches, particularly Learning History Regular meetings of the multidisciplinary team involved: sharing of academic perspectives across 'normal' boundaries
Third-person method	Publication and dissemination of stories of change Regular dialogue conferences involving all contributors to the learning histories and other interested parties Presentation of research findings as stores and quotes rather than formal report
Theoretical underpinning	Theories of technological change – Lock-In, the Social Shaping of Technology, Socio-technical Transition Framework Critical theory Relational theory
Findings/insight	Social, organisational, technological and economic factors are systemically linked and combine in particular ways to produce change at a certain time Effective action involves seizing or creating sometimes brief opportunities when these elements align

QUALITY AND VALIDITY

From the discussion above it will be clear that addressing questions of validity in this type of research is not straightforward. AR, like other approaches that may be seen as postmodern rather than positivist, rejects the concept that the world is a fixed entity external to the researcher, waiting to be discovered and against which claims to truth can be tested. The conventional route to establish validity is through objectivity, generalisability and repeatability. For the action researcher, all knowing is seen as contextual and emergent, so 'findings' will always have a contingent quality – reflecting the messiness of real life. AR is concerned with actionable knowledge in particular places, and what that has to say in relation to wider bodies of theory. For this reason, the whole concept of validity becomes open to question – a puzzle to grapple with, rather than an edict to follow.

Attention to quality in this type of work is, however, important. If it is to be taken seriously as a form of research, action researchers need to be able to show that their practice is rigorous and that claims are based on evidence, even if that evidence may be drawn from a more diverse range of data than is conventionally the case. The processes through which quality is established and shown involve *transparency* about *choices* – overtly discussing and demonstrating what has been done. As Reason says:

> There are in the end no clear foundational grounds. The best we can do is to offer our choices to our own scrutiny, to the mutual scrutiny of our co-researchers, to the wider community of inquirers, and to the interested public at large. Quality rests not so much on getting it right but on stimulating open discussion. (2006: 199)

Showing quality in AR involves thoughtfully answering these sorts of questions:

- What are the epistemological assumptions that this work is based on?
- What is the intent of the work, and how has that been established?
- What precise first-, second- and third-person methods have been chosen, and on what basis?
- In what ways does the work demonstrate actionable knowledge, and what grounds are being used to make that judgement?
- How is the participative process being demonstrated, and what grounds are being used to make that judgement?
- In what ways can AR be said to be making a generative, worthwhile contribution to the issue or problem that is being addressed, and what grounds are being used to make that judgement?

CONCLUSION: CHALLENGES AND STRENGTHS

There are, then, some challenges associated with this approach, which the practitioner–researcher needs to bear in mind. From the discussion above it will be clear that AR sits somewhat uncomfortably with conventional academia. The case for its academic contribution is often made (see e.g. Coghlan, 2011), but the practical orientation and alignment with particular sorts of outcomes contravene some deeply held academic norms. AR produces knowledge that cannot be generalised in the way normally expected of research results, and is not repeatable in the same manner by other people at a different time. This in turn places a burden on the researcher who wants to use AR for research in a university setting to argue their case and justify their choices, procedures and validity criteria. Finally, to be an action researcher requires a set of skills that are wider than those of a conventional researcher, since the AR cycle involves acting, in collaboration with others, as well as planning, reflecting and theorising. New researchers can find it difficult to muster the confidence to convene an inquiry group and the capacity to create 'communicative space'. However, these are things that are learned by doing, and practitioner–researchers are often helped in the process by their maturity and work-based experience.

For practitioner-led research, however, AR offers a distinctive route with some clear strengths. Firstly, it addresses real problems: its whole orientation is around engagement with the world as it is rather than as it is theorised. Secondly, it fully embraces mess and complexity; AR does not aim to produce one single answer to a question, and recognises the contingency of human understanding of our world. Research from this perspective involves engaging with and articulating that complexity, particularly with respect to the aspects that are routinely overlooked or seen as of little value. Thirdly, it offers opportunities for personal and practice development, since in AR the researcher is a participant rather than an outside observer, and is inevitably and rightfully impacted and changed by the work. This is a form of research that invites the practitioner to step into the areas of their own uncertainty and not-knowing, with an attitude of inquiry, to discover what to do, in collaboration with others. And finally, AR makes the role of the insider–researcher an asset rather than a problem: attachment to the issue, providing it is reflexively worked with, becomes part of the process rather than something that needs to be countered.

Key Points

Action research involves finding out about issues and then actively working to bring about change in practice.

There are a variety of models of action research but the following characteristics are common to all models:

- A primary concern with practical issues.
- It is concerned with human development.
- Participation and partnership of all involved are integral to the research process.
- It fits into the knowledge action domain.

There are three levels of focus, which interact: 'for me', 'for us' and 'for them'.
It is important for the researcher to determine and explain their position or stance.

ANNOTATED BIBLIOGRAPHY

Bradbury, H. (ed.) (2015). *The Sage Handbook of Action Research* (3rd edn). Los Angeles: Sage.

The third edition of this comprehensive handbook begins with a useful introduction on how to situate and define action research. It contains a wide range of examples of action research practices from around the world, demonstrating the diversity of interpretation and application that fall within the overall approach. It also includes sections on aspects of action research theory and skills.

Coghlan, D., & Brannick, T. (2014). *Doing Action Research in Your Own Organization* (4th edn). London: Sage.

This book is an essential guide for anyone who is involved in being an 'insider–researcher'. It covers the theory and principles of action research with an emphasis on the epistemology of practical knowing, and considers the challenges and dilemmas posed by organisational research in the place where you work, including important questions of power, politics and ethics.

Herr, K., & Anderson, G. L. (2014). *The Action Research Dissertation: A Guide for Students and Faculty* (2nd edn). Thousand Oaks, CA: Sage.

As the title suggests, this book is specifically for those who are putting together doctoral (or masters) dissertations in formal academic settings. Although situated within academia in the United States, the discussion about how to negotiate some of the pinch-points faced by action researchers is applicable to universities in most parts of the world. It covers writing research proposals, quality criteria, ethical approval processes and the practicalities of conducting the research.

McNiff, J. (2014). *Writing and Doing Action Research*. London: Sage.

Another book aimed at those who are doing masters and doctoral degrees using action research, this time from a UK perspective. McNiff began her action research work in teacher education, and her books aim to provide practical and straightforward help for research practitioners. This one includes chapters on what makes good writing in action research, for the researchers themselves as well as for the reader, and how action research may be taken into journal publication and other forms of academic writing.

REFERENCES

Argyris, C. (2003). Actionable knowledge. In T. Tsoukas, & C. Knudson (Eds.), *The Oxford Handbook of Organization Theory* (pp. 423–52). Oxford: Oxford University Press.

Bradbury, H., Roth, G., & Gearty, M. (2015). The practice of learning history: local and open systems approaches. In H. Bradbury (ed.) *The Sage Handbook of Action Research* (3rd edn, pp. 17–30). London: Sage.

Brown, J., & Isaacs, D. (2005). *World Cafe: Shaping Our World Through Conversations than Matter*. San Francisco: Berrett-Koehler.

Burns, D. (2015). How change happens: the implications of complexity and systems thinking for action research. In H. Bradbury (ed.) *The Sage Handbook of Action Research* (3rd edn, pp. 434–45). Los Angeles: Sage.

Burns, D., & Worsley, S. (2015). *Navigating Complexity in International Development*. Rugby: Practical Action Publishing.

Capra, F. (1997). *The Web of Life: A New Synthesis of Mind and Matter*. London: HarperCollins.

Carr, W., & Kemmis, S. (1986). *Becoming Critical: Education, Knowledge and Action Research*. Basingstoke: Falmer Press.

Carr, W., & Kemmis, S. (2005). Staying critical. *Educational Action Research*, 13(3), 347.

Chambers, R. (1997). *Whose Reality Counts? Putting the First Last*. London: Intermediate Technology Publications.

Checkland, P., & Poulter, J. (2006). *Learning for Action: A Short Definitive Account of Soft Systems Methodology, and its Use for Practitioners, Teachers and Students*. Hoboken, NJ: Wiley.

Coghlan, D. (2011). Action research: exploring perspectives on a philosophy of practical knowing. *Academy of Management Annals*, 5(1), 53–87.

Coghlan, D., & Brannick, T. (2010). *Doing Action Research in Your Own Organization* (3rd edn). Thousand Oaks, CA: Sage.

Coleman, G. (2015). Core issues in modern epistemology for action researchers: dancing between the knower and the known. In H. Bradbury (ed.) *The Sage Handbook of Action Research* (3rd edn, pp. 392–400). Los Angeles: Sage.

Cooperrider, D. L., & Srivastva, S. (1987). Appreciative inquiry in organisational life. In R. W. Woodman, & W. A. Pasmore (eds) *Research in Organizational Change and Development* (Vol. 1 ed., pp. 129–70). Grenwich, CT: JAI Press.

Denzin, N. K., & Lincoln, Y. S. (2005). *Handbook of Qualitative Research*. Thousand Oaks, CA: Sage.

Embury, D. C. (2015). Action research in an online world. In P. Reason & H. Bradbury (eds) *The Sage Handbook of Action Research* (2nd edn, pp. 529–35). London: Sage.

Etherington, K. (2004). *Becoming a Reflexive Researcher: Using Our Selves in Research*. London: Jessica Kingsley.

Flood, R. (1999). *Re-thinking the Fifth Discipline: Learning Within The Unknowable*. London: Routledge.

Gamin, B., & Fox, S. (1999). *Visual Journaling: Going Deeper Than Words*. Wheaton, IL: Quest Books.

Gaventa, J., & Cornwall, A. (2015). Power and knowledge. In H. Bradbury (ed.) *The Sage Handbook of Action Research* (3rd edn, pp. 465–71). London: Sage.

Gergen, K. J., & Gergen, M. M. (2015). Social construction and research as action. In H. Bradbury (ed.) *The Sage Handbook of Action Research* (3rd edn, pp. 401–08). Los Angeles: Sage.

Gustavsen, B. (2003). Action research and the problem of the single case. *Concepts and Transformation* 8(1), 93–9.

Habermas, J. (1984). *The Theory of Communicative Action: Reason and the Rationality of Society*. Boston, MA: Beacon Press.

Heron, J. (1996). *Co-operative Inquiry: Research into the Human Condition*. London: Sage.

Heron, J. & Reason, P. (2005). Extending Epistemology within a Co-operative Inquiry 366 John Heron and Peter Reason (366–380). In P. Reason and H. Bradbury (eds) *The SAGE Handbook of Action Research*. Thousand Oaks, CA: Sage.

Ison, R. (2010). *Systems Practice: How to Act in a Climate Change World*. London: Springer.

Kemmis, S. (2001). Exploring the relevance of critical theory for action research: emancipatory research in the steps of Jurgen Habermas. In P. Reason & H. Bradbury (eds) *The Sage Handbook of Action Research: Participative Inquiry and Practice* (2nd edn). London: Sage.

Ludema, J. D., Cooperrider, D. L., & Barrett, F. J. (2001). Appreciative inquiry: the power of the unconditional positive question. In P. Reason, & H. Bradbury (eds) *Handbook of Action Research: Participative Inquiry and Practice* (pp. 189–99). London: Sage.

Marshall, J. (1999). Living life as inquiry. *Systemic Practice and Action Research*, 12(2): 155–71.

Marshall, J. (2004). Living systemic thinking: exploring quality in first-person action research. *Action Research*, 2(3), 305–25.

Marshall, J. (2016). *Living Life as Inquiry*. London: Sage.

Marshall, J., Coleman, G., & Reason, P. (2011). *Leadership for Sustainability: An Action Research Approach*. Sheffield: Greenleaf Publishing.

McArdle, K. L. (2008). Getting in, getting on, getting out: on working with second-person inquiry groups. In P. Reason & H. Bradbury (eds) *The Sage Handbook of Action Research* (602–614). London: Sage.

McNiff, J. and Whitehead, J. (2010). *You and your action research project*. Abingdon: Routledge.

Midgley, G. (2008). Systems thinking, complexity and the philosophy of science. *Emergence: Complexity and Organization, 10*(4), 55.

Owen, H. (1997). *Open Space Technology: A User's Guide*. San Francisco: Berrett-Kohler.

Reason, P. (2006). Choice and quality in action research practice. *Journal of Management Inquiry, 15*(2), 187–203.

Reason, P., & Bradbury, H. (eds) (2001). *Handbook of Action Research: Participative Inquiry and Practice*. London: Sage.

Reason, P., & Bradbury, H. (eds) (2008). *The Sage Handbook of Action Research: Participative Inquiry and Practice* (2nd edn). London: Sage.

Reason, P., & Marshall, J. (1987). Research as personal process. In D. Boud & V. Griffin (eds) *Appreciating Adults Learning: From the Learner's Perspective* (pp. 112–26). London: Kogan Page.

Reason, P., Coleman, G., & Ballard, D. (2009). *Insider Voices: Human Dimensions of Low Carbon Technology*. Bath: University of Bath Centre for Action Research and Professional Practice.

Rorty, R. (1999). *Philosophy and Social Hope*. London: Penguin Books.

Rudolph, J. W., Taylor, S. S., & Foldy, E. G. (2001). Collaborative off-line reflection: a way to develop skill in action science and action inquiry. In P. Reason & H. Bradbury (eds) *The Sage Handbook of Action Research: Participative Inquiry and Practice* (pp. 405–12). London: Sage.

Seeley, C., & Reason, P. (2008). Expressions of energy: an epistemology of presentational knowing. In P. Liamputtong, & J. Rumbold (eds) *Knowing Differently: Arts-based and Collaborative Research*. New York: Nova Science Publishers Inc.

Senge, P. M. (1990). *The Fifth Discipline: The Art and Practice of the Learning Organization*. New York: Doubleday.

Senge, P. M., Kleiner, A., Roberts, C., Ross, R. B., & Smith, B. J. (1994). *The Fifth Discipline Fieldbook: Strategies and Tools for Building a Learning Organization*. New York: Doubleday.

Stenhouse, L. (1983). Authority, Education, and Emancipation: A Collection of Papers. Portsmouth, NH: Heinemann.

Stringer, E. T. (2007). *Action Research* (3rd ed). Los Angeles; London: Sage.

Swantz, M. (2008). Participatory action research. In P. Reason, & H. Bradbury (eds) *The Sage Handbook of Action Research* (2nd ed, pp. 31–48). London, Thousand Oaks, NewDelhi: Sage.

Torbert, B. (2004). *Action Inquiry: The Secret of Timely and Transforming Leadership*. San Francisco: Berrett Koehler.

Toulmin, S., & Gustavsen, B. (1996). *Beyond Theory: Changing Organizations Through Participation*. Amsterdam: John Benjamins.

Turner-Vesselago, B. (2013). *Writing Without a Parachute*. Bristol: Vala Publishing Co-operative.

Weisbord, M.R. (2012). *Productive Workplaces: Dignity, Meaning and Community in the 21st Century*. San Francisco: Jossey-Bass,.

Wicks, P. G., & Reason, P. (2009). Initiating action research: challenges and paradoxes of opening communicative space. *Action Research, 7*(3), 243–62.

Yorks, L., Aprill, A., James, L., Rees, A., Hoffman-Pinilla, A., & Ospina, S. (2008). The tapestry of leadership: lessons from six co-operative inquiries groups of social justice leaders. In P. Reason, & H. Bradbury (eds) *The Sage Handbook of Action Research* (2nd ed, pp. 487–98). London, Thousand Oaks, New Delhi: Sage.

Zuber-Skerritt, O. & Perry, C. (2002) Action research within organisations and university thesis writing. *The Learning Organization, 9*(4), 171–79.

Zuber-Skerritt, O. (ed.) (2012). *Action Research for Sustainable Development in a Turbulent World*. London: Emerald.

10

CASE STUDY

Catherine Hayes

KEY TERMS

Case study: a systematic inquiry that investigates a contextually specific phenomenon of relevance to current practice, using multifaceted approaches to the collation of evidence and where there is often evident ambiguity between the phenomenon and the context.

Phenomenon: anything observable or that can be studied, exhibiting specificity or being atypical from the norm, which by its very nature might be fundamentally unique, challenging to interpret and difficult to articulate.

Constructionism: the internal or creative interpretation of the outside world that necessitates differentiation between elements and the fundamentally changeable connections or interrelationships they share.

Positivism: the philosophical stance acknowledging that which is scientifically verifiable via logical and systematised means of proof.

INTRODUCTION

This chapter provides an overview of the philosophical backdrop of case study as a method of inquiry. The first half of the chapter focuses on methodological design whereas the second half is focused on pragmatic execution of the method. Emphasis is placed upon the key uses of case study design, and through the worked example of educational research undertaken with work-based professional doctorate students, the purposefulness and the practicalities of its execution are outlined. The whole concept of case study as an independent method of inquiry is then refined by examining the specific contexts for its implementation in practice. The development of theory as an analytic process that can be subject to rigorous quality assurance is discussed through description of the author's own educational research execution. Discussion of reaching theoretical saturation and the iterative process of developing new hypotheses as a tangible outcome of the work are also considered so that readers can logically progress into the relative complexity of theory building from case study findings. The chapter draws on the seminal work of authors whose insight into case study research has defined and shaped a generation of expectation about an often unnecessarily overlooked and undervalued research method.

When using case study research there are a number of choices which have to be made: one's epistemological or philosophical position; the extent or range of the case study; and the basic purpose of the research. These will have implications for the design of the study.

WHAT IS THE PHILOSOPHICAL STANCE?

In Chapter 2 the philosophical basis of research and the choices which may have to made were explored and a broad division was made into positivism and constructionism; when using case study as a methodological approach there is a case tradition in both positivism and constructionism.

Positivism became the prevailing and most significant of all epistemological approaches in social research until the mid-1960s. The prevailing focus was that social worlds are external to the researcher, with logical, systematic, tangible and hence observable criteria. It negated the need for values, which characterise so many fundamental pieces of case study research. The main issue with this approach is the fact it negates knowledge that cannot be tested by empirical measure or formulation or generalised to wider populations and subjected to scientific parameters or laws.

Yin (2013) has written extensively on the use of case studies as a methodological approach and his approach to the case study is largely positivist, the assumption being that there is a particular reality which exists and the researcher is attempting to explore and uncover this reality. He emphasises its strengths as: it deals with practicalities of everyday life; it has ambiguities which may need to be unpicked; it requires the use of several data sources; and there is potential for a theoretical exploration which goes beyond the superficial. To put this in another way, it gathers a richness of data and in applying theory allows one to go well beyond the superficial. The case study approach can generate new hypotheses which can lead to further research. It allows for inductive and deductive approaches in the same study, that is the testing of ideas derived from theory (deductive) and the development of theoretical ideas from the practical situation (inductive).

Case study research has also been firmly placed in constructionism, an epistemological standpoint that transcended the need for the pure objectification of both what is observable and empirical measurement. At the heart of all interpretation lies the social construction of reality, a defining feature of case study design, which is reliant on the projection of meaning by the participant and the capacity of the researcher to interpret, translate and articulate this meaning-making in a systematic and analytic approach. Hume's seminal argument for the fact that we cannot ever directly observe theories and that they can only ever be interpreted and articulated through human discourse is the basis of explaining the temporal nature of cause rather than a definitive or statistically metric measure of it. Case studies, as a result, often generate more questions than they answer or illuminate, in contrast to objective approaches which may answer the '*how*' but not the '*why*' of human experience. Since constructivism provides a truth that is fundamentally relative and entirely dependent on the interpreter's own stance or perspective, emphasis can be placed equally on the subjective nature of meaning-making and the place that this occupies when object and subject need to be defined and delineated.

Activity

Think about your own professional field. Where might its underpinning philosophy fit with the concept of case study research? How much will this matter?
Possible areas for consideration might be:

1. Is your professional field aligned to a discipline that is a purist empirical science, a social science or neither?
2. Are there any accepted social or cultural norms that might influence your decision making?

Once you have done this, think of an area or topic you would like to explore in the context of the study. Are there any contradictions within your professional field? Does it necessitate a very different approach?

WHAT IS THE EXTENT AND RANGE OF THE CASE STUDY?

If you decide to use case study as an approach you firstly need to decide what is your case. Stake (1995) identified the main approaches to case study as intrinsic, instructional and collective (Table 10.1).

Table 10.1   Stake's approaches to case study

Intrinsic	This means studying a situation (e.g. a hospital ward or a school because they are using a new or novel approach or are of interest) An exemplary case might be chosen or one in which people are struggling or dealing with difficult issues and problems
Instructional	Rather than a specific situation, a concept or a particular phenomenon is explored across several sites; for example, how assessment is approached might be examined across several schools
Collective	One or more sites might be explored to gain an understanding of a phenomenon; collective is like intrinsic but rather than one site, the issue might be explored across several sites

Once having established what your case will be, you then need to state what the purpose of the research is. Simons (2009) poses the typology in Table 10.2.

Table 10.2 Simon's typology

Theory-led, or theory-generated case studies	This is led by a theoretical idea, and either it is tested or theory is developed from the case study. This would work best when there is a basic idea
Evaluative case studies	This could be chosen when you wish to look at a development or innovation which has been introduced in practice
Ethnographic case studies	The ethnographic tradition is followed and a setting or an issue is explored across several settings in some detail; if you wish to explore an area in detail and find out more about it then this might be the approach to choose

Activity

Think of the purpose of your study and what you want to find out about in the context of the study. Using the grid below, indicate where you think your study best fits:

	Intrinsic	Instructional	Collective
Theory-led, or theory- generated case studies			
Evaluative case studies			
Ethnographic case studies			

The next decision is to consider the methods you will use to gather the information. Case study as a methodology is fairly eclectic in that it allows for a range of data to be collected depending on the overall purpose of your study. The remainder of this chapter explores the practicalities of using case study as a methodological approach.

USING CASE STUDY RESEARCH IN THE CONTEXT OF A PROFESSIONAL DOCTORATE

Many professional doctorate (PD) programme teams reconcile tension around the role that PDs play in development and progression in terms of practical excellence, particularly in disciplines where this impact needs to be measurable and staff need to be accountable (predominantly health and education). Often PD projects embrace case study as a mechanism of translating experiential and tacit knowledge into practice and this becomes a key part of how practitioners generate new and valuable 'professional knowledge' (Burgess and Wellington, 2010). For this work to have a strategic relevance and influence in professional circles, it needs to have an evidence base, which undertaking case study research can often fulfil. This may stem from the collation of narratives and discourses around practice development or where there may be elements of dissonance which serve to form the basis of further research in practice.

The permutations of building a theory with case study research data are numerous. Table 10.3 outlines an adaptation of a recognised model, which rationalises the implementation process and provides a clear framework for undertaking it in practice.

THEORY BUILDING WITH CASE STUDY RESEARCH DATA

Table 10.3 Adaptation of Eisenhardt's (1989) process of building theory from case study research

Stages	Processes	Rationale for implementation
Stage 1: Initiation	• Clear framing and operational definition of research phenomenon • Acknowledgement of the existence of a priori construct • Consideration of how an existing theory or hypothesis could impact the focus of inquiry	✓ Reduces ambiguity and provides methodological focus ✓ Enables constructs to be grounded in the published or acknowledged extant evidence base ✓ Maintains and develops theoretical flexibility
Stage 2: Case selection and sampling technique	• Define a specific research population • Operationalise a theoretical sampling technique	✓ Enhances the external validity of the findings ✓ Provides a focused emphasis on those specific phenomena that can prove, extend or develop further an existing evidence base
Stage 3: Developing the specifics of research design and methodology	• Implementation of multiple data collection methods/ mixed methods approaches • The combined impact of qualitative and quantitative data established • The inclusion of multiple investigators	✓ Provides a mechanism of triangulating data so that theoretical emergence can be clearly grounded in theory ✓ Strengthens grounding of theory by triangulation of evidence ✓ Combined and synergistic perspectives are facilitated in relation to the collated evidence base ✓ Facilitates the notion of divergent perspectives and strengthens the methodological process of grounding

(Continued)

Table 10.3 (Continued)

Stages	Processes	Rationale for implementation
Stage 4: Initial data collection	• Synergised data collection, transcription and analysis • Implementation of potentially flexible and opportunistic data collection methods	✓ Enables data enrichment via a focused thematic adjustment to interview schedules/data collection ✓ Enhances the analysis phase speed and provides purposeful adjustments to the data collection process ✓ Allows investigators to exploit emergent themes and fundamentally unique characteristics of the specific case under investigation
Stage 5: Data analysis	• Case analysis (phenomena specific) • Identification of emergent theory from the potential crossover of methodological approaches	✓ Gains familiarity with data and preliminary theory generation ✓ Researcher moves beyond superficial thematic analysis to deep conceptual explanation of theoretical emergence
Stage 6: Framing and establishing testable hypotheses	• Attempted repeatability rather than the sampling of cases and the application of systematic logic across the process of framing and establishing testable hypotheses • Examination of specific causation factors in relationships and interactions (i.e. the 'why' rather than the 'how' of the specific case)	✓ Provides conclusive confirmation, extends knowledge and provides a strategic focus for theoretical postulation ✓ Provides enhanced levels of internal validity to the case study
Stage 7: Embedding extant literature	• Iterative comparison with opposing and contested viewpoints from the extant literature and affirmation of consistency with that which is in the same field	✓ Enhances the degree of apparent internal validity ✓ Highlights and extends the claim of external validity
Stage 8: Theoretical saturation and case completion	• Statement of completion of theoretical saturation where this is possible	✓ Provides closure to the case at the point where no more can be added

STAGE 1: INITIATION

Eisenhardt's seminal work established that there are three fundamental aspects of initiating a case study. These are: (a) clear framing and operational definition of research phenomenon; (b) acknowledgement of the existence of a priori construct; and (c) consideration of how an existing theory or hypothesis could impact the focus of inquiry (Eisenhardt, 1989).

(a) Clear Framing and Operational Definition of Research Phenomenon

Operationally defining the research phenomenon is fundamental to the establishment of a case not shrouded in ambiguity. Yin highlighted that the sheer volume of data it is possible to collect means that, without a clear focus, the process of analysis can become simply overwhelming (Yin, 2011).

Work-based PDs have necessitated challenging the legitimacy of academic findings from traditional universities. In the context of public discourse, 'research' generally requires no differentiation of practice-based or theoretical research and, for the first time, this has become a focal point of debate around the value of research in practice. This has important ramifications for the research-contingent areas of academic curricula and the programmes that working professionals seek to access. It focuses on the holistic, societal, civic and corporate worth of education beyond individual benefit alone. Case studies therefore have the potential to serve in the capacity of illuminating and illustrating key aspects of practical life and as such are inherently valued to how this can be achieved in practice.

Case Study Vignette from Practice: Integration of a Dialogic Feedback Loop with Professional Doctorate Students

I undertook a small case study with PD students to emphasise the need for them to engage with the process of feedback on formative assessment. The specific intent of my own study was to provide a depth of understanding of how dialogic feedback loops could reinforce our teaching team's collective understanding of formative feedback implementation. I did this by researching a mechanism of completely different delivery of feedback than any other we had used before. At a much more focused level, my own contribution to ascertaining this level of understanding was directed at being able to identify an explanation of the 'how' and 'why' of doctoral students engaging or not engaging with processes of interim formative feedback. To achieve this objective, I stated two highly interrelated research questions: *'What is the orthodoxy that frames how students perceive mechanisms of feedback on their formative work?'* *'How and why do doctoral students react to the provision of dialogic feedback loop in practice?'* As explained below, these research questions provided a well-defined focus to our research and allowed us to specify the kind of data to be gathered.

(b) Acknowledgement of the Existence of a Priori Construct

In the use of extant theoretical constructs to guide my approach in theory-building research, I had to consider two individual potential approaches that I could adopt (Moore et al., 2015). It is useful to examine each in turn to see the impact of each approach.

1. The Provision of a Specific and Explicit Conceptual Framework

There was the option to use a conceptual analytical framework to make explicit theoretical statements in relation to the notion of using dialogic feedback loops as part of formative assessment with doctoral students (Miles and Huberman, 1994). This would have provided a means of visibly 'mapping' major concepts simultaneously so that the interrelationships in the phenomena could be clearly seen and articulated (Saldaña, 2015).

2. Not Being Constrained by the Existence of Prior Theory

This is where the iterative development of theoretical emergence and hypothetical understanding underpin and provide purposefulness to the case study research.

This second option was to attempt not to be constrained by the existence of prior theory. Instead I needed to regard the development of theoretical emergence, potential hypotheses and conceptual possibilities in a topic area that already had been the focus of much pedagogic research (Cohen et al., 2013).

There were evident parallels in grounded theory approaches to research and the development of constructivist grounded theory (Charmaz, 2014). I actually combined both approaches since the intention of my study was to provide a new perspective in an already-established research field (i.e. my focus was on theory building rather than theory testing). I could therefore undertake this knowing that the constructs were embedded within the conceptual framework and in accordance with Yin's recommendations; any exploratory case study research undertaken ought to make use of a conceptual framework to define categorically the priorities of the case study (Yin, 2013). In my own study this provided the assurance that I did not overlook significant issues, that I could make meaning of occurrences and that I could clearly define the priorities. Doing this subsequently provided a clear set of constructs for investigation and which ultimately guided and facilitated my sense of focus.

Using my established research questions as a guide, my conceptual framework was used comprehensively to group constructs related to the contextual conditions influencing the implementation of the dialogic feedback loop (e.g. the resources necessary; context of the feedback; supplementary annotation on formative work; metric data). As a researcher, I paid attention to the context and interaction between myself and the doctoral students, within which human action was one of the most significant factors. Eisenhardt (1989) posited that the identification of constructs is tentative in theory-building research, something I found accurate in the context of this research when new contributing factors were revealed during iterative data collection, which needed to be added to the process of data analysis.

(c) Consideration of how an Existing Theory or Hypotheses could Impact the Focus of Inquiry

Eisenhardt's proposition is that research detailing theoretical emergence must start with a *tabula rasa* and allude to the ideal of no former theoretical consideration since any pre-contemplated phenomena may skew the interpretation of a fresh data set and potentially limit the findings. I followed this to a certain extent by not explicitly identifying specific relationships between the constructs identified in my conceptual framework, where I adopted the teleological view advocated by Knobe and Samuels (2013). It was here that this teleological theory reflected my basic assumptions regarding the phenomena under scrutiny and that which reflected what was known in the extant literature. The adoption of this teleological view of the implementation of a dialogic feedback loop enhanced my capacity as a researcher to understand how a specific intervention could be used to gain an insight into processes of student learning and engagement.

STAGE 2: CASE SELECTION AND SAMPLING TECHNIQUE

Theoretical sampling lies at the heart of purist case study research (Yin, 2013). This is a means of collecting data with the specific purpose of generating theory via the concurrent collection and analysis of data. The researcher moves to the most purposive area for data collection in light of what initial analysis reveals. This enriches the theory as it is revealed from one data set to the next. My unit of analysis in the study was related to the way the research questions were operationally defined and the generalisations I needed at the end of the study (Yin, 2011). The unit of analysis in my study could be defined as the dialogic feedback project, or, to be even more specific, the procedural steps taken during the implementation.

STAGE 3: DEVELOPING THE SPECIFICS OF RESEARCH DESIGN AND METHODOLOGY

The potential to triangulate the process of data collection was important to the study. It permitted a much more robust formulation of constructs and hypotheses. It has also been posited that the collection of data via a variety of means ensures that a fuller picture of the phenomena under scrutiny can be achieved. The primary goal of data collection was via a semi-structured questionnaire and a series of short interviews, for which interview guides were developed for use with the doctoral students. I adopted the stance of Kaplan and Maxwell (1994) and Joukes et al. (2016), ensuring that the primary goal of my interviews was to elicit the respondent's views and experiences in my own terms, rather than to collect data sets designed to collate responses from specific pre-established response categories. The initial stage of the research process was interviewing the doctoral students on a one-to-one basis. The interview provided a context for explanation and discussion of the purpose of the inquiry and was designed to engage doctoral students and to motivate them to be interested in the processes of assessment and feedback across the work-based PD programme. Bias was minimised by not providing an extensive insight into the conceptual framework underpinning the study.

The qualitative data sets were used only to suggest theoretical arguments which could then be strengthened (or weakened) by quantitative support. A survey instrument in the form of a questionnaire was developed to collect data that would either confirm or refute the interpretation of the data. Respondents were the same students who had taken part in the initial semi-structured interviews. Collating both quantitative and qualitative evidence aided the research process in illuminating the level of interpretive consistency between myself and the doctoral students in relation to my capacity as a researcher and their capacity to articulate their experiences.

STAGE 4: INITIAL DATA COLLECTION

Eisenhardt (1989) originally noted the increasing degree of overlap in instances where data collection and data analysis take place concurrently. I implemented Ritchie and Spencer's qualitative framework analysis (2002), which is outlined below. This was a pragmatic means of ensuring I could become familiar with the data I had collected, and identify thematic sufficiency to the point where I could move to the next interview, adapting the schedule as necessary. It facilitated the process of actively exploring the similarities and differences in the data, and the overall relationships within and between them (Duff and Anderson, 2015). I bridged this gap through the use of memos and field notes as advocated by Charmaz (2003) which permitted me to maintain a record of what Van Maanen (2011) would later term the 'streaming consciousness' of key significance to the research process. This process also enhanced my capacity to make meaning of the data sets collected since they were contextualised and framed in the memos and field notes (Fink, 2013). The net outcome of this stage was the active enrichment of collected data.

STAGE 5: DATA ANALYSIS

Ritchie and Spencer's framework analysis was used as a mechanism of data analysis in this study for purely pragmatic reasons (Table 10.4).

Table 10.4   Ritchie and spencer's qualitative framework analysis

Step 1: Familiarisation with the data set

Through immersion in the raw data, it is possible to manually become familiar with each data set (termed familiarisation). It was a combinatorial process of re-listening to audio recording files and the extensive reading and rereading of transcripts and field notes

Step 2: Identifying a thematic framework

Following familiarisation with the data, the key issues and themes that have been identified form the basis of a thematic framework. This is carried out through a deductive process drawing on a priori issues that form the aims of the study as well as issues raised by the participants that recur in the data. At a result, a detailed index of the data will be developed, thus allowing data to be labelled and explored

Step 3: Indexing

The thematic framework will be applied and all data contained in the transcripts indexed against the codes. This allows for the identification of portions or sections of the data that correspond to a particular theme or concept in the thematic framework

Step 4: Charting

The data that has been indexed will then be rearranged to form charts of the themes. Charts will be produced for key themes with entries from the data, linked to individual participants

Step 5: Testing of emergent themes

The emergent theory was then used to devise the questionnaires, which formed an integral part of data triangulation processes for the study

In keeping with Yin's recommendation that all case studies should have an embedded analytical strategy to guide the process of deciding what ought to be analysed, the data was sorted pragmatically in conjunction with the process of familiarisation (Yin, 2011). Whereas Yin presents three definitive analytic strategies (i.e. pattern matching, explanation building and time-series analysis), I decided that I would remain faithful to Ritchie and Spencer's framework analysis on the basis of its making the data I had collected highly accessible. In order to understand the *how* and *why* associated with each dialogic feedback project, with the intention of providing direct answers to initial and established research hypotheses and research statements, I implemented an approach which allowed the co-construction of answers within a framework that ensured analytical process. This was a decision based on the pragmatics of prioritising and categorising the most salient findings of the study from the initial data sets.

STAGE 6: FRAMING AND ESTABLISHING TESTABLE HYPOTHESES

The next stage of the iterative process in the case study research was to establish the degree of alignment or refutability between the existing evidence bases and to see whether there was any degree of strategic fit with the most salient findings of my own study. The focus here was to ensure that, theoretically, findings could be coherently aligned to the data set, in accordance with the seminal work of Eisenhardt (1989). This raises important considerations in how the quality of my case study is assessed by any outsider and is best articulated as in Table 10.5.

Table 10.5   Criteria of quality evaluation in case study design

Research quality criterion	Description	Implementation process
Criterion 1: Construct validity	• The provision of clear operational definitions at the initial introduction of the case study research	• Triangulation of several sources of evidence • Review of data (check of content validity) interpretation by participants • Engagement of both qualitative and quantitative methods in a mixed methods design

(Continued)

Table 10.5   (Continued)

Research quality criterion	Description	Implementation process
Criterion 2: Internal validity	• Ensuring and validating causal relationships through active comparison, rather than creating unlinked relationships in the data sets	• Analytical approach to co-constructing meaning within an established framework of logic • Content validity check repeated by research participants • Contextual significance of case findings is articulated • Integration of several illustrative citations in the final case study research report • Formulation of a database of findings to act as a checklist • Linking new theoretical propositions iteratively to the extant literature as they emerge
Criterion 3: External validity	• Clear identification of the parameters of research to which the findings of the study can be generalised	• Analytically generalising findings within an established methodological framework • Explicit linkage of theoretical propositions/emergence to the extant literature
Criterion 4: Reliability	• Ensuring repeatability of the procedural elements of the study. (When working with spoken discourse, this can be replaced by the concepts of 'Trustworthiness' and 'Authenticity' since the case study will provide snapshots at any given time, which are essentially non-repeatable due to the dynamic and ever-changing features of human opinion)	• Validation of the systematic framework analysis tool • Case study research design and methodology as expressed by a stipulated protocol

STAGE 7: EMBEDDING EXTANT LITERATURE

In order to build theoretical propositions it is necessary to make an active comparison of the most salient conceptual or hypothetical findings with the extant published evidence base (Eisenhardt, 1989). Within the context of my own study, I needed to ask fundamental questions about what knowledge my findings consolidated, refuted and in some cases bore no relevance to whatsoever.

STAGE 8: THEORETICAL SATURATION AND CASE COMPLETION

Reaching the point of closure in the emergence of new themes was outlined by Eisenhardt (1989) as the point to end the study and draw together the most salient findings. The possibility of further incremental or iterative learning at this stage is minimal since all notable phenomena have been identified and examined already (Glaser and Strauss, 1967). Within my own study, as with many others conducted in practice, there was a pragmatic decision of when to end case collection, another reason why I adopted a theoretical sampling technique, so that I could account for how many cases I would have even before data collection began.

Activity

Use the following exercises and questions, based on what has been outlined in this chapter, to begin framing your own approaches to case study research:

- Think about your own professional discipline. Where might its underpinning philosophy fit with the concept of case study research? How much will this matter?
- Consider how you will begin to frame your case. Pay particular attention to the concepts of time and activity and how these fit with definition and context.
- Begin to categorise your own focus for case study research. Where will it best fit in relation to the classification systems offered by Stake and by Simons?
- How or why will the notion of 'soft positivism' matter to your proposed case study? Where will you position your inquiry methodologically?
- Consider the three conceptual lenses outlined in this chapter. Which will be most significant to your own case study research and why?
- Why might the issues that Flyvbjerg (2006) highlights be of significance to your case study research? How will you defend the stance you take?
- Think about the concepts of theory, reliability and validity in your case study research proposal. How will you address each one?
- How far would a *tabula rasa* be possible in your case study research? How will you articulate this in justification of your own methodological approach?
- Critique the illustrative case study outlined in this chapter in terms of its methodological allegiance to case study research. How might it have been better executed?
- Where does the notion of 'streaming consciousness' fit in relation to previous research that you have undertaken? How do you make meaning of the issues you interpret in everyday life?
- How far do you agree with Yin's proposition that all case studies should have an embedded analytical strategy? What are the challenges of implementation?
- Debate how much pragmatism might influence the decision of when you will draw your own case study research to a conclusion. How far is this dependent on the practicalities of your research execution?
- What do you think are the greatest challenges of case study research?
- What would you do to address these challenges?
- How will you disseminate your work?

Key Points

- The use of case study research enables the in-depth systematic interpretation of policy, experience and context.
- Case study research provides a means of examining the functional dynamics of experience as well as providing a lens to identify the processes of active implementation of phenomena.
- It also provides a mechanism of making research data accessible to a wide audience and for reflection and adaptation to events.
- The co-construction of reality with participants means knowledge and who controls it can be accounted for and readily established. Epistemologically this is significant in the establishment of and development of core knowledge of a specific case.
- Case study research emphasises the value of processes of self-regulation and reflexivity, on behalf of the researcher and the research participants, which can be mutually beneficial.
- The temporality of case study research means it is not dependent on time or constrained by methodological approach and method, which is responsive to a shift in focus and unanticipated developmental progression.

ANNOTATED BIBLIOGRAPHY

The following citations provide a useful accompaniment to this chapter and have been selected on the basis of their accessibility and potential for integration and articulation into applied practice projects such as the professional doctoral thesis.

Busk, P. L., & Marascuilo, L. A. (2015). Statistical analysis in single-case research. *Single-Case Research Design and Analysis (Psychology Revivals): New Directions for Psychology and Education*, 159.

While this text is predominantly pitched towards the academic and applied disciplines of psychology and education, it has a great degree of relevance for doctoral candidates from an array of professional disciplines who may be intellectually contending the place of statistical analysis in case study design and methodology. The authors highlight the reliance of case study researchers on interpretive analysis lacking any validation and provide an informed discussion of the relative merits of increasing relative degrees of validity in data capture and the greater credibility with which findings can be transferred to other relevant contexts in cases of apparent ecological validity. Most valuably, though, this chapter complements the main chapter on case study methods in methodologies for practice development by extending the reach of professional doctorate researchers whose inquiry may well lend itself to a more analytical approach than that which characterises traditional interpretive approaches.

Palinkas, L. A., Horwitz, S. M., Green, C. A., Wisdom, J. P., Duan, N., & Hoagwood, K. (2015). Purposeful sampling for qualitative data collection and analysis in mixed method implementation research. *Administration and Policy in Mental Health and Mental Health Services Research*, 42(5), 533–44.

This paper provides a valuable insight into the notion of purposeful sampling in the context of implementation research. It is particularly useful in providing a taxonomy of purposeful sampling strategies and suggestions for an exceptionally pragmatic approach to the alignment of methodological approach with the central aims of an inquiry. Emphasis is firmly placed on the need for a question-led rather than a methods-driven approach, which so often leads to issues of concern during professional doctorate viva voce examinations. This is a particularly useful paper for those in the early planning stages of case study research who are seeking a pragmatic yet methodologically robust approach. It also incorporates a structured and unambiguous mechanism of matching single or multistage strategies to study aims and quantitative, rather than qualitative, methodological designs.

Thomas, G. (2015). *How to Do Your Case Study*. London: Sage.

This publication provides a really eclectic insight into the application of case study methods beyond the traditional parameters of sociology as an academic discipline. Thomas succeeds in providing a means of capturing the generic transferability of case study as a methodological approach to interdisciplinary contexts that reflect well the professional practice of professional doctorate candidates. Particularly useful is the section detailing processes of constant comparison and the development of rich description. The book also incorporates a means of addressing the construction of narrative from emergent theory and a consideration of how best case study findings can be articulated and pitched to reflect methodological rigour. For those embarking on case study research for the first time, there is also an exceptionally sound overview of procedural ethics in relation to case study design and execution, which would make valuable reading for all those preparing formal research protocol documentation for ethical approval. As such it is uncomplicated yet thorough in ensuring that any potential ethical implications of undertaking case study research are fully addressed.

Yazan, B. (2015). Three approaches to case study methods in education: Yin, Merriam, and Stake. *The Qualitative Report*, 20(2), 134–52.

Yazan provides an exceptionally clear overview of key authors on case study, namely Yin, Merriam and Stake. Far from being a purely narrative overview, Yazan aims at and successfully undertakes a scrutiny of areas where these authors' perspectives diverge, converge and complement one another in varying dimensions of case study research. This is a particularly accessible text for those from professional contexts who may wish to adopt a combinatorial approach to the integration of case study methods in practice. It is also a paper that provides consolidation of the literature available which is useful and practical in aiding professional doctorate students to discern a single overarching research methodology, which in turn makes the constructive alignment of their methods far more straightforward.

REFERENCES

Burgess, H., & Wellington, J. (2010). Exploring the impact of the professional doctorate on students' professional practice and personal development: early indications. *Work Based Learning e-Journal International*, 1(1), 160–76.

Charmaz, K. (2003). Grounded theory: Objectivist and constructivist methods. In N. K. Denzin, & Y. S. Lincoln (eds) *Strategies for Qualitative Inquiry* (2nd edn, pp. 249–91). Thousand Oaks, CA: Sage.

Charmaz, K. (2014). *Constructing Grounded Theory*. London: Sage.

Cohen, L., Manion, L., & Morrison, K. (2013). *Research Methods in Education*. London: Routledge.

Duff, P. A., & Anderson, T. (2015). Case-study research. In J. D. Brown & C. Coombe (eds) *The Cambridge Guide to Research in Language Teaching and Learning* (p. 112–18). Cambridge: Cambridge University Press.

Eisenhardt, K. M. (1989). Building theories from case study research. *Academy of Management Review*, 14(4), 532–50.

Fink, C. K. (2013). Consciousness as presence: an exploration of the illusion of self. *Buddhist Studies Review*, 30(1), 113–28.

Flyvbjerg, B. (2006). Five misunderstandings about case-study research. *Qualitative Inquiry*, 12(2), 219–45.

Glaser, B., & Strauss, A. (1967). *The Discovery of Grounded Theory: Strategies of Qualitative Research*. London: Weidenfeld & Nicolson.

Joukes, E., Cornet, R., de Bruijne, M. C., & de Keizer, N. F. (2016). Eliciting end-user expectations to guide the implementation process of a new electronic health record: a case study using concept mapping. *International Journal of Medical Informatics*, 87, 111–17.

Kaplan, B., & Maxwell, J. A. (1994). Qualitative research methods for evaluating computer information systems. In J. G. Anderson, C. E. Aydin, & S. J. Jay (eds) *Evaluation Health Care information systems: Methods and Application*. California. Sage.

Knobe, J., & Samuels, R. (2013). Thinking like a scientist: innateness as a case study. *Cognition*, 126(1), 72–86.

Miles, M. B., & Huberman, A. M. (1994). *Qualitative Data Analysis: An Expanded Sourcebook*. Beverly Hills, CA: Sage.

Moore, G. F., Audrey, S., Barker, M., Bond, L., Bonell, C., Hardeman, W., & Baird, J. (2015). Process evaluation of complex interventions: Medical Research Council guidance. *British Medical Journal*, 350, h1258.

Ritchie, J., & Spencer, L. (2002). Qualitative data analysis for applied policy research. *The Qualitative Researcher's Companion*, 573, 305–29.

Saldaña, J. (2015). *The Coding Manual for Qualitative Researchers*. London: Sage.

Simons, H. (2009). *Case Study Research in Practice*. London: Sage.

Stake, R. E. (1995). *The Art of Case Study Research*. Thousand Oaks, CA: Sage.

Van Maanen, J. (2011). *Tales of the Field: On Writing Ethnography*. Chicago: University of Chicago Press.

Yin, R. K. (2011). *Applications of Case Study Research*. Beverly Hills, CA: Sage.

Yin, R. K. (2013). *Case Study Research: Design and Methods*. Beverly Hills, CA: Sage.

11

WORKPLACE INQUIRY: USING AN INTEGRATED METHODOLOGY FOR MIXED METHODS RESEARCH

David Plowright

INTRODUCTION

In many of the other methodologies discussed in this book, undertaking research has involved collecting both qualitative and quantitative data. Generating different types of data in the same study is usually described as mixed methods. It can also be used as an overarching framework to undertake empirical research. This particularly applies in the workplace. The approach is based on the principles of pragmatism: that is, what is the best approach to getting the most appropriate information we need to deal with a real-world practical problem? This chapter aims to explore the use of an integrated mixed methods approach to the design of your research. It introduces you to a different way of thinking about the research process, including data collection.

Research is firmly embedded in a conservativism that can lead to a confused understanding of both the practicalities and the conceptualisation of the research process. There is no doubt a variety of reasons for this. It may be the reluctance of methodology tutors, supervisors and researchers to let go of their cherished positions held over many years. It might also include a lack of confidence, time, incentive or interest to challenge the traditional perspectives ubiquitous in methodology publications and research cultures in higher education.

Whatever the reasons, this chapter argues that research methods rely, for their understanding, on a number of myths. The biggest myth of all is the use of the traditional distinction between qualitative research and quantitative research.

THE CHALLENGE

Understanding research methods is a demanding task. To begin with, they have a dual function: firstly, as a clearly identified subject in its own right; and, secondly, as an instrumental means to an inquiry end. They are used as a tool, in a similar way a mechanic might use a range and variety of tools alongside their own expertise and experience to help them work on a project. Hence the focus of this book: that the researcher is a *Bricoleur*, a worker who makes use of the available tools to undertake a task (Kincheloe and Berry, 2004). The *Bricoleur* draws on the techniques and objects to hand in order to solve a problem and construct a representation of the world under scrutiny (Denzin and Lincoln, 2011).

However, it is easy to forget that those tools and techniques employed in the activities of the *Bricoleur* are well-established, tried and trusted approaches. In the past, they have been shown to be reliable, trustworthy and fit for purpose. That is because the *Bricoleur*'s:

> universe of instruments is closed and the rules of his [sic] game are always to make do with 'whatever is at hand', that is to say with a set of tools and materials which is always finite and is also heterogeneous because what it contains bears no relation to the current project. (Lévi-Strauss, 1966: 17)

But the world is changing, including that of research. The hegemony of inward-looking, discipline-based scholarship is increasingly giving way to practically useful, instrumental mode 2 knowledge that can be put to good use to address workplace issues and real-world problems. The approaches of the past, therefore, may no longer be appropriate for those of the present or the future. They may not always fit well with the kind of research that leads to useful, practical solutions (Plowright, 2016b).

POSTGRADUATE RESEARCH

One of the aims of research is to provide timely answers and solutions to pressing questions and problems. In workplace research, the priority will be to getting things done in order to improve a situation with an eye on organisational success.

Postgraduate degree candidates have very often been drawn to undertaking research as a result of an interest in the practicalities of a professional situation. Their motivation is very rarely as a result of the theoretical and conceptual challenges they have discovered in the scholarly literature. In addition, many are often confused by the sophisticated methodological and conceptual principles that they are required to draw on when they eventually embark on their academic research programme. However, it is not surprising that such ideas are a high priority for a postgraduate dissertation or thesis, and are particularly important, of course, in the examination process.

TRADITIONAL DISTINCTIONS

One thing all research has in common is the requirement to employ appropriate research methods and methodologies. However, it is surprising that the paradigmatic distinction between quantitative and qualitative research is still being used as a framework for both teaching and research at postgraduate level. The principles that are traditionally associated with the two different paradigms, referred to in this chapter as the Q words, are shown in Table 11.1, where this information is seen in various guises in many texts.

Table 11.1 Traditional approaches to research

	DOMAINS OF RESEARCH	
	Quantitative research	Qualitative research
Experiential location	Etic – outside	Emic – inside
Research problem	Presented as a hypothesis	Presented as a question
Role of theory	Theory-informed inquiry	Theory-emergent inquiry
Contextual factors	Marginalised or ignored	Integral to the research
Role of researcher	Non-involved neutralised spectator	Involved and reflexively participating
Case selection	Probability sampling	Non-probability sampling
Sample to population characteristics	Representativeness	Typicality or individualistic

(Continued)

Table 11.1   (Continued)

	DOMAINS OF RESEARCH	
	Quantitative research	Qualitative research
Methods	Quantitative: experiment and observation	Qualitative: case study and naturalistic observation
Type of data	Interval and ratio data based on counting and measuring	Nominal and ordinal data based on categorising and ranking
Data analysis	Statistical analysis	Description and theme analysis
Generalisability	Sample to population	Theoretical or resonant
Ontology	Mind independent	Mind dependent
Epistemology	Objective	Subjective
Values	Value free	Value based
Knowledge application	Universal	Particular
Knowledge type	Nomological	Idiographic
Phenomena	Discovered	Constructed
Inferential reasoning	Deductive	Inductive
Rationale	Test theory	Develop theory
Understanding	Valid	Authentic

QUANTITATIVE

Traditionally, research in the quantitative domain is 'etic' in its experiential location: that is, it is outsider research. It draws on scientific research as a model and
presents the research problem as a hypothesis informed by theory derived from
previous and similar research.

Contextual factors are marginalised or are seen as being irrelevant and the voice
of the researcher, a non-involved neutral spectator, is silent throughout the project
and the reported outcomes of the research. Case selection uses randomised, probability sampling with the aim of creating a sample that is representative of a wider
population. Experiment and observation are deployed in order to collect interval
and ratio data created through counting and measuring. Data are analysed statistically in order to generalise from a sample to a population.

Research in this domain traditionally draws on a mind-independent ontology
where the reality under study has an existence external to and independent of
human thought or consciousness. Epistemologically, this type of research aims for
objectivity that is value free, with an emphasis on arriving at universally applied,
extrapolated claims.

The type of knowledge produced because of the claims made is nomological and
forms the basis of identifying lawful relationships between events, processes and
phenomena. Overall, the intention is to discover order and pattern in the world. It

achieves this through deductive inferential reasoning which tests theory. The outcome results in research accounts that provide valid descriptions corresponding to the phenomena being investigated.

QUALITATIVE

The traditional view of research in the qualitative domain is 'emic' in its experiential location: that is, it is insider research. It draws on naturalistic, ethnographic-type research as a model. It presents the research problem as a question or issue and is more concerned with theory building than theory testing.

Context plays an important role and is seen as being integral to the research. The voice of the researcher, an involved and reflexive participant, can be identified throughout the project as well as the account that reports the outcomes of the research. Case selection uses purposive, non-probability sampling with the aim of creating a sample that is either typical of the wider population or individually unique to itself. It aims to achieve this by deploying case study and naturalistic observation in order to collect nominal and ordinal data based on categorising and ranking. Data are analysed thematically in order to describe and understand the experience of the particular cases under study. In addition, resonant generalisation is also used to relate the findings to other situations or groups whose experiences will resonate with the experiences of those involved in the research (Plowright, 2007).

Research in this domain traditionally draws on a mind-dependent ontology where reality is created by human cognition. Epistemologically, qualitative approaches acknowledge that undertaking research is a subjective, social activity and therefore the values of the researcher are important considerations. The aim is to make claims that are particular to the research context and location. The type of knowledge produced is idiographic in focus, identifying characteristics of specific and particular events, processes and phenomena.

Overall, the intention is the construction of the individual realities that are unique to specific contexts, locations and experiences. It aims to achieve this through inferences based on induction, where the purpose is to develop theory. The outcome is the construction of a detailed, rich understanding through accounts that provide authentic and genuine insight into particularistic experiences.

NOT COHERENT

So far so good, but despite what appears to be persuasive and well-established approaches developed over many years, research methods described as qualitative and quantitative are far from coherent strategies. There is not the space to offer a full critique of the characteristics listed under each of the domains in Table 11.1 but the information shows the serious confusions around how we think, talk and write about the research process (Plowright, 2013).

Two important issues stand out. The first is that the claim that the two domains are incompatible arises from ambiguities of language and its imprecise use and meaning. For example, take the qualitative domain. Terms such as qualitative research, approaches, paradigms, strategies, methods and methodologies are used interchangeably but are rarely explained adequately or comprehensively. The term qualitative research is used as a shorthand way of summarising the activities and concepts found in this domain. The same problem applies to the quantitative domain. This creates a lack of clarity, if not confusion, especially since the terms qualitative or quantitative should rightly only be used to describe the types of data that are collected during research.

The second issue that stands out from the two lists in Table 11.1 is that assumptions are made that research in a particular domain necessarily requires using the listed characteristics from that domain. This is not supported by the practice of undertaking research. As Gurtler and Huber point out, both approaches:

> rarely highlight the fact that terms and techniques from the other domain are widely used, and sometimes even play an important part as a sort of hidden but seldom explicitly labelled agenda. On the other hand, various researchers from both fields are aware that their scientific work depends on concepts and constructions from the other domain. (2006: 315)

For example, a hypothesis can be presented as a research question and vice versa. Research from the qualitative domain often includes the collection of data based on counting and measuring: in a questionnaire survey open questions are frequently used as well as closed questions. In the quantitative domain, qualitative descriptions are used when interpreting and discussing the results. Theory will and should inform all meaningful, postgraduate research, whether it is quantitative or qualitative research, and, in addition, theory emerges inductively from quantitative research, as the history of science and social science can testify. Contextual factors are important in all workplace research, whatever the domain, otherwise it would be impossible to understand what the research applied to.

An interesting distinction in Table 11.1, and one that is crucial in the perpetuation of the mythology of research, is the type of data that is *supposed* to be collected in each domain of research. A traditional experiment, again supposedly, deals in quantitative data based on counting and measuring. This implies that qualitative data can play no part in an experiment. However, this is untrue. The comparison of findings from, say, an experimental group and a control group can reveal important insights into attitudes and values expressed through participants' written or spoken responses to open-ended interview questions. Generation and collection of this nominal data will not involve either counting or measuring, nor need the analysis lead to the use of statistics or any numerical information in the presentation of the conclusions.

It appears, therefore, that the labels *quantitative* and *qualitative* are not very helpful when it comes to describing the characteristics of the research process. Indeed, the labels are misleading and are, at times, simply inaccurate.

Activity

We have considered the so-called differences and similarities between the traditional duality of qualitative and quantitative research. Based on your reading and experience, what do you think are the issues associated with using the Q words to describe research?

MIXED METHODS RESEARCH

One apparent solution to the inadequacies of the use of qualitative and quantitative distinctions lies with mixed methods. However, this approach has created further problems and confusions despite its recently becoming more prevalent (see e.g. Gorard and Taylor, 2004; Plano Clark and Creswell, 2008; Tashakkori and Teddlie, 2010).

Proponents of this 'third way' or 'third methodological movement' (Teddlie and Tashakkori, 2003) argue that both qualitative and quantitative approaches can be used in the same study. Therein, however, lies the problem: the use of mixed methods continues to draw on the terminology and concepts of a traditional qualitative/quantitative explanation. Such explanations draw on, often without question or reflexivity, the well-used principles and methods from each domain of research. The effect is that, despite claims that using mixed methods frees researchers from the constraints of the qualitative/quantitative divide, it 'can actually reinforce the binary positioning of the qualitative and quantitative paradigms' (Symonds and Gorard, 2010: 133). A brief look at the definitions of mixed methods supports this view. For example:

> A mixed methods study involves the collection or analysis of both quantitative and/or qualitative data in a single study in which the data are collected concurrently or sequentially, are given a priority, and involve the integration of the data at one or more stages in the process of research. (Creswell et al., 2003: 212)

The use of traditionally opposing domains of research can be seen in the following definition, where mixed methods involves: 'The incorporation of various qualitative or quantitative strategies within a single project that may have either a qualitative or quantitative theoretical drive' (Morse, 2003: 190). Greene offers a more sophisticated explanation, arguing that mixed methods is:

> the planned and intentional incorporation of multiple mental models – with their diverse constituent methodological stances, epistemological understandings, disciplinary perspectives, and habits of mind and experience – into the same enquiry space. (2007: 13)

Plowright's alternative, although still simplified, definition explains that:

> Mixed methods is the collection of different types of data using more than one method, approach or strategy derived from more traditional research paradigms or perspectives that draw on different epistemologies and explanations that inform and underpin knowledge claims. (2013: 67)

To illustrate this approach, imagine a postgraduate researcher who has used a traditional mixed methods approach. Alex, a professional doctorate student, was looking at the way staffing levels were organised in healthcare settings. In particular, she wished to establish a way of improving morale in the workplace. She knew that everyone had their own ideas about how this should be addressed. She first organised a series of focus groups with key members of staff generating and collecting qualitative data through using open questions. She then designed and produced a questionnaire based on the responses from the focus groups. Detailed statements were formulated which participants were asked to rate on a six-point scale. The resulting quantitative data were then statistically analysed. As a result of her research, Alex was able to establish a model of workforce planning and development aimed at contributing to the improvement of staff morale.

It is clear, therefore, that mixed methods is still dominated by the two traditional research domains. The mixed approach remains restricted to, and constricted by, the conceptual and practical characteristics of qualitative and quantitative research. It has some way to develop if it is to meet Onwuegbuzie and Leech's suggestion that both approaches 'can be blended or integrated in such a way that reference to the terms "quantitative" and "qualitative" is no longer needed' (2005: 276). In other words, what is needed is to be able to address the problems of thinking, talking and writing about the research process without falling into the trap of reinforcing the long-held myths associated with the two apparently opposed domains. It will be based on characteristics of holistic, coherent integration and not just using one type of research alongside the other. It is:

> an idea of research that gives up a number of the old distinctions such as values/facts, objective/engaged, researcher/practitioner, concept/fact and qualitative/quantitative/interpretive. (Smeyers, 2008: 698)

The challenge will be to offer an approach that is appropriate for scholarly empirical research *and* meets the demands of undertaking rigorous and systematic workplace inquiry in the public, private and non-profit sectors. The approach recommended in this chapter is that based on the FraIM (Plowright, 2011), whose main characteristic is the rejection of the use of the Q words with their confusing conceptual, methodological and practical pedigrees.

THE FraIM: A BRIEF DESCRIPTION

The FraIM (Frameworks for an Integrated Methodology) shown in Figure 11.1 is the overall design of the research project. The basic structure is relatively straightforward. It is appropriate for carrying out any type of empirical investigation that is aimed at evaluating, developing and improving an understanding of practice. It can be applied to doctoral research undertaken for a programme of study in a higher education setting. It can also be deployed in a variety of professional, vocational and workplace contexts and locations.

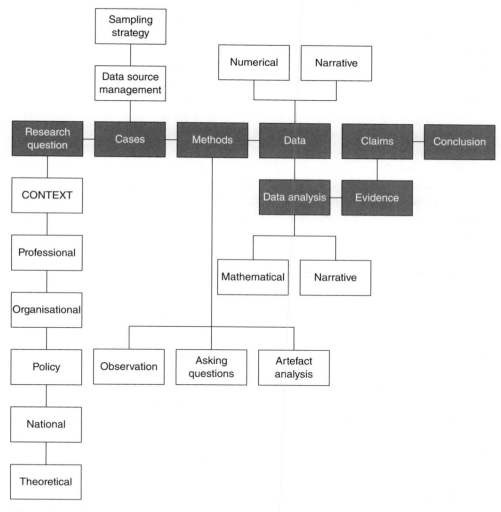

Figure 11.1   The FraIM

(Source: Plowright, 2011: 9)

THE RESEARCH QUESTION AND ITS CONTEXTS

Using the FraIM, the research process begins with the main research question, which has a central role in research that systematically employs empirical data to answer an explicit research question (Punch, 2009). All research questions, from whichever domain, are embedded in a contextual milieu that can include, *inter alia*, professional, organisational, policy, national and theoretical contexts. The contexts play an important role in enabling readers to understand fully, and challenge, the salience and potential impact of the research.

The *professional context* reports information about the researcher and the subject or professional area within which the research is undertaken. The research may take place in a particular *organisational context*. The size, culture and type of organisation may have an impact on the type of research that might be undertaken and may foreground issues around insider and outsider research (Hellawell, 2006). It has been argued that all social research takes place in a *policy context* (Clough and Nutbrown, 2002). It is likely, therefore, that taking the policy context into consideration will inform the researchers' understanding of the issues they are investigating. It may also help to formulate more appropriate research questions.

Research is increasingly international in scope, focus and audience. An international audience will need information about the national characteristics of the location in which the research was conducted. This might include the social and economic structures, the culture and the history of the geographical area. The theoretical context involves undertaking a literature search and writing a literature review that provides the theoretical context to the research. This enables the researcher to provide a conceptual framework for the thesis, dissertation or other type of research report.

A CONTEXT FOR ALL RESEARCH

Usually, a traditional view gives prominence to contextual factors only in research within the qualitative domain (Stephens, 2009). The FraIM, however, argues that context is important for *all* research and especially that aimed at evaluating, developing and improving an understanding of practice in the workplace.

The balance and emphasis of each of the different contexts will, of course, vary across different research enquiries. For example, at times, the policy context may have a high priority since the research may rely on a detailed understanding of the historical development of government policy over a period of time. Whatever the focus and purpose of the research, contextual factors are important and need to be taken into account when planning the data collection and interpretation of the findings.

CASE SELECTION

Case selection involves two stages: the first is the data source management, followed by the second stage, the sampling strategy. These are integrated decisions that need to be taken into account as part of the research.

Data Source Management

It should be noted that the three data source management terms (Table 11.2) represent case selection decisions. They do not refer to the overall design of the research project, as they would in conventionally conceptualised research that draws on the two traditional domains. The design is the FraIM.

Table 11.2 Data source management characteristics

	Experiment	Survey	Case study
Level of control	High	Medium	Low
Ecological validity	Low	Medium	High

Data source management consists of three choices: (1) experiment, (2) survey and (3) case study (Hammersley, 1992). Among the characteristics for these are, firstly, the level of control that the researcher has over which cases are allocated to the groups in the research and, secondly, the degree of naturalness (i.e. the ecological validity) of the groupings and their activities. Table 11.2 shows how these characteristics are associated with data source management decisions.

Level of control concerns the responsibility the researcher has in the allocation of individual cases to the group(s) in the research. In case study, control will be low since the case or cases already exist before the research is undertaken. For example, the case under study might be a senior management team in a school or it could be the school itself. In experiment, degree of control is high, since the researcher decides which cases are allocated to, say, either a control group or an experimental group.

Survey falls between experiment and case study since the groups in the research are likely to already exist outside the research situation, for example in research about supervisors and postgraduate researchers in a university department. However, unlike case study, the survey researcher has some control over how the groups in the research are constituted. For example, each of the two survey groups might be subdivided into gender, prior qualifications or undergraduate degree class as comparative variables. This decision is under the control of the researcher and will be dependent, of course, partly on the research focus and the main research question.

Ecological validity is concerned with the naturalness of the part played by the cases or participants in the research situation. If the researcher determines the often contrived role of the participants, as in a laboratory experiment, the level of ecological validity is low. In a case study it is more likely to be high, since the case or cases are studied in their natural context without researcher intervention in the behaviour of the cases or participants. In relation to ecological validity, survey again falls between experiment and case study.

The characteristics represented in Table 11.2 challenge a number of received arguments about case selection decisions. A traditional perspective expects that case study is a qualitative method (see e.g. Bassey, 1999). In fact, it is neither qualitative nor a method.

By rejecting this view, the door is opened to collecting data that are quantitative, or, in the terms of the FraIM, numerical. In addition, a traditional view requires experiment to collect quantitative data, which does not necessarily happen in practice. In addition, postgraduate research reports will sometimes state emphatically that the research is qualitative and employ a survey which then surprisingly contains closed and open questions, thus generating both types of data. So why, then, is this a 'qualitative method'?

Whatever the detail of the criticism that can be made about traditional qualitative and quantitative approaches to research, there is one important characteristic that should not be overlooked. Each data management decision can be integrated with each other. For example, survey and experiment might be used as part of a case study while a survey might be deployed as an integral part of an experiment.

Sampling Strategy

Whatever the data source management employed in the research, the second stage in case selection is the sampling strategy. This will include a justification for who or what the cases/participants are, how they were selected, why they were selected and how access was gained and maintained.

Depending on the research problem or question, the contexts, the location and the purpose of the research, the researcher may have limited choice about who or what the cases are. This is especially so with workplace research where the focus may be on a particular group of participants. It is probably true to state, therefore, that most workplace research is undertaken using non-probabilistic convenience and purposive sampling strategies. This may not apply, however, to all workplace research. Probabilistic randomisation might be built into the case selection process if the total number of participants in the organisation is too large for the researcher to manage and therefore sampling needs to be undertaken. Further, it is not just a matter of either/or. An integrated methodology supports any sampling strategy that might be included in data source management decisions, depending of course on the main research question and the aims and purpose of the research.

METHODS OF DATA COLLECTION

One of the myths of research is that methods of data collection are either qualitative or quantitative. Conceptually and practically this distinction has little meaning. Using the FraIM relieves researchers of trying to squeeze an explanation of the practicalities of their research into these two unhelpful perspectives.

In the FraIM, there are three generic methods of data generation and collection. They lie on a continuum from observation through asking questions to artefact analysis. All methods of data collection can be subsumed within these three generic approaches. Observation includes not only seeing and hearing, but also tasting, smelling and being in physical contact with the surrounding environment. Asking questions involves, for example, the use of a questionnaire, face-to-face and telephone interviews, texting questions and focus group discussions.

Researchers will be familiar with observation and asking questions, but less so with artefact analysis. An artefact might be a radio or TV programme or perhaps the presentation of the characteristics of international schools on school websites. They may also be documents that are produced by an organisation to communicate its purpose and aims. The researcher's task is to undertake a detailed description and analysis of the values and ideological messages conveyed by the artefacts. It is a method that is used not only in social and education research but also in media studies, communication studies and cultural studies research.

Rather than basing the methods of data collection on the Q words, the FraIM argues that the characteristics of the different methods are based on the following two criteria: firstly, the level of mediation; and secondly, the degree of structure of the methods.

LEVEL OF MEDIATION

Level of mediation is the proximal/distal location in time and space of the researcher to an event or process that is under study. It is a continuum, from observation through asking questions to artefact analysis.

Observation has a low level of mediation since the researcher is usually physically and temporally closer to the phenomena being studied: it is more about the here and now of data collection compared to the other two methods. Asking questions lies at the next level of mediation. The questioning is likely to be about, say, an event, experience or process that has already taken place and is removed in time and place from the researcher. Artefact analysis has the highest level of mediation due to the intervening stages in the production of the artefact and its analysis by the researcher. This removes the analysis even further from the original event or process, compared to observation and asking questions.

All methods of data collection, of course, involve meditational issues. There will always be an element of interpretation by the researcher, whatever the method of data collection. It can be argued, however, that it is less severe in observational approaches compared to asking questions that, in turn, is less severe than in artefact analysis. Being aware of mediational issues provides the researcher with an insight into the potential problems associated with data collection and the interpretation of the data. In other words, the more mediated the method, the increased potential there will be for factors to influence and inevitably bias the research.

Activity

We have discussed the generic approaches to data collection that include observation, interviews and artefact analysis. Thinking about your own research, list the ways in which you can use these approaches and the extent to which they can be integrated into a coherent strategy.

DEGREE OF STRUCTURE

A second characteristic of data collection methods is *degree of structure*[1] that is, again, a continuum. At one extreme, the process is highly structured and, at the other, less structured. It applies in the FraIM to each of the three methods of data collection and is a common idea in the introductory methodology literature (see e.g. Blaikie, 2000; Bryman, 2008; Robson, 2002). However, it is very rarely referred to as the *main* criterion on which to base an explanation of methods of data collection since authors usually fall back onto using the Q words.

A low degree of structure in, for example, asking questions is characterised by open questions and a lower level of 'pre-structuring' of data. This results in a lower level of predictability of the data to be collected. An example might be the use of an informal interview based on asking only two open questions about participants' views of a methodology workshop.

On the other hand, a higher degree of structure uses closed questions, where the data have a higher level of pre-structuring and therefore a higher level of predictability over what data will be collected. An example would be a questionnaire that asked for *Strongly agree – Agree – Disagree – Strongly disagree* responses. The consequences of the degree of structure for participants and the researcher are important for the data collection procedure and these are outlined further in Table 11.3 for asking questions. A similar table can be constructed, showing how the degree of structure can be applied to both observation and artefact analysis.

Table 11.3 Degree of structure: asking questions

Lower degree of structure	◄———►	Higher degree of structure
Open questions	Questions	Closed questions
Lower level of pre-structuring of data	Data	Higher level of pre-structuring of data
Lower level of predictability over data *to be* collected	Data	Higher level of predictability over data *to be* collected
Responses to questions are not predetermined.	Participant	Responses to questions will be predetermined
Increased choice of participant response during data collection	Participant	Limited choice of participant response during data collection
Higher level of participant control about how to respond to questions during data collection	Participant	Lower level of participant control about how to respond to questions during data collection
Lower level of researcher control during data collection	Researcher	Higher level of researcher control during data collection
Researcher has more choice over how the data are managed and analysed	Researcher	Researcher has less choice over how the data are managed and analysed

(Source: After Plowright, 2011: 54)

---

[1]Note that 'unstructured' is not used, since this has little meaning in practical terms. It would be impossible to detect anything that has no structure and would probably not exist anyway.

The final point to make about the three different generic research methods is that each method can collect both types of data, namely numerical and narrative. It does not make sense, therefore, to refer to methods of data collection as being either qualitative or quantitative.

DATA

The next element of the FraIM concerns the data that will be collected as part of the research. There are two generic categories of data, numerical and narrative, which are alternative labels for the traditional categories of quantitative and qualitative data.

The FraIM employs the terms numerical and narrative since they do not have the long pedigree, history and connotations of the Q words that channel researchers into a set way of thinking about undertaking research. Published texts about research methods, including mixed methods, still explain these as being numbers and words. This, again, is an unhelpful description that does not provide an adequate outline of the distinction between the two. For example, narrative data can also include illustrations, performance, sculpture and audio presentations.

An alternative and potentially more detailed and useful explanation of the difference between the types of data is based on the idea of the *codification* of knowledge. This relies on the systematic application of a code or rules of representation and interpretation in order to encode and decode information.

Research data draw on two types of major codes that represent the two generic types of data. Numerical data involves counting and measuring and is informed by the logical code or rules of mathematics (Guiraud, 1975) or science (Chandler, 2001). The data are often seen as unambiguous, fixed and non-negotiable and are very often analysed using statistical testing. Narrative data draw on relatively more constructed or 'poetic' codes of meaning (Guiraud, 1975). Such codes – or rules of representation and interpretation – are based on the use of language or perhaps still and moving imagery. The data are often more complex, ambiguous and uncertain. Of course, both types of data can be generated and collected using each or all of the three types of data collection methods.

Once the data have been collected then it can be analysed mathematically and/or narratively. In other words, items in narrative data can be counted and/or measured and numerical data can be discussed and explained using narrative analysis to present understandings and interpretations. Which approach is taken will be determined by the research question and the purpose of the research, rather than a restricted view of what an imagined qualitative or quantitative research supposedly demands.

WARRANTABILITY OF RESEARCH

An important issue in the planning and undertaking of any type of research is the *warrantability* (Toulmin, 2003) of the research. This applies equally to scholarly research as well as work-based corporate research.

The FraIM can be used to undertake research that is aimed at making evidentially supported claims about the cases without recourse to traditional perspectives confusingly based on the research domains outlined earlier in Table 11.1. The purpose is to undertake and report on research that leads to warrantable or justifiable conclusions. Such warrants or justifications rely on an inferential process based on C. S. Peirce's pragmatism. The procedure progresses from abduction, through deduction and ends with induction as integral and necessary stages of *all* research enquiries (Plowright, 2016a). This challenges a myth of methodology and the conventional view that research is either deductive or inductive.

The aim is to arrive at valid and warrantable conclusions to the research. Such conclusions, will, of course, be tentative and open to being questioned. The researcher, therefore, will be expected to approach these in a sceptical and critical attitude and thus challenge the interpretation of the findings (Gorard and Taylor, 2004). Alternative explanations based on counter-arguments for the warrants proposed can then be considered which, if more plausible and persuasive, can lead to the rejection of the initial conclusions. If the alternative explanations are subsequently rejected, however, then the warrant for the research can be accepted as the most appropriate available at the time.

The focus on warrantability does not ignore the importance of epistemological questions. However, use of the term and its underlying concepts does at least avoid the irresolvable arguments about truth resulting from a correspondence theory of ontological veracity. In its place, Peirce's pragmatism argues that truth involves a community of enquirers arriving at an agreement about an issue or understanding over a period of time. He argued:

> Different minds may set out with the most antagonistic views, but the progress of investigation carries them by a force outside of themselves to one and the same conclusion .... The opinion which is fated to be ultimately agreed to by all who investigate, is what we mean by the truth. (Peirce, 1878: para 407)

This can only be achieved by undertaking investigative enquiries that produce warrantable results that can be shared, challenged and developed further by others. In other words, Peirce argued for a *rigorous and systematic* approach that can be applied not only to scientific investigations but also to philosophy, day-to-day living and other social inquiry. Peirce's work and ideas, drawn from his pragmatism, are highly relevant to using an integrated methodology.

INTEGRATED MATRIX

It is apparent from the above discussion that the FraIM is more than simply a mixed methods strategy for undertaking research. It provides a more holistic and coherent approach that integrates the different and disparate elements of a research inquiry. It rejects the use of the Q words as a description of two different types of research and acknowledges that the practicalities of research rarely fit the two domains that were outlined at the start of the chapter in Table 11.1. Such a traditional approach to research is confusing, often inaccurate and therefore unhelpful when undertaking empirical research.

In its place, the FraIM offers an alternative means of conceptualising the methodological perspective of an investigation as well as practically structuring the research activities. The purpose is to ensure a warrantable outcome to the research. It achieves this by justifying the claims made through providing evidence selected from the data generated by using appropriate methods, collected from the cases and drawing on supporting contextual factors.

The main elements of the empirical research activity, therefore, form a three-dimensional matrix that provides an insight into the opportunities and possibilities for undertaking workplace inquiry using an integrated methodology for a mixed methods strategy. This is shown in Figure 11.2.

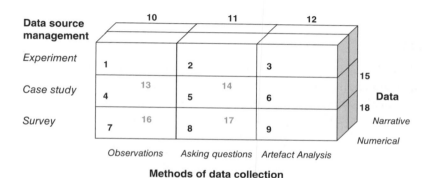

Figure 11.2   The integrated matrix: opportunities and possibilities

(Source: Plowright, 2011: 19)

Rather than there being only two approaches to undertaking empirical research (i.e. qualitative and quantitative), the integrated matrix highlights the possibility of deploying 18 different strategies. Each can be used on its own or in different combinations with each other. For example, a research project could involve an investigation of gender issues in the use of language in the classroom. Using the matrix in Figure 11.2, data source management using experiment might compare purposively selected participants allocated to two groups, aimed at exploring the use of different teaching materials to portray gender.

The materials might be a written vignette that tells a brief story depicting the experiences of a fictitious character. In the material given to one group, the character is described as she/her and to the second group as he/him. However, the description of the events depicted are identical. The only difference is in the reference to the gender of the character. The method of data collection involves asking the two groups to describe the lifestyle of the character. The written descriptions from participants in each of the two groups are then collected and compared.

The independent variable is gender identification and the dependent variable the written accounts produced by the participants. The type of data collected will be narrative data, so placing the investigation firmly in cell 17 of the integrated matrix: Experiment × Asking questions × Narrative. The data would be analysed narratively, despite a traditional perspective, no doubt, claiming that experiment necessitates the collection of statistically analysable numerical data.

There are many benefits to deploying the FraIM as the research design for the structure of an inquiry or investigation. Most important of all, as in the above example, it avoids use of the Q words and acts as a liberating influence on how we think about, talk about and write about the process and the practicalities of undertaking empirical research.

FINALLY

Plowright's (2011) FraIM has the ability to make a contribution to meeting the needs of postgraduate researchers, and in particular workplace research, that is both useful and methodologically rigorous. In addition, it goes some way to mitigating against a number of misleading and erroneous ideas about research, embodied in the use of the Q words and perpetuated by the so-called third way of mixed methods. The FraIM is highly appropriate for undertaking strategically purposed workplace inquiry that aims to evaluate, develop and improve practice in identified contexts.

Key Points

- In dealing with practice-based issues it is helpful to use an integrated mixed methods strategy to address or answer the problems that can arise.
- The FraIM offers an alternative means of conceptualising the methodological perspective of an investigation as well as practically structuring the research activities.
- The research begins with an explicit research question rather than a choice of qualitative or quantitative approaches.
- The research will be located within a number of different contexts which, therefore, determine the selection of participants that, in turn, enable you to choose the methods of data generation and collection.
- Rather than qualitative and quantitative methods, it is more helpful to think of structured and less structured approaches to data collection using the generic approaches of observation, asking questions and artefact analysis.

- An important element of the research process is that the data provide the evidence to support the warrantable claims and conclusions of the research study.
- It achieves this by justifying the claims made through providing evidence from the analysis of the data collected by appropriate methods from selected cases and drawing on supporting contextual factors.

ANNOTATED BIBLIOGRAPHY

Bergman, M. M. (ed.) (2008). *Advances in Mixed Methods Research*. London: Sage.

The title of this book may lead readers to expect an account of innovative developments in either thinking and/or practice in undertaking mixed methods research. It contains neither. The editor appears to be both critical and frustrated at the lack of developments in mixed methods. He believes the differences between qualitative and quantitative research (expressed in the usual way as QUAL and QUAN) are overstated, with claims and arguments that are not sustainable. Most important of all, however, is the questioning of the legislative connection between philosophy and methodology. He points out that 'No empirical evidence and no theoretical structure can determine which precise ontological and epistemological position researchers should take. Instead, researchers must and do make this decision based on their habits, training, and other concerns' (p. 16). The editor acknowledges that much more could be written to dispel the myths of the duality of qualitative and quantitative research but ironically perpetuates those myths in his opening chapter and the selection of the other chapters in the book. It provides no evidence that mixed methods has advanced beyond using so-called qualitative and quantitative approaches in the same study. It is worth reading, if for no other reason than to witness the hegemonic trap that social science authors and researchers have created for themselves.

Kuhn, T. S. (1966). *The Structure of Scientific Revolutions* (3rd edn). London: University of Chicago Press.

This is an essential book for anyone interested in understanding how a paradigmatic research perspective influences our thinking and practice in social and educational research. Although predominantly about science research, the book nevertheless is pivotal to understanding how the paradigms we use draw on the ubiquitous rules and standards that are applied to research. More importantly, it raises both explicit and implicit questions about whether the social sciences have yet acquired paradigm status. The book provides an insight into how professional socialisation prepares new researchers, whether undergraduate students or doctoral candidates, to accept unquestionably the paradigm in which they are working.

Law, J. (2004). *After Method: Mess in Social Science Research*. London: Routledge.

This is an important book that challenges the hegemony of conventional social science research methodologies. The author argues that the rules on which research is based are too restrictive since they no longer meet the needs of the present day. They draw on qualitative and quantitative methods that are found by teachers and students to be at best marginally relevant to the research process. At worst, the methods are restraining and blinkered. They presuppose and enact particular metaphysical assumptions, which, the author argues, should be challenged and questioned through using a 'method assemblage' in which research is both reality *detector* and reality *amplifier*. The aim is to acknowledge and accept that social science research is messy and our current approaches are unable to make sense of the world we study.

REFERENCES

Bassey, M. (1999). *Case Study Research in Educational Settings*. Buckingham: Open University Press.

Blaikie, N. (2000). *Designing Social Research*. Cambridge: Polity Press.

Bryman, A. (2008). *Social Research Methods* (3rd edn). Oxford: Oxford University Press.

Chandler, D. (2001). *Semiotics: The Basics*. London: Routledge.

Clough, P., & Nutbrown, C. (2002). *A Student's Guide to Methodology*. London: Sage.

Creswell, J. W., Plano Clark, V. L., Gutmann, M. L., & Hanson, W. E. (2003). Advanced mixed methods research designs. In A. Tashakkori & C. Teddlie (eds) *Handbook of Mixed Methods in Social and Behavioral Research* (ch. 8). London: Sage.

Denzin, N. K., & Lincoln, Y. L. (2011). Introduction: the discipline and practice of qualitative research'. In N. K. Denzin & Y. L. Lincoln (eds) *The SAGE Handbook of Qualitative Research* (ch. 1). London: Sage.

Gorard, S., & Taylor, C. (2004). *Combining Methods in Educational and Social Research*. Maidenhead: Open University Press.

Greene, J. C. (2007). *Mixed Methods in Social Inquiry*. San Francisco: Jossey-Bass.

Guiraud, P. (1975). *Semiology*. London: Routledge.

Gurtler, L., & Huber, G. L. (2006). The ambiguous use of language in the paradigms of QUAN and QUAL. *Qualitative Research in Psychology*, *3*(4), 313–28.

Hammersley, M. (1992). *What's Wrong with Ethnography?* London: Routledge.

Hellawell, D. (2006). Inside-out: analysis of the insider-outsider concept as a heuristic device to develop reflexivity in students doing qualitative research. *Teaching in Higher Education*, *11*(4), 483–94.

Kincheloe, J. L., & Berry, K. S. (2004). *Rigour and Complexity in Educational Research: Conceptualising the Bricolage*. Maidenhead: Open University Press.

Lévi-Strauss, C. (1966 [1962]). *The Savage Mind (Le Pensée Sauvage)* (trans. from the French). London: Weidenfeld & Nicolson.

Morse, J. M. (2003). Principles of mixed methods and multimethod research design. In A. Tashakkori & C. Teddlie (eds) *Handbook of Mixed Methods in Social and Behavioral Research* (ch. 7). London: Sage.

Onwuegbuzie, A.J. and Leech, N.L. (2005). Taking the 'Q' out of research: teaching research methodology courses without the divide between quantitative and qualitative paradigms. *Quality and Quantity*, *39*(3), 267–96.

Peirce, C. S. (1878). How to make our ideas clear, *Popular Science Monthly*, *11*(January), 286–302. In C. Hartshorne & P. Weiss (eds) (1935) *Collected Papers of Charles Sanders Peirce*, Vol. 5, *Pragmatism and Pragmaticism*. Cambridge, MA: Harvard University Press.

Plano Clark, V. L., & Creswell, J. (2008). *The Mixed Methods Reader*. London: Sage.

Plowright, D. (2007). Self-evaluation and Ofsted inspection: developing an integrative model of school improvement. *Educational Management Administration & Leadership*, *35*(3), 373–93.

Plowright, D. (2011). *Using Mixed Methods: Frameworks for an Integrated Methodology*. London: Sage.

Plowright, D. (2013). To what extent do postgraduate students understand the principles of mixed methods in educational research? *International Journal of Multiple Research Approaches*, *7*(1), 66–82.

Plowright, D. (2016a). *Charles Sanders Peirce: Pragmatism and Education*. New York: Springer.

Plowright, D. (2016b). Developing doctoral research skills for workplace inquiry using an integrated methodology. In M. Fourie-Malherbe, C. Aitchison, R. Albertyn & E. Bitzer (eds) *Postgraduate Supervision: Future Foci for the Knowledge Society* (ch. 16). Stellenbosch: African SUNMedia.

Punch, K. F. (2009). *Introduction to Research Methods in Education*. London: Sage.

Robson, C. (2002). *Real World Research* (2nd edn). Oxford: Blackwell.

Smeyers, P. (2008). Qualitative and quantitative research methods: old wine in new bottles? On understanding and interpreting educational phenomena. *Paedagogica Historica*, 44(6), 691–705.

Stephens, D. (2009). *Qualitative Research in International Settings: A Practical Guide*. London: Routledge.

Symonds, J. E., & Gorard, S. (2010). Death of mixed methods? Or the rebirth of research is a craft. *Evaluation and Research in Education*, 23(2), 121–36.

Tashakkori, A., & Teddlie, C. (eds) (2010). *Handbook of Mixed Methods in Social and Behavioral Research*. London: Sage.

Teddlie, C., & Tashakkori, A. (2003). Major issues and controversies in the use of mixed methods in the social and behavioral sciences. In A. Tashakkori & C. Teddlie (eds) *Handbook of Mixed Methods in Social and Behavioral Research* (ch. 1). London: Sage.

Toulmin, S. E. (2003). *The Uses of Argument* (2nd edn). Cambridge: Cambridge University Press.

12

TRANSLATIONAL RESEARCH IN PRACTICE DEVELOPMENT

John Fulton

INTRODUCTION

This chapter explores translational research as a methodological approach for a professional doctorate; as the name suggests, it is about the translation of research findings into practice. Practice and practice development are integral to the professional doctorate, as is translational research. It is therefore an appropriate approach to the professional doctorate: it requires an understanding of practice and of the knowledge which is valued in that practice area. Medicine is its main exponent but it is becoming increasingly commoner in other areas.

The first consideration is what exactly translational research is; almost all professions are committed to practising from a strong evidence base and translational research is concerned with translating research into practice. A definition of translational research is: 'effective translation of the new knowledge, mechanisms, and techniques generated by advances in basic science research into new approaches for prevention, diagnosis, and treatment of disease is essential for improving health' (Fontanarosa and DeAngelis, 2002: 1728). The term is used most commonly in medicine and primarily refers to the translation of laboratory findings to the clinical setting or to the bedside. It is also used in public health concerning the findings of epidemiological surveys and other research, and how the surveys and other research can be translated to public health strategies, affecting the health of populations. Translational research also has implications for professional practice in a wider sense; it is not healthcare which has the drive for evidenced-based practice but other disciplines such as education and business which also strive to make their practice more strongly focused on evidence. The focus of this chapter will be to consider translational research from this perspective and the ways in which it can enhance other professional groups.

It might seem relatively straightforward to base one's practice on evidence, and this is also the case on a larger scale, but it is an area fraught with potential problems. Importantly one must ensure the evidence is sound and robust. Secondly, one must be sure it can be applied in different settings. An additional issue is that much of the rhetoric in evidenced-based healthcare is around quantitative research and more specifically randomised control trials, while other disciplines may use a variety of research approaches and much of their evidence base may be around qualitative studies, which make little if any claim to transferability. On a more practical level, managers and other stakeholders need to be convinced that the associated cost and benefit will be worth the effort.

Chafouleas and Riley-Tillman (2005) argue that there is no effective mechanism for the dissemination of research findings and their subsequent evolution in practice. In building an evidence base various disciplines have progressed at very different levels and in different ways. One thing they all have in common, however, is that the process of translating the findings into practice can in itself be a major piece of work and one which needs to be done in a rigorous and systematic manner. This is an important issue which is highlighted by many writers (Greenhalgh and Wieringa, 2011). Translational research does not equate to applying research findings in an ad hoc or individualistic manner but rather in an organised, rigorous and systematic way. This translation should be at the level of the organisation or at least a clearly defined practice area. Although there is a very clear model of translational research in evidenced-based healthcare, this chapter will considerably broaden the perspective from healthcare to a variety of disciplines and the different approaches which may be relevant. As such the chapter, in considering a variety of disciplines, outlines some of the general principles inherent in translational research and will conclude by identifying the key considerations which should be taken into account in translational research.

TYPES OF KNOWLEDGE

Before thinking about the translation of research findings, it is important to consider the types of knowledge and the associated research on which the practice is focused. All of these will have implications for the transferability of the research to practice. Ward et al. (2009) discuss three types of knowledge (these are often referred to as paradigms) which can be translated into practice: research evidence; tacit knowledge; and novel ideas and innovations. Deetz (1996) further explored the types of knowledge which are relevant to practice, and he added dialogic (or postmodernist approaches) and critical theory. These areas will now be considered sequentially.

RESEARCH-BASED EVIDENCE

Research-based evidence is the commonest use of the term, mainly because of its use in healthcare settings. The type of evidence considered is heavily influenced by the randomised control trial and qualitative research; however, there is some acknowledgement of the significance of qualitative approaches. The underlying premise is that the goal of evidenced-based research is to find this evidence and translate the findings into practice. In medicine, this occurs at the level of the individual clinician who is trained to determine evidence and implement the findings in their clinical practice.

Drawing from medical research in terms of the translation of research findings on a slightly larger scale, the translation can occur on three levels: translation of basic science to the design of diagnostic tests and treatments and the subsequent translation of these tests into everyday clinical practice (Woolf, 2008), referred to as T1 and T2 approaches; and, thirdly, the type of translational research (T3) which is the translation of findings from epidemiological studies into public research strategies. There is a growing body of literature which discusses strategies for the translation of scientific (T1) to clinical practice (T2) and epidemiological studies into public health strategies. In this approach the research is pre-existent and is not generated as part of the study, but rather the focus is on the implementation of the research findings, the aim of which is to bring about change in practice.

While medicine and healthcare have the most clearly defined strategy, other professional groups, such as education, are equally as concerned with establishing an evidence base for their practice. The issue with this is that, for many disciplines, much of the evidence base lies in qualitative studies which by definition are developed in a very specific area of practice and as such can be context specific, although it can be argued that the detailed context-specific nature of qualitative research allows for a comparison to be made. Strategies for the translation of research are less clearly defined and often need to be established rather than using, as in the case of healthcare, a pre-existing model.

TACIT KNOWLEDGE

Tacit knowledge stems from the work of Polanyi (2009) and the central idea is that many of the skills (and associated knowledge) found in practice are executed unconsciously and can therefore be said to be instinctive. Polanyi uses the example of riding a bicycle to illustrate this point: if you know how to ride a bicycle it is easy to do but hard to explain. This principle applies to many of the skills used in everyday life. There is also a great deal of theoretical knowledge integrated with practical skills. Making this more widely known is not without its challenges as it can be very difficult to translate into practice, when often stopping to think about what we are doing holds everything up. To return to the example of the bicycle, as soon as we start to think about what we are doing when riding a bicycle we fall off! Tacit knowledge can be summarised as people working in practice creating knowledge through their day-to-day activities.

A central challenge lies in making tacit knowledge explicit. While there are challenges in applying established research to practice, there are certain guidelines which can be followed. Applying tacit knowledge to practice is less clearly defined, and importantly this raises the question of how good is the original tacit knowledge? All practice is not at an optimal level and people can develop ways of 'doing', which contradicts evidence. So perhaps in translational research an appropriate focus is on tacit knowledge which has been validated by research studies. However, in articulating tacit knowledge the main approach is qualitative research and this raises issues about the generalisability of the work. This needs to be given careful consideration. In the translation of research findings into practice, tacit knowledge is important and is part of the skill package of translational research.

CRITICAL APPROACHES

Deetz (1996), in his discussion of the relationship of theory and practice, takes the discussion a stage further and introduces critical approaches. By this he means that, far from a harmonious site, the workplace can be a place of potential struggle with conflicted positions and views held by the workers. Alvesson and Deetz (2006) discuss the philosophical position of these approaches and in doing so emphasise the importance of knowledge–power relations and the long-standing conflict arising from the various class positions of the individuals, as well as the ways in which experience and society construct reality. It is worth examining this area in some detail. Deetz places tacit knowledge and evidenced-based approaches in the consensus paradigm and, while this is not to ignore tensions which can be involved in the changing of practice, it is assumed that there is an underlying and overall agreement that those involved have the same aims and are basically moving in the same direction. Critical approaches challenge the so-called consensus and acknowledge the underlying tensions that exist in the workplace.

Critical studies are concerned with disadvantaged groups and the righting of inequalities in both the workplace and the practice area. A focus is on the relative position of various groups with some being more advantageous than others; practices and the structure of the organisation can in many ways conspire against certain groups and certain individuals within those groups. Critical studies can inform practice and its development, both in terms of workplace practices and in terms of service delivery.

An example of this is demonstrated in education at all levels where in many UK institutions there are large numbers of overseas students. A critical approach would be to examine how these students are treated, and uncover patterns which may show discrimination, such as particular groups underperforming. The next step would be to identify strategies which may address these issues. An example there is a body of literature around culturally sensitive teaching, mostly developed from work with American students in the United States (Gay, 2010). This would need to be translated into a particular practice setting; issues around transferability of these findings and the particular nuances would need to be established before the implementation could be fully identified in any real sense.

POSTMODERN APPROACHES

Postmodernism is a notoriously difficult term to define but covers an approach which spans a variety of disciplines and is characterised by a rejection of grand narratives or universal rules or laws. It sees knowledge as being socially constructed and as arising out of a particular set of circumstances at a particular historical point. To put this in another way, the prevalent discourses can determine the direction and shape of the discipline and its particular emphasis and type of knowledge which is valued. Discourses are the ways in which particular issues are represented at both a popular level and an academic level. This representation can give rise to knowledge construction.

In discussing translational research, postmodernist approaches may seem like a contradiction in terms, but are important for several reasons. The prevalent discourses will determine the knowledge and research findings which will be valued by an organisation at a particular point in time. This determination of the discourses will determine the ability of the organisation to take on new ideas and approaches.

Five very different types of knowledge have been explored: research-based evidence, tacit knowledge, innovative thinking, critical theory and dialogic theory, as the basis for the translation of knowledge into practice. The term knowledge is used rather than research as not all types of knowledge involve research which is tested and rigorous. The type of knowledge which is used depends on the type of knowledge which is valued within the discipline. Tacit knowledge is dependent on exploration by, usually, qualitative research, and on this basis it can be applied to practice. Critical approaches and dialogic approaches are focused on an understanding of the organisational context in terms of the relative advantaged and disadvantaged positions of the various groups. Dialogic knowledge is focused on language and the discourses which can shape the practice areas. While innovation underlies, at some point, all the other types of knowledge, this refers to creativity and the trying out of novel ideas as the translation of knowledge into practice. In undertaking translational research it is important to position ourselves in one of these domains or paradigms and be very clear about what it is we wish to translate into practice.

However, reality is complex and multidimensional and professional groups do not exist in a vacuum. While we need to be very clear about the knowledge domain which we will translate into practice, this does not mean to say that the other types of knowledge will not be of use in the process of translation. Tacit knowledge, for instance, will interact with research knowledge, and practitioners when faced with 'new evidence' will consider it against their experience and will also consider the implementation against their experiences. Similarly with innovation, in translating findings an innovative approach or the making of creative links can make the process considerably more effective. An awareness of this can speed up the process of translational research.

INNOVATIVE THINKING

Now technically all of translational research is innovative in that it brings about change in an area of practice and as such it can be said to be a novel approach. In the context of organisational research, innovations refer to ideas and knowledge which are either completely novel or taken and transferred from a very different source. However, the argument central to this chapter is that the research which is being transferred must be from well-designed and reliable studies whether qualitative or quantitative. Innovation in this context is about the transfer of ideas.

In the business world, innovative and creative thinking are highly valued. In other domains such as healthcare, creative ideas are the starting point for rigorous research. It would be unthinkable to commence a treatment regime in medicine on the basis that it is an innovative idea which might work! Whereas in some businesses, and in art and design, good and fairly off-beam ideas are the staple diet, often success is only known if they are tried out.

Activity

We have looked at the different types of knowledge inherent in practice.

Write down your understanding of each one and how it applies to your practice area

Term	Definition	Implications for your practice
Evidenced-based research		

Term	Definition	Implications for your practice
Tacit knowledge		
Critical knowledge		
Postmodern approaches		
Innovation		

HOW DO YOU KNOW THAT RESEARCH CAN BE APPLIED TO PRACTICE?

This is an important issue in translational research and comes back to the generalisability of findings across areas and from the (often) artificial world of the research setting to the practice setting with all its nuances and changes. In quantitative studies, a key issue around generalisability is around the representativeness of the sample. The focus on considering the validity of research findings has been largely on internal validity (Glasgow and Green, 2007) and, in the evidence-based healthcare movement, external validity. How generalisable the findings are has been largely ignored. The assumption is that if internal validity is achieved then external validity will automatically follow.

Internal validity is concerned with how well the study is designed and whether external explanation for the phenomena is controlled. To give an example of internal validity, in evidenced-based healthcare the gold standard is the randomised control trail through the control of extraneous variables. The factor which is being investigated is isolated and this allows the establishment of a causal relationship. For example, a randomised control trial exploring the effectiveness of a new type of toothpaste would establish a group which would use the new toothpaste and a second group which would use a conventional one. By measuring predetermined variables such as dental carries, whiteness and overall satisfaction of the user, the effectiveness (or lack of) could be determined. This assumes all other explanations are controlled: for instance, both groups were comparable in terms of dental health, eating patterns were similar and the groups cleaned their teeth with similar timing and technique. Thus, there is a high degree of internal validity, but how applicable it is to areas other than where the research has been carried out is very important: it is essential to ensure the research is well constructed and has high reliability and validity.

If the study is well designed and reliable and valid, is that enough to assume it is fine to apply it to practice? This is where the idea of internal validity comes into play. Campbell (1986), one of the earlier theorists to discuss external validity, outlines two models: the sampling model and the proximity similarity model. The sampling model is concerned with how representative the sample is of the population, and the size of the sample. The basic idea of the proximity similarity model is to consider how similar the setting is to the area in which the findings will be transferred and the more similar the setting, the more applicable the findings will be. Glasgow et al. (2003) discuss efficacy and efficiency: efficiency trials are highly controlled studies, whereas efficiency trails are concerned with the effect under less ideal circumstances. This is an issue which must be considered as many trials are carried out in ideal conditions and of course in day-to-day practice things can be messy and can be more difficult. This is what is meant by external validity and it is an important consideration. It is useful to have an explicit criterion as indicated above on which to base the transferability. Also, the tacit knowledge of your practice is important as experience can tell you what might work and what might not.

An important development which has affected the generalisability of findings is the systematic review. There are an increasing number of systematic reviews which combine the findings of a series of studies and these often include a meta-analysis where all the results are combined and consistent patterns can be established over a series of studies. This adds to the generalisability of the findings. To return to the toothpaste example, if a series of studies were carried out and consistent results were obtained then we would be more comfortable about its translation to practice. Yet, clinicians are always advised to use their judgement and think very carefully if this approach is applicable to their client group. In other types of research one issue is the transferability from the laboratory to the real world: for instance, in psychological research which can be undertaken in the laboratory setting, how applicable is this to the natural setting?

Qualitative research, while not claiming generalisability, does explore the natural setting in considerable detail and, through what Geertz (1994) calls rich description, allows the reader to determine its representativeness and then compare it to their setting and determine if the findings can easily be translated into practice. This is not too dissimilar to the clinician using their judgement to determine the applicability of findings to their practice. This is referred to as the transferability of the findings.

Glasgow et al. (1999) discuss the *Re aim* framework a criterion for the application of research to the practice setting. They are writing from the perspective of public health and on the translation of findings into practice from this perspective.

However, the areas they consider are important and can be applied to other settings, which can be useful criteria when considering the application of the research to practice. A summary of their criteria is as follows. *Reach* – the setting of the research is considered in detail and how representative it is; specifically, how similar it is to the area of research is considered in some detail, and the *effectiveness* of the intervention. The staff undertaking the implementation and their readiness to *adopt* and *implement* it are also considered. Specific outcomes should be established and long-term effects should also be considered (*maintenance*).

ROLES IN TRANSLATIONAL RESEARCH

Translation of research into an area can be fraught with problems and it is important to determine the role and responsibilities of the key players. Broekkamp and van Hout-Walters (2007) discussed the various roles in relation to the implementation of research findings to practice. They are:

- The researcher
- The practitioner
- The mediator (more commonly referred to as the knowledge broker)
- The policy maker.

These roles are not mutually exclusive and one individual may take on several roles; this is particularly relevant to the professional doctorate where the practitioner–researcher is the norm rather than the exception. However, in terms of all of the roles the researcher is usually an academic carrying out original research both within and without the practice setting. The practitioner is someone who is working in the practice setting and is the one who will implement the research findings into this practice. The policy maker is usually concerned with the overall management or strategic direction of service, may commission the research and/or is becoming increasingly common, particularly in the health service in commissioning the development of evidenced-based protocols. Hammami et al. (2013) emphasise the point of the organisation in translational research and the need to ensure that the aims and directions of the strategy match the ethos of the organisation.

The roles and models of translational research are very important because in any situation change can be difficult and there can be tensions between those taking the different roles. In the case of translational research the mediator or broker has a central role to play in the process of the translation of research findings into practice. Lomas puts this rather well:

> decision makers – the patients, the care providers, the managers, and the policy makers – tend to see research as a product they can purchase from the local knowledge store, but too often it is the wrong size, needs some assembly, is on back order, and comes from last year's fashion line. (Lomas, 2007: 130)

In the case of the professional doctorate, the candidate will usually be the mediator, although this may be combined with other roles. The mediator is a term used interchangeably with knowledge broker. Malinovskyte et al. (2016) proposed that the term knowledge broker can be used in two ways: firstly, that of translating knowledge into practice and in doing so devising a strategy to take account of social differences (Lomas, 2007), while the second approach concerns innovation and the role of the broker is to promote innovation within the organisation (Hargadon, 2002). The ways in which the mediator is used can vary from professional setting to professional setting. In business, for example, Hargadon (2002), discussing the business setting, sees the role of the knowledge broker as focusing on innovation, and innovation in a very broad sense which includes trying previous strategies in new contexts. According to Hargadon, the knowledge broker is expected to assist the organisation in its organisational learning. In different settings the knowledge broker can take on very different roles, for example in discussing the research practice setting. Bulterman-Bos (2008) discusses the tension between practitioners and researchers and sees the role of the academic as working with practice both to develop practice-based research and to implement previously established research.

Activity

Think of an issue of research which you think you might apply to your practice area. If you were to apply it, what would the process be like?

What particular stages would you follow?

Write these down and as you read the next section draw comparisons with the recognised approach outlines.

THE PROCESS OF TRANSLATIONAL RESEARCH

Ward et al. (2009), on the basis of their review, outline three models of the knowledge transfer process: a linear model, a cyclical process and a dynamic multidimensional process. These broadly equate to the models of Broekkamp and van Hout-Walters (2007) and Ball (2012) who discuss models of translational research in relation to their implantation strategies.

The approaches outlined, in the previous section, were concerned primarily with roles of the key players in the translation process. An alternative approach is a focus on the actual process of the research and its stages and components. Ward et al. (2009) outline three main approaches to the structural organisation. It must be emphasised that the review was concerned with the translational process within the context of medicine and health. The three processes are:

- A linear process
- A cyclical process
- A dynamic multidimensional process.

The linear model examines the ways in which research derived from previous empirical studies, and often studies independent of the direct practice setting, can be applied to practice. In this the role of the mediator is very important and the dissemination is through secondary papers and guidelines. This is a linear chain, in which basic research is tested or developed into concepts more applicable to practice. The mediator then through reports and the development of protocols disseminates the findings as an appropriate basis for practice. A good example of this is the concept of deep and surface learners. This was originally derived from the work of Marton and Säljö (1976a; 1976b) who through psychological experimental research illustrated that people could learn in a surface or superficial manner or in one which was more meaningful and involved changes to cogitative structures. This basic concept was taken up by higher education researchers such as Biggs and Tang (2011) and Entwistle (2013) who tested the idea in higher education settings and developed a learning inventory which determined the learning strategies of individuals. They also linked the learning styles to the wider learning environment. In this instance, the mediator would assist with the development of protocols, assessment strategies and would work with the practitioners in their implementation.

The cyclical process is much less linear, diminishes the role of the mediator and focuses on collaboration between the researchers, practitioners and policy makers. These roles can be carried out by one person who, in the context of the project, can undertake all these roles.

The model outlined by Ward et al. (2009) in Figure 12.1 is very complex, and as such is a multi-dimensional model which reflects the process of translational research with all its complexities. The problem or proposed developmental area needs to be outlined, as does the knowledge/research which will address the issue identified earlier in the process. The target group and the key roles also need to be articulated, as do the facilitating and potential barriers. The dynamic nature of the process is established in this model, as is diagrammatically illustrated, and the ways in which each component affects and interacts with each other, which means in practice that modifications and adjustments will be continually made.

To illustrate the point, this section will consider an example of a research study which could be linked to and used to develop an area of practice. Lisa Alcorn, a professional doctorate student at the University of Sunderland, while not framing it as such, used a model of translational research in the development of her doctoral studies (Alcorn, 2017). Lisa is an operational manager, working in an

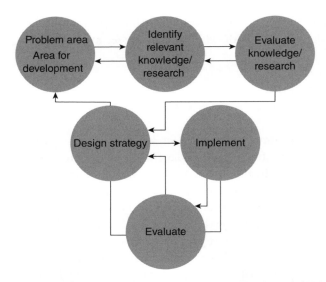

Figure 12.1   Model of translational research based on Ward et al. (2009)

organisation which provides services for people with autism. She was concerned with improving what was good service but wanted to bring about lasting change within her organisation. Lisa had a national role and as such covered a wide geographical area. The problem area within autism demonstrated that much of the behaviour could be challenging and practice involved restraining individuals to protect them from self-harm or for the safety of others. While this, so to speak, was unavoidable, Lisa was convinced that there must be a better approach to the management of such behaviour. She was aware of the government report 'Positive and Proactive Care: reducing the need for restrictive interventions ' (DOH, 2014) and wished to implement the strategy in her area. What follows below is an indication of the way in which Lisa approached this task and the way in which she structured her approach.

The *problem area* was the need to consider the clients in a more holistic way and, rather than deal with their behaviour, create a climate in which people could flourish, thus reducing the need for problematic behaviour. The premise was that behaviour expresses a need and if needs were being met then people would behave in more a purposeful way.

The *context/barriers/support* ... the context was a national group of care homes where Lisa could not be present all the time. Although she visited the settings regularly, she had to rely on the support of others to implement the strategy. The positive aspect was that the staff all wanted to develop and improve the service, but the barrier was that in dealing with the large number of staff the message could become diluted. Lisa decided that the focus would be on work with the managers of the individual settings who could then cascade the message down to the individual carers.

An important issue was that the *intervention* was done in a rigorous and systematic manner and while implementing research the process of the implementation was treated as a research study. The first thing she did was to carry out a comprehensive literature review, and although she found that there was not a strong evidence base, her tacit knowledge and experience told her that this was an appropriate approach. Importantly, it was in keeping with her ethical values. She also needed fully to assess the environment and, in particular, to examine the macro (the larger forces impinging on the service), meso (the organisational level) and micro (the level of worker–client interaction) levels. Using the framework of situational analysis (Clarke, 2005), Lisa thoroughly explored the situation and established some key areas which would influence it: namely, social care influences and impact on practice, the economic situation, invisible institutional policy, policy and procedure drivers, professional practice standards, quality-of-life outcomes. She further developed managers' thinking through a series of focus groups. On this basis she produced a series of standards which were adopted both as a philosophy and as a means of ensuring a rigorous adherence to the principles and practice of Positive Behaviour Support (PBS). The standards Lisa developed with the managers are listed in Table 12.1.

Table 12.1   Practice standards (Alcorn, 2017)

Leaders demonstrate a commitment to PBS and have an effective governance framework founded on transparency and accountability for quality and safe practice.

Organisational policies are consistent with the PBS framework and promote the principles of reducing restrictive physical intervention and promoting the rights of service users.

Promoting the ethical and attitudinal foundation of PBS.

An individualistic holistic assessment is undertaken and is continually monitored, reviewed and measured through consultation and collaboration with a multi-disciplinary team.

Person-centred PBS plan is developed from assessment information and through the involvement of the service user and those around them.

Risk management plans developed and fundamentally embedded into the PBS plan and reviewed, evaluated and measured alongside plan by MDT. Restrictive physical interventions, risk assessments have been completed by the PBS team and will be distributed following bespoke training.

Effective data, reporting, recording and reviewing practice is in place to inform practice and organisational priorities which are aimed at reducing restrictive physical interventions.

An effective PBS practice development–training framework that promotes a broad holistic programme is central to workforce development if safe and good practice is to be promoted.

These practice standards shaped and focused the form and direction of the intervention. Lisa was not 'hands off' but involved herself in the training and support of staff at all levels, where the standards developed from her own research provided clear focus and direction. The practice standards derived from her own original research provided very clear guidance to all the staff involved and a shape and focus for the intervention.

The final stage lay in the *utilisation* and implementation of the strategy. Lisa carried out an evaluation with the managers as well as examining indicators involving the clients, such as challenging behaviours, and found some positive changes as well as increased staff job satisfaction.

This was a very successful implementation and as stated was not treated as an explicit piece of translational research even though the research was carried out in a rigorous and systematic manner. While it has been described as a linear process it was very much as outlined in Figure 12.1 as much more of an interactive process between the various stages.

CONCLUSION

In this chapter translational research as a research approach in its own right has been considered. The range of knowledge/research which can be translated into practice has been explored in terms of empirical research studies and tacit knowledge validated by research. Critical and dialogic studies, which take an analytical perspective on the workplace, have also been explored, and innovations have also been considered in some detail.

An important consideration concerns what is to be transferred into practice and to consider the applicability of the knowledge/research. The roles involved in translational research were outlined and the role of the mediator (or knowledge broker) was also considered. In the case of practice-based research, often these roles are combined. A model of implementation needs to be established very clearly and this should involve both a clear strategy and a model of evaluation.

Key Points

- Translational research, the translation of research findings into practice, is itself a research study.
- There are different approaches to knowledge, all of which have implications for practice.
- In translational research, it is important to think of the role the researcher takes, which is often that of a knowledge broker.
- It is also desirable to do this in a rigorous and systematic manner using recognised models.
- Finally, to determine how to evaluate the process as well as the product.

ANNOTATED BIBLIOGRAPHY

Deetz, S. (1996). Crossroads-describing differences in approaches to organization science: rethinking Burrell and Morgan and their legacy. *Organization Science*, 7(2), 191–207.

This is an excellent paper which outlines underlying philosophical assumptions which underpin the uses of knowledge in practice. It considers the approaches which are outlined in this chapter in more detail and is an excellent starting point if you wish to explore any of the issues further.

Geertz, C. (1994). Thick description: toward an interpretive theory of culture. In M. Martin & L. C. McIntyre (eds) *Readings in the Philosophy of Social Science*. Cambridge, MA: A Bedford Book.

Geertz is writing about and primarily for the ethnographer, but his work raises many valuable points for practice-based research and the professional doctorate candidate. Through thick description, much of what may seem strange becomes understandable. The translation of research findings into practice can be challenging to many deeply held beliefs, and practice gaining an understanding of the rational and logic of practice is important when trying to challenge and bring about change.

Hargadon, A. (2002). Brokering knowledge: linking learning and innovation. *Research in Organizational Behavior, 24*, 41–85.

This paper focuses on the business world and discuses innovation, implementation and knowledge brokerage. It is very readable and is of interest because it discusses organisational learning and knowledge brokerage in a general context and raises many issues which apply across a spectrum of disciplines. It is also useful for comparing the issues raised with the literature which specifically focuses on medicine and health settings.

Ward, V., House, A., & Hamer, S. (2009). Developing a framework for transferring knowledge into action: a thematic analysis of the literature. *Journal of Health Services Research & Policy, 14*(3), 156–64.

This is a very good consideration of the transferring of knowledge into practice; it reviews the literature and then suggests a model. Like the paper by Deetz (1996) it informed much of this chapter, and although its focus is healthcare it does outline the key principles which can be transferred to any area of practice. It is well written and contains much valuable information. I would recommend it to anyone who is taking this approach.

REFERENCES

Alcorn, L. (2017). *Development and National Integration of a Positive Behaviour Support Holisitic Practice Framework for Autism Practitioners*. Doctoral thesis, University of Sunderland.

Alvesson, M., & Deetz, S. (2006). 1.7 critical theory and postmodernism approaches to organizational studies. *The Sage Handbook of Organization*. Thousand Oaks, CA: Sage.

Ball, A. F. (2012) To know is not enough: knowledge, power, and the zone of generativity. *Educational Researcher, 41*(4), 283–93.

Biggs, J., & Tang, C. (2011). *Teaching for Quality Learning at University: What the Student Does*. Maidenhead: Open University Press.

Broekkamp, H., & van Hout-Wolters, B. (2007). The gap between educational research and practice: a literature review, symposium, and questionnaire. *Educational Research and Evaluation, 13*(3), 203–20.

Bulterman-Bos, J. (2008). Will a clinical approach make education research more relevant for practice? *Educational Researcher, 37*(7), 412–42.

Campbell, D. (1986). Relabeling internal and external validity for applied social scientists. *New Directions for Program Evaluation, 31*, 67–77.

Chafouleas, S.M. and Riley-Tillman, T.C. (2005). Accepting the gap: An introduction to the special issue on bridging research and practice. *Psychology in the Schools*, 42(5), 455–8.

Clarke, A.E. (2005). *Situational Analysis. Grounded Theory after the Postmodern Turn*. Thousand Oaks, CA: Sage.

Deetz, S. (1996). Crossroads-describing differences in approaches to organization science: rethinking Burrell and Morgan and their legacy. *Organization Science*, 7(2), 191–207.

Department of Health (2014). *Positive and Proactive Care: Reducing the Need for Restrictive Interventions*. London: Department of Health.

Entwistle, N. (2013). *Styles of Learning and Teaching: An Integrated Outline of Educational Psychology for Students, Teachers and Lecturers*. London: Routledge.

Fontanarosa, P. B., & DeAngelis, C. D. (2002). Basic science and translational research in *JAMA*. *Journal of the American Medical Association*, 287(13), 1728.

Gay, G. (2010). *Culturally Responsive Teaching: Theory, Research, and Practice*. New York: Teacher's College Press.

Geertz, C. (1994). Thick description: toward an interpretive theory of culture. In M. Martin & L. C. McIntyre (eds) *Readings in the Philosophy of Social Science*. Cambridge, MA: A Bedford Book.

Glasgow, R., Vogt, T., & Boles, S. M. (1999). Evaluating the public health impact of health promotion interventions: the RE-AIM framework. *American Journal of Public Health*, 89(9), 1322–7.

Glasgow, R., & Green, L. (2007). A focus on external validity. *Evaluation & the Health Professions*, 30, 115–17.

Glasgow, R.E., Lichtenstein, E., & Marcus, A.C. (2003). Why don't we see more translation of health promotion research to practice? Rethinking the efficacy-to-effectiveness transition. *American Journal of Public Health*, 93(8), 1261–7.

Greenhalgh, T., & Wieringa, S. (2011). Is it time to drop the 'knowledge translation' metaphor? A critical literature review. *Journal of the Royal Society of Medicine*, 104(12), 501–9.

Hammami, H., Amara, N., & Landry, R. (2013). Organizational climate and its influence on brokers' knowledge transfer activities: a structural equation modelling. *International Journal of Information Management*, 33(1), 105–18.

Hargadon, A. (2002). Brokering knowledge: linking learning and innovation. *Research in Organizational Behavior*, 24, 41–85.

Lomas, J. (2007). The in-between world of knowledge brokering. *British Medical Journal*, 334(7585), 129–32.

Malinovskyte, M., Mothe, C., & Rüling, C.-C. (2016). *Knowledge Brokerage: Towards an Integrative Conceptual Framework*. www.strategie-aims.com/events/conferences/24-xxiiieme-conference-de-l-aims/communications/3166-knowledge-brokerage-towards-an-integrative-conceptual-framework/download. Accessed 27 June 2018.

Marton, F., & Säljö, R. (1976a). On qualitative differences in learning: I – Outcome and process. *British Journal of Educational Psychology*, 46(1), 4–11.

Marton, F., & Säljö, R. (1976b). On qualitative differences in learning: II – Outcome as a function of the learner's conception of the task. *British Journal of Educational Psychology*, 46(2), 115–27.

Polanyi, M. (2009). *The Tacit Dimension*. Chicago: University of Chicago Press.

Ward, V., House, A., & Hamer, S. (2009). Developing a framework for transferring knowledge into action: a thematic analysis of the literature. *Journal of Health Services Research & Policy*, 14(3), 156–64.

Woolf, S. H. (2008). The meaning of translational research and why it matters. *Journal of the American Medical Association*, 299(2), 211–13.

13

THEORY OF CHANGE: THE REAL THING AND HOW TO DESIGN SUCCESSFUL SOCIAL CHANGE PROJECTS

Heléne Clark

INTRODUCTION

The first goal of this chapter is both to introduce theory of change (ToC) as a concept with various participatory methodologies and to clarify the term. The term has become faddish, and with that has come both increased demand (great!) and lots of lesser knock-offs that do not have the quality of a 'real' ToC (terrible). Following such clarification, the next goal is to present how to use a ToC in practice. To that end, there is a brief discussion and examples of using a ToC for strategic planning, workplans and evaluation. Finally, the chapter will identify a number of resources on ToC, including web-based software to create them and communities of interest and best practice.

Hopefully, you are by now asking 'but what *is* a theory of change'? My favourite description predates ToC but is perfect:

'Would you tell me, please, which way I ought to go from here?'

'That depends a good deal on where you want to get to.'

(Lewis Carroll, *Alice in Wonderland*)

What is a Theory of Change

A theory of change is a totally *practical* and *grounded* concept which posits that it is necessary to show *how* and *why* a goal can be reached and under what conditions.

It is represented graphically as a flow of logic from start to finish, and then summarised into plain language narrative.

'A Theory of Change is an initiative's own "theory" or "story" of how they will make change in the world' (Clark and Grimaldi, 2013).

BASIC COMPONENTS OF A THEORY OF CHANGE

There are many names being used that are 'sort of' like a ToC (see Funnell and Rogers, 2011) for a comprenhensive list, and even more various depictions of graphics and descriptions actually labelled 'Theory of Change' which are not. The variety of names is not very problematic, except they can cause confusion. But all the names – programme theory, theory of action, logicial framework and dozens more – do have their own specific meaning and they are related to ToC. So, no reason to get rid of them. They all have a purpose. But the serious problem is calling things a ToC which do not have all of the components or the logical coherence. That is where ensuring all of the components are included and the concept well understood is critical.

ToC is not a difficult concept to understand but it is challenging to implement as it involves hard thinking. There are many methods to articulate a rigorous ToC. The basic components are simple, but harder to flesh out comprehensively in practice. The components are as follows.

Basic Components of a Theory of Change

1. Outcomes and preconditions, modelled in causal pathways
2. Indicators
3. Rationales
4. Assumptions
5. Interventions (activities), leading to the relevant outcome(s)
6. Narrative.

BASIC DEFINITION OF THEORY OF CHANGE

A ToC spells out initiative or programme logic. Confusingly, it is *not* a logic model as that term is traditionally used,[1] but it depends on logic and on a complete-as-possible identification of conditions that need to change before a long-term goal can be reached. It defines long-term goals and then maps backwards to identify changes that need to happen earlier (preconditions). For example, an education initiative in a school that has a long-term goal of 100 per cent graduation may agree that a certain level of attendance is a necessary precondition. There are many others, usually that involve changing the school climate, parent involvement, teacher cultural competency and more. All of those, in turn, do not happen automatically. They have prior changes that need to occur.

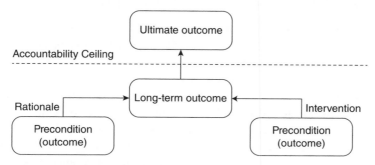

Figure 13.1   Visual language of ToC

---

[1]See Clark and Anderson's (2004) presentation on theories of change and logic models; and Tools4Dev (2016) for clear descriptions and depictions of the differences.

The identified changes are mapped graphically in causal pathways of outcomes, showing each outcome in logical relationship to all the others. Interventions, which are activities and outputs of any sort, are mapped to the outcomes pathway to show what stakeholders think it will take to effect the changes, and when (see Figure 13.1). ToC provides a working model against which to test hypotheses and assumptions about what actions will best bring about the intended outcomes. A given ToC also identifies measurable indicators of success as a roadmap to monitoring and evaluation.

ToC is both process and product: the process of working out the theory, mainly in group sessions of practitioners and stakeholders led by a capable facilitator; and, as the product of that process, a document of the change model showing how and why a goal will be reached. There is a good deal of discussion as to which provides more value – the group process of reflecting on the work, surfacing assumptions, creating transparency and building consensus; or the product, a sound and complete plan with plausible potential for producing the change desired.

ToC turns conventional planning on its head because it pushes groups to work out first their goals or desired impact and work backwards on outcome pathways rather than engage in conventional forward-oriented 'so that' reasoning. As an example of such reasoning, a grantee decides to increase media coverage on the lack of health insurance among children *so that* public awareness increases *so that* policy makers increase their knowledge and interest *so that* policies change *so that* more children have health insurance. In ToC, by contrast, the group begins not with its intervention but with its long-term goal and outcomes and then works backwards (in time) towards the earliest changes that need to occur. Only when the pathway has been developed is it time to consider which interventions will best produce the outcomes in the pathway.

THEORY: EACH COMPONENT DEFINED

1. OUTCOMES PATHWAY: TOC'S BASIC STRUCTURE

A ToC models **outcomes** in an **outcomes pathway**. Outcomes in a ToC represent changes in condition of some kind – whether a policy, law, behaviour, attitude, knowledge, state of the environment – among people, institutions and environments. Outcomes are the building blocks of a ToC. An outcome is never something like 'hold trainings on student-centred learning', or 'call parents'. However, 'Teachers are trained and practise student-centred learning' may be a valid outcome.

The outcomes pathway is a set of graphically depicted building blocks ordered and connected through a causal chain (see Figure 13.2). Outcomes along the pathway are also preconditions to outcomes above them. Thus early outcomes must be in place for intermediate outcomes to be achieved; intermediate outcomes must be in place for the next set of outcomes to be achieved; and so on. An outcomes pathway therefore represents the logic (or hypotheses) about why, for example, attendance is necessary to reach graduation and is articulated in assumptions and rationales, which become part of the ToC graphic.

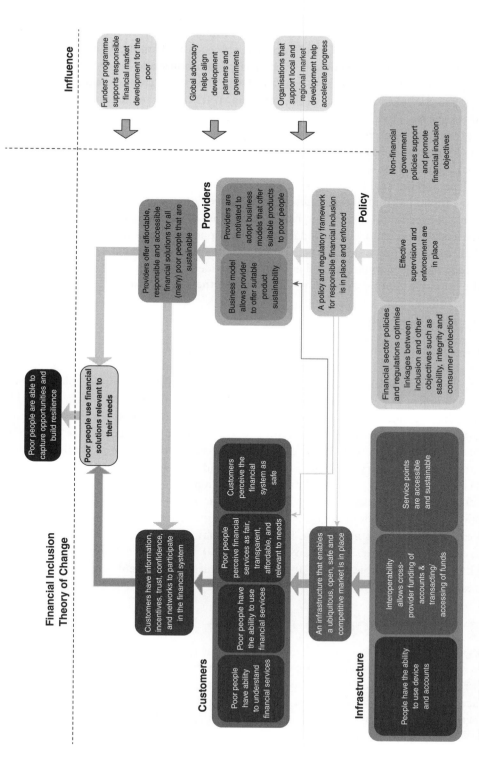

Financial Inclusion Theory of Change

Influence

Funders' programme supports responsible financial market development for the poor

Global advocacy helps align development partners and governments

Organisations that support local and regional market development help accelerate progress

Providers

Providers offer affordable, responsible and accessible financial solutions for all (many) poor people that are sustainable

Providers are motivated to adopt business models that offer suitable products to poor people

Business model allows provider to offer suitable product sustainability

Policy

A policy and regulatory framework for responsible financial inclusion is in place and enforced

Non-financial government policies support and promote financial inclusion objectives

Effective supervision and enforcement are in place

Financial sector policies and regulations optimise linkages between inclusion and other objectives such as stability, integrity and consumer protection

Poor people are able to capture opportunities and build resilience

Poor people use financial solutions relevant to their needs

Customers

Customers have information, incentives, trust, confidence, and networks to participate in the financial system

Poor people have ability to understand financial services

Poor people have the ability to use financial services

Poor people perceive financial services as fair, transparent, affordable, and relevant to needs

Customers perceive the financial system as safe

Infrastructure

An infrastructure that enables a ubiquitous, open, safe and competitive market is in place

People have the ability to use device and accounts

Interoperability allows cross-provider funding of accounts & transacting/ accessing of funds

Service points are accessible and sustainable

Figure 13.2 ToC example outcomes framework

Outcomes include long-term outcome and intermediate/short-term outcomes. The term 'impact' is often reserved for the ultimate goal of an initiative, but is not a measurable outcome of that initiative alone. For example, if an organisation works to provide job training, education programmes and career counselling, it may be that the ultimate reason for doing this is to create sustainable family incomes and reduce poverty in the community. It was the reduction in poverty that drove the initiative, but the organisation may not be directly accountable for reducing poverty. What an organisation usually decides to be directly accountable for is the long-term outcome. This is a clearly stated, focused, measurable and plausible goal for the organisation.

The impact level is distinguished from the long-term outcome and its preconditions by an 'accountability ceiling', which may be drawn in the form of a dashed line. The accountability ceiling can be moved up or down as the group developing the ToC gathers more knowledge about the opportunities and limits of the work. Add more partners, and perhaps a higher target can be reached. Conversely, the ceiling may need to be lowered if it becomes evident that many systemic factors that the initiative cannot work on will impinge on the level of success.

2. INDICATORS

Every outcome (and preconditional outcome) in a ToC needs to be demonstrated in some way. Indicators are evidence that tell you if an outcome has been reached at your target level. Indicators which refer to measurable and observable information monitor the achievement of outcomes and can show quickly where trouble may be encountered. Stakeholders choose the best indicator(s) for each outcome, often with the help of their evaluator. An indicator may be quantitative (e.g. number of new jobs created) or qualitative (a description of new knowledge or attitudes). For every indicator, the group (and evaluator) identifies four things: (1) Who or what is going to change? (2) How many of them will change? (3) How much will they change? (4) By when will the change be realised? So, in the sentence 'Eighty per cent of fourth graders will read at grade level by the end of the second year of the programme', the indicator itself may be reading test scores, the 'who' is fourth graders, the 'how many of them' is 80 per cent, the 'how much will they change?' is being able to read at grade level, and the 'by when' is at the end of two years of the programme.

3. INTERVENTIONS

Generally, stakeholders are eager to talk about their activities, and therefore this step, in practice, often occurs right after the pathways of outcomes are constructed. But, in reality, it is only possible to choose the best intervention or activity once you have decided on a target and a threshold. This means that an activity depends on how many people it needs to reach and at what level of quality. For example, a project that aims at financial inclusion of low-income people for all of Africa will need different interventions than one aimed at financial inclusion of low-income people in one neighbourhood. That is the target. As to quality (or the threshold to be reached), financial inclusion that is defined as women are allowed to own land will need policy changes, whereas financial inclusion defined only as residents have access to bank accounts may not need a focus on women's rights. So, we recommend attempting to set targets and thresholds before identifying interventions. However, ToC must be a flexible process that meets people where they are, and this may mean letting people discuss their activities and then asking if these activities actually will bring about the outcome as they desire it.

The definition of **interventions** is the work undertaken within an initiative or programme that lead to the desired outcomes. In a ToC, the term 'intervention' may refer to single activities or whole programmes, depending on how specific the group wants to be and how it wants to use the theory with respect to a strategic plan or theory of action. Mapping interventions to the outcomes pathway has the effect of revealing strategy: it shows the theoretical linkages between actions and results all along the way.

Interventions can be located on an outcomes framework by means of symbols positioned along the connectors between the outcomes, illustrating that the intervention can begin once Outcome A is realised, and that its successful completion is necessary to producing Outcome B. The logic for placing an intervention is as follows: Outcome A sets up the conditions that allow Outcome B to unfold. Nevertheless, Outcome A (and other outcomes in the same phase of work) may not in itself be sufficient for Outcome B to transpire. Therefore, to achieve Outcome B, we need intervention #1. The intervention, or symbol for that intervention, is placed on the connector between Outcome A and Outcome B.

4. RATIONALES

Rationales explain why the outcomes will occur if the preconditions identified, and the interventions proposed, happen as planned. It is the rationales the provide the logic and theory of a ToC. A practical tip here is that many rationales will be expressed as people discuss and argue the placement and definition of outcomes. Having someone take notes on the conversation can save having to go back and query 'why?' will this happen later.

5. ASSUMPTIONS

One of the many important and valuable aspects of ToC is in challenging stakeholders to make explicit the assumptions (and risks) inherent in an initiative. The process of identifying clear outcomes and their preconditions involves an elaboration of the reasons why the group thinks the theory will work in practice. **Assumptions** may be based on the empirical knowledge of expert practitioners or in research evidence. They are primarily *about context*.

The full definition can be stated as: 'Assumptions are implicit beliefs about the context or environment within which the initiative will operate. Assumptions involve beliefs about conditions that exist in the context/environment which are critical to the theory' (Taplin et al., 2013). As assumption may be that Internet service is available for credit transactions in remote areas of Africa. It is an assumption if that is likely or known to exist. If it is known as not existing, and necessary to the success of the initiative, it would be a precondition. As a precondition, you are making it explicit that it is a condition that needs to be brought about as it does not already exist. As an assumption, you hold the belief that it is not problematic. When an initiative does not achieve success, it is critical to test the assumptions. Perhaps the unproblematic condition changed, that is a new government or provider eliminated Internet service from certain areas.

Exposing assumptions involves a certain risk. Programmes often fail by one or more measures. ToCs make the expected how and why of change processes explicit, and the clearer one can be in outlining a change process, the greater the risk that failures can be attributable to the initiative. Without a clear change model, results are abstracted from the specifics of the initiative; results are not monitored, and failures and successes cannot easily be tied to the effort. With theory-based initiatives, the specifics are all laid out, results are measured, and failures are easier to identify and evaluate. The more explicit the theory, including all its assumptions, the more failure can be tied to mistaken assumptions. Despite this risk, ToC increases the chance of sustained success. Failure in reaching goals is almost guaranteed in the absence of a clearly developed model of change. Failures in the context of a ToC can be opportunities to learn from the experience, recalibrate and return to the field with more effective interventions.

ToC allows proponents and stakeholders the means to challenge their assumptions continually and, in doing so, refine and sharpen their strategies for greater success. In considering a given outcome, one might ask 'What will happen if this outcome does *not* come about?' If its absence leaves a hole in the logic, or points to a 'missing middle' where the outcome pathway seems to take a leap over necessary steps, you will have identified a gap in the model. You will need to work to understand and identify what is necessary to fill in the missing steps.

6. NARRATIVE

The **narrative** is simply a plain language summary of the theory that explains the overall logic, highlights major assumptions, and presents a compelling case as to how and why the initiative is expected to work. The purpose of the narrative is twofold: (1) to convey the major elements of the theory easily and quickly to others; (2) to communicate how the elements of the theory work as a whole. The narrative is a natural companion to the visual elements of the theory as they reinforce each other (Taplin et al., 2013).

Activity

Choose a long-term goal from your own work or a subject you care about and work in a small group to discuss what conditions need to change before your goal can be reached.

Draw a basic outcomes framework (as in Figure 13.2).

THREE BASIC PURPOSES AND TIMES FOR THEORY OF CHANGE

While it has been most common to develop ToC of existing initiatives for evaluation, and increasingly popular to use ToC to plan new initiatives, there is a middle ground. Many organisations with programmes that have been operating for years want to develop a ToC to help them understand and possibly change what they do. In such cases, organisations want to revisit long-term goals and challenge their assumptions about what is needed to reach those goals. Here then are the three basic applications of ToC:

- evaluation
- conceptualising and planning initiatives
- revisiting goals, assumptions and activities of an existing initiative (especially if things seem to be not going as well as hoped).

Organisations may have other reasons to develop ToCs, but these will be sub-categories of the three basic applications of the method. For example, moving an existing strategic plan into a ToC belongs to the third basic use, that of revisiting the goals, assumptions and activities of an existing initiative.

USING A THEORY OF CHANGE IN PRACTICE

CREATING ACTION PLANS AND WORKPLANS

The most common problem initiatives have with a ToC approach is how to fit the theory into the existing practices of an organisation. Most organisations already have procedures and templates in place for creating workplans and action plans. So, it is important to commit, with leadership, at the outset, that the ToC process is intended not just to create a theory but to *use* it. Figure 13.3 is an example of a successful and simple workplan format where outcomes are the starting point for deciding who does what, and interventions match those on the ToC diagram.

Outcomes: chronic absenteeism (ToC)	Proposed programmes, services, activities and events	Outcome indicators and potential impact	Staff responsible (school and/or lead agency)	School, student, family and/ or community involvement
Students maintain good attendance				
Effective communication between teachers and parents/ families on attendance				
Parents/families understand policies on attendance				
School is aware of and implements district attendance policies				

Figure 13.3   Creating a workplan from a ToC

MONITORING AND EVALUATION

Testing theories of change through monitoring and evaluation can furnish powerful evidence of the success or failure of initiatives. Coupling monitoring and evaluation to ToC can bring a better understanding of how to improve the design and implementation of ongoing initiatives, and how to scale initiatives up or out.

ToC can begin at any stage before, during and after the lifetime of an initiative, depending on the intended use. A theory developed at the outset is best at informing the conceptualisation and planning of an initiative. As monitoring and evaluation data becomes available, stakeholders can periodically refine the ToC based on evidence. A ToC can also be developed retrospectively by reading programme documents, talking to stakeholders, and using monitoring and evaluation data. This is often done during evaluations or for a reflective process of learning about what has worked and why, in order to understand the past and to plan for the future.

Figure 13.4 presents an example of using a ToC to create a results framework.

Theory of Change-Context of Each Outcome in its Pathway

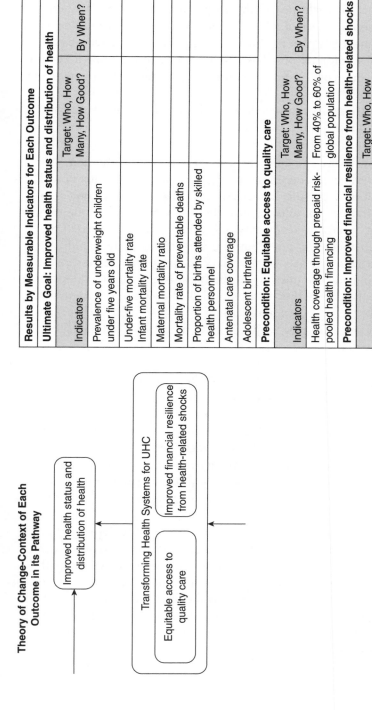

Improved health status and distribution of health

Transforming Health Systems for UHC

Equitable access to quality care

Improved financial resilience from health-related shocks

Results by Measurable Indicators for Each Outcome

Ultimate Goal: Improved health status and distribution of health

Indicators	Target: Who, How Many, How Good?	By When?	Grants/Activities
Prevalence of underweight children under five years old			
Under-five mortality rate			
Infant mortality rate			
Maternal mortality ratio			
Mortality rate of preventable deaths			
Proportion of births attended by skilled health personnel			
Antenatal care coverage			
Adolescent birthrate			

Precondition: Equitable access to quality care

Indicators	Target: Who, How Many, How Good?	By When?	Grants/Activities
Health coverage through prepaid risk-pooled health financing	From 40% to 60% of global population		

Precondition: Improved financial resilience from health-related shocks

Indicators	Target: Who, How Many, How Good?	By When?	Grants/Activities
Out-of-pocket payments	Global/ % decrease	2015	
Impovershment due to catastrophic out-of-pocket health-related payments	Global/ % decrease	2015	

Figure 13.4 Creating a results frame for evaluation

MATCHING THE SCOPE OF THE TOC WITH ITS PURPOSE

The scope of a ToC is a key decision to be made when starting. The definition of the scope is really simply how comprehensive the theory will be in accounting for how to reach a goal. It must, of course, be of sufficient scope to be plausible. However, if the impact is world peace, the scope cannot possibly account for every condition and activity needed. (That is why 'world peace' would never be the long-term outcome of a theory, but can only be an impact above the accountability ceiling – you may do what you are doing in the hope it contributes to world peace, but your initiative cannot be accountable for achieving such a lofty goal.)

The scope of any outcomes pathway will resemble one of the four basic types, as follows (from Clark, 2004):

Narrow and shallow pathways show the least amount of information. This scope identifies relevant preconditions to the long-term goal, but not all necessary preconditions. Usually it focuses 'narrowly' on those preconditions which the initiative can address directly. For example if a long-term goal is employment, a narrow scope may only identify the skill-related preconditions to employment and not identify things like available child care, stable lives, or attitudes that may be necessary for people to get and retain jobs, but that are outside the purview of the initiative. Similarly, the pathway is 'shallow' in that the pathways are not drilled down to the beginning (where the initiative would start); and perhaps multiple outcomes are summarized for simplicity. This type of pathway is useful as a summary of a project or an evaluation.

Narrow and deep pathways, like narrow and shallow pathways, develop only that part of the pathway that is most central to the organization's work. The narrow and deep pathway, however, drills deep so that that every intermediate outcome is identified. This scope provides enough detail for the initiative to make decisions within the narrow pathway it identified, and leaves out any parts of the pathway it does not control. The narrow and deep scope may be appropriate for an initiative that relies relatively little on partners or on influencing other actors in the arena, or for single small programs.

In Broad and shallow pathways all preconditions to the long-term goal are identified, including those not within the expertise and influence of the proponent organization, but the pathway is not drilled deeply. A shallow pathway paints goals with a broad brush and leaves the granular preconditions for others to define. A good match for this type is the funder that seeks to drive change toward particular goals. This funder recognizes that there may be many routes to those goals and leaves it to the grantees to try out and demonstrate the effectiveness of various alternatives.

Narrow and shallow (least detail)	Broad and shallow
Narrow and deep	Broad and deep (most detail)

Figure 13.5 Examples of alternatives

Broad and deep pathways are the most detailed and useful. Pathways of this scope identify all the preconditions to change, and drill the pathways deeply enough to identify necessary preconditions at all levels. This scope provides a level of detail that allows for the most organisational learning and strategy development, and a finely honed evaluation that can sort out what is really happening. The breadth of the pathway can be contingent on partner relationships. Sometimes certain outcomes or pathways are left to one side of the diagram and greyed out. Such outcomes are necessary to the long-term goal but are beyond the capacity of the proponent organisation to carry out or are beyond the scope of the initiative. In cases where partnerships resolve the question of who will carry out such necessary work, the outcomes pathway can be relatively broad, if not deep, so as to represent the work of the different partners in co-operation and in making distinct yet necessary contributions to a long-term goal.

While a broad and deep scope is our favourite, in the real world a programme may be very limited in its focus, or a funder may not be one to prescribe hypotheses beyond the very immediate conditions they wish to see. In these cases, a more limited scope is most appropriate.

Activity

Using the long-term goal from the first activity, attempt to construct an outcomes framework of the four different scopes described here.

Discuss the pros and cons of each scope for a given type of organisation or initiative.

SNAPSHOT OF THE PROCESS OF CREATING A THEORY OF CHANGE

An important first step in the process is identifying a workable long-term goal and outcome. The long-term outcome should be something the initiative can realistically achieve and that everyone involved understands. A trained external facilitator is best to lead the group to consensus and specificity in this process.

Once identified, the group then considers, 'What outcomes must be brought before we can achieve the long-term outcome?' These outcomes – shorter-term preconditions to the long-term outcome – are then placed directly underneath the long-term outcome. The process continues, drilling down the pathway by posing fundamental questions, such as 'What has to be in place for this outcome to be achieved?' and 'Are these preconditions sufficient for the outcome to be achieved?'

Traditionally, this process occurs by gathering a group of stakeholders with different roles and perspectives who have expert knowledge or interest in aspects of the theory, but are willing and able to see the big picture. As ToC has expanded its reach, some creative methods have been tried, often very successfully:

- Remote convenings through webinars where stakeholders based all over the world can participate.
- Convening multiple groups to deal with issues of power and then having the facilitator synthesise the results.
- Sending out online surveys with ToC questions (good examples exist at the Center for Theory of Change, 2018) and compiling the answers into a draft graphic to begin.
- Using the online web-based platform Theory of Change Online (www.theory-ofchange.org) to build the theory in real time during either in-person or web discussions. (The author's organisation, ActKnowledge, created Theory of Change Online).

TIPS ON SUCCESS IN CREATING A THEORY OF CHANGE

Our experience in using a ToC approach across many topics, many geographies and all types of organisations has led to some useful lessons. In practice, developing a ToC will be more likely to be successful if:

1. Leadership of an initiative or organisation has to have buy-in and ownership of the ToC. We have often helped staff keen to have a ToC, only for it not to be well used or integrated into planning, implementation, monitoring, evaluation or communication.
2. Theory development begins as the planning stage to design an initiative and before deciding on activities. Evaluators should be at the table at the beginning to help develop measurable indicators and advise on feasibility. It is fine to take on a ToC process mid-stream for learning and mid-course corrections. In fact, ToC was first developed as an evaluation methodology (see Connell et al., 1995; Fulbright-Anderson et al., 1998). But in an ideal situation, it is used as a planning tool.

3. If there are known 'paths' to reach goals in your topic area, use them and contextualise them. There is no need to reinvent the wheel. Many areas, such as education, public health, international development and environment conservation, have particularly strong literatures that already provide parts of a theory you can use.

On the other hand, Forti (2012) has identified six pitfalls to avoid in undertaking a ToC:

1. Confusing accountability with hope. Define results in a way that forces your organisation to get real about the impact you can feasibly achieve, not just what you would like to accomplish.
2. Creating a mirror instead of a target. Do not reflect on what you are already doing. Choose a goal and work backwards to create a plan for how to make change.
3. Failing to take context into account. No theory can really exist without stakeholders understanding the context of the subject and the region.
4. Not confirming the plausibility of your theory. It takes time, but stakeholders need to be convinced the theory makes logical sense and has no gaps. All theories are made to be changed and improved, but start with something that everyone agrees is comprehensive and plausible.
5. Creating a theory that is not measurable. Testing, refining and improving a theory requires that you can observe and measure what change is occurring.
6. Assuming you have figured it all out. To get the most out of a ToC, do not assume it is static. It should change as you learn. It should become dog-eared with constantly checking in to see if your assumptions were correct, if your targets are being reached, and changing the theory to account for changing circumstances and what you learn on the ground. (List from Forti, 2012; explanations added)

CONCLUSION

As Carol Weiss said back in 1995, and it the most important point about ToC to make today, 'there is nothing as practical as a good theory'. I hope this chapter has laid out what must be in a ToC to make it rigorous and worthy of the name. In sum:

> Creating a ToC requires forethought, participation and transparency. A well-designed ToC will focus participants to reach agreements on end goals: how they know if they have achieved those goals or not; what intermediate steps can be expected; what initial processes should be put in place; what is doable; and who are the stakeholders. A ToC has to fill out the 'missing middle'. (Clark and Collins, 2013)

In other words, there must be a detailed sequence of preconditions outlined from the present problem to the long-term goal.

It has to be clear from the ToC who is to do what, including who or which organisation will drive the whole process. It has to be clear what effective implementation looks like (Clark and Collins, 2013).

By ensuring that the components and considerations above are part of a theory development process, a rigorous and useful theory will be produced. This chapter will not make you automatically a good ToC facilitator – only practice will do that. But knowing your topic thoroughly is half the battle.

Key Points

- Theory of change (ToC) is a well-used and often demanded process nowadays in social change, social research and philanthropy, but there is great confusion as to what it actually entails.
- A true ToC describes all the necessary and sufficient conditons for change needed to reach a long-term goal.
- There are key components that make a ToC rigorous and thorough. They must be present and complete and logical.
- There are many methods that can be used to capture the theory, both in-person and remotely. But it is always a participatory process.
- A ToC is only useful if it is used – to make decisions on implementation, for ongoing monitoring, to develop workplans and to design evaluations.
- The amount of a problem and the path to its solution that is necessary to be successful depend on the goal, the size of the initiative and the type of the organisation.

ANNOTATED BIBILOGRAPHY

Center for Theory of Change (2018). Resources section for multiple presentations and articles. www.theoryofchange.org. Accessed 27 June 2018.

The Center for Theory of Change is the only repository for almost every book, article and example written on ToC. It includes examples and access to Theory of Change Online. It is a superb one-stop website for all things ToC.

Clark, H. (2004). *Deciding the Scope of a Theory of Change*. New York: ActKnowledge.

This article focuses on how large or comprehensive a ToC should be in certain circumstances and how to choose.

Connell, J., Kubisch, A., Schorr, L., & Weiss, C. (eds) (1995). *New Approaches to Evaluating Community Initiatives: Concepts, Methods and Contexts*. Washington, DC: The Aspen Institute.

Fulbright-Anderson, K., Kubisch, A., & Connell, J. (eds) (1998). *New Approaches to Evaluating Community Initiatives: Vol. 2, Theory, Measurement and Analysis*. Washington, DC: The Aspen Institute.

These two volumes are the seminal work on ToC, with articles on its defintion and many examples. It focuses on comprehensive community initiatives and evaluation, so it is dated in ToC use but absolutely essential reading and up to date on understanding the ToC concept.

Taplin, D. H., Clark, H., Collins, E., & Colby, D. (2013). *A Series of Papers to Support Development of Theories of Change Based on Practice in the Field (Tech.)*. New York: ActKnowledge.

A series of papers on many ToC topics can be found under Resources at www.theoryof-change.org.

www.theoryofchange.org (2018). *Theory of Change Online*. New York: ActKnowledge.

The website of the Center for Theory of Change, which houses ToC resources and is listed here particularly as the portal to access Theory of Change Online web-based software to create, store and share ToCs.

REFERENCES

Center for Theory of Change (2018). Resources section for multiple presentations and arti-cles. www.theoryofchange.org. Accessed 27 June 2018.

Clark, H. (2004). *Deciding the Scope of a Theory of Change*. New York: ActKnowledge.

Clark, H., & Anderson, A. (2004). Theories of change and logic models: telling them apart. Presentation at American Evaluaton Association, Atlanta, Georgia.

Clark, H., & Collins, E. (2013). Evaluation design and implementation considerations in community school settings. In N. Trépenier (ed.) *Making a Case for Community Schools*. Montreal: Éditions Nouvelle.

Clark, H., & Grimaldi, C. (2013). Evaluation of children's aid society community schools. In J. Dryfoos, J. Quinn & C. Barkin (eds) *Community Schools in Action*. New York: Oxford University Press.

Connell, J., Kubisch, A., Schorr, L., & Weiss, C. (eds) (1995). *New Approaches to Evaluating Community Initiatives: Concepts, Methods and Contexts*. Washington, DC: The Aspen Institute.

Forti, M. (2012). *Six Theory of Change Pitfalls to Avoid*. Stanford, CA: Stanford Social Innovation Review.

Fulbright-Anderson, K., Kubisch, A., & Connell, J. (eds) (1998). *New Approaches to Evaluating Community Initiatives: Vol. 2, Theory, Measurement and Analysis*. Washington, DC: The Aspen Institute.

Funnell, S. C., & Rogers, P. J. (2011). *Purposeful Program Theory: Effective Use of the Models*. San Francisco: Jossey-Bass.

Taplin, D. H., Clark, H., Collins, E., & Colby, D. (2013). *A Series of Papers to Support Development of Theories of Change Based on Practice in the Field (Tech.)*. New York: ActKnowledge.

Tools4Dev (2016). Theory of Change vs. Logical Framework – What's the Difference? www.tools4dev.org/resources/theory-of-change-vs-logical-framework-whats-the-difference-in-practice. Accessed 21 August 2018.

Weiss, C. (1995). Nothing as practical as good theory: exploring theory-based evaluation for comprehensive community initiative for children and families. In J. Connell, A. Kubisch, L. Schorr & C. Weiss (eds) *New Approaches to Evaluating Communith Initiatives: Concepts, Methods and Contexts*. Washington, DC: The Aspen Institute.

www.theoryofchange.org (2018). *Theory of Change Online*. New York: ActKnowledge.

ADDENDUM A: TERM DEFINITION

Accountability ceiling A dashed line drawn horizontally across an outcomes pathway. All outcomes below the accountability ceiling, whether medium-term changes or changes in state and condition, represent changes for which an initiative or programme will hold itself accountable. The accountability ceiling separates outcomes from impact.

Activities The action taken by the initiative or programme to deliver outputs and bring about outcomes and impact.

Assumption Assumptions are always made about the context or environment within which the initiative will operate, but are often left implicit. If such assumptions involve things necessary to the theory and not yet attained, they are naturally treated as outcomes. If they are thought to be in place already and likely to be sustained, they should be noted but not put on the pathway as outcomes. As an example, proponents of an employment training programme may assume jobs will be available in the occupations for which people are being trained. In developing the ToC, the group must consider whether that is a safe assumption. If not, it should be treated as a precondition, even if jobs in those occupations are available at present.

Backwards mapping The process of beginning with a long-term goal and working 'backwards' through a chain of outcomes towards the earliest changes that need to occur. In backwards mapping one builds the outcomes pathway starting at the top, most general and longest term outcome, then 'drills down' by identifying each set of pre-conditions, ending at the most particular, immediate and short-term outcomes to be achieved.

Baseline A measure of population for any indicators at the outset of the initiative, used for comparison as evaluation data is analysed.

Core Planning Group The group within the initiative or programme or other lead organi-sation who will be responsible for development of the theory.

Facilitator The person who runs the participatory theory of change development sessions. The facilitator should have good facilitation skills – able to keep people engaged and focused on outcomes, be responsive to the group dynamics, etc. The facilitator should also have a good grasp of theory of change concepts, terms and practice.

Goal A desired condition among people, institutions, environments (e.g. good health, literacy, gender equality). A goal implies a relatively broad and distant outcome and is usually synonymous with 'impact' and 'outcome'.

Indicator	Measurable evidence of meeting a goal. Indicators are visible signs (e.g. legislation enacted, landmark publications, participation in a joint learning network) of the outcomes. Indicators can be either quantitative or qualitative. An indicator has four components: population, target, threshold, and timeline (see their definitions also). These answer the questions: • Who or what is to reach this goal? (Population) • How many among that population do we need to have reached the goal? (Target) • How much does the target group need to change (or to what level) does it need to have reached? (Threshold) • By when does this goal need to be reached? (Timeline)
Inputs	The funds and human resource capacity invested/allocated by the initiative or programme to address a development problem.
Intervention	The set of actions undertaken in an initiative to realise outcomes.
Long-term outcome(s)	The final outcome represented in the outcomes pathway before the impact/goal level. The long-term outcome is the most general of all the outcomes the foundation expects to achieve primarily through its work and the work of its grantees and partners.
Narrative	A prose summary of a theory of change. The narrative succinctly explains the logic of the outcomes pathway and key assumptions. It may include some contextual and background information.
Organisational capacity	The skills and resources the initiative or programme needs to carry out the activities identified in a theory of change.
Outcome	Outcomes in a theory of change represent desired changes in condition of some kind – whether a policy, law, behaviour, attitude, knowledge, state of the environment – among people, institutions and environments. Outcomes include immediate and intermediate changes in behaviour, attitudes or knowledge or other state or situation.
Outcomes pathway	Also causal pathway, results chain map: The graphic, diagrammatic representation of a theory of change, consisting of outcomes arranged and connected in causal pathways, with activities, assumptions and justifications keyed to the diagram.
Outputs	The tangible products or services that a grantee, partner or the initiative team deliver. These products and services are the deliverables and milestones that a grantee and its partner are accountable for according to an agreed schedule.
Population	As one dimension of a target or indicator, the aggregation of people among whom change will be effected.

Precondition	All outcomes in an outcomes pathway that contribute to outcomes above them in the hierarchy are preconditions. They are called preconditions because they are conditions that must exist, or pre-requisites, for the next outcome in the pathway to be achieved.
Rationale	A rationale explains the logic and/or evidence base for a given connection between outcomes in a pathway. Rationales can also be used to explain why an activity or set of activities is necessary to attain an outcome.
Scope	The degree of inclusion of domains and conditions that have some bearing on the long-term outcome; also the level of detail provided. In the breadth of an outcomes pathway, a theory of change may be framed to include pathways that lie outside the foundation's work but are to some extent necessary to achieve the long-term or ultimate outcomes. Similarly, a deep scope will have the pathway drilled down to level of detail that shows present and short-term conditions of change. Different scopes are appropriate for different purposes.
Strategy	The optimal combination of opportunity, leverage and capability to be employed by an initiative in attaining desired outcomes. Strategy is inherent in a theory of change.
Target	As one dimension of an indicator, how many among a given population must show the desired change for the outcome associated with the indicator to be considered fulfilled.
Theory of change	Broadly, a set of beliefs and assumptions about what changes need to happen, and how to bring them about, to reach a stated goal. As a methodological practice, theory of change is a process through which participants construct a descriptive model (both graphic and narrative) that explains the outcomes sought, why they are needed, how they will be achieved, and how progress on them can be monitored.
Threshold	As one dimension of an indicator, the level of change that needs to be observed among the target population for the associated outcome to be considered fulfilled. Simply put, 'How good is good enough?'
Timeline	As one dimension of an indicator, the time by when the threshold and the target are to be met.

(Source: Adapted from Taplin et al., 2013)

ADDENDUM B: ADDITIONAL RESOURCES

ActKnowledge & The Aspen Institute (2003). *Tips and Challenges on Team Building with Theory of Change* (Working paper). New York: ActKnowledge.

ActKnowledge & The Aspen Institute (2003). *Making Sense: Reviewing Program Design with Theory of Change* (Working paper). New York: ActKnowledge.

Aspen Institute (1997). *Voices from the Field*. Washington, DC: The Aspen Institute.

Blamey, A., & Mackenzie, M. (2007). Theories of change and realistic evaluation. *Evaluation*, *13*(4), 439–55.

Breuer, E., Silva, M. J., Fekadu, A., Luitel, N. P., Murhar, V., Nakku, J., & Lund, C. (2014). Using workshops to develop theories of change in five low and middle income countries: lessons from the programme for improving mental health care (PRIME). *International Journal of Mental Health Systems*. www.ncbi.nlm.nih.gov/pmc/articles/PMC4012094/. Accessed 28 June 2018.

Brides, G. N. (2015, May 3). *A Theory of Change on Child Marriage – Girls Not Brides*. www.girlsnotbrides.org/theory-change-child-marriage-girls-brides/. Accessed 28 June 2018.

Bullen, P. B. (2013, April 2). *Creating theories of change with the Theory of Change Online (TOCO) Software*. www.tools4dev.org/resources/theory-of-change-online-toco-software-tec. Accessed 28 June 2018.

CARE International UK (2012). *Defining Theories of Change*. London.

Clark, H., & Anderson, A. A. (2004, November). *Theories of change and logic models: telling them apart*. Lecture presented at American Evaluation Association, Atlanta, Georgia.

Connell, J. P., & Klem, A. M. (2000). You can get there from here: using a theory of change approach to plan urban education reform. *Journal of Educational and Psychological Consultation*, *11*(1), 93–120.

Connell, J. P., & Kubisch, A. C. (1998). *Applying Theory of Change Approach to the Evaluation of Comprehensive Community Initiatives: Progress, Prospects, and Problems* (Working paper). Washington, DC: The Aspen Institute.

De Silva, M. J., Breuer, E., Lee, L., Asher, L., Chowdhury, N., Lund, C., & Patel, V. (2014, July 5). *Theory of Change: a theory-driven approach to enhance the Medical Research Council's framework for complex interventions*. http://trialsjournal.biomedcentral.com/articles/10.1186/1745-6215-15-267. Accessed 21 March 2017.

Developing a Theory of Change (Issue brief) (2015). The Management Center.

Developing a Theory of Change: A Framework for Accountability and Learning for Social Change (Issue brief). (2009). London: Keystone.

Flynn, M., Treasure-Evans, J., Fraser, S., Green, D., & Vogel, I. (2012). Theory of Change: what's it all about? *The Newsletter of Intrac*, No. 51, May.

Guidance for Developing a Theory of Change for Your Programme (Issue brief) (n.d.). Nesta.

Guijt, I., & Retolaza, I. (2012). Defining 'Theory of Change', *E-dialogues* (March), 1–7. The Hague: Hivos.

How to Apply a Theory of Change in Country Programmes and Programmes and Projects (Issue brief) (n.d.). Copenhagen: DANIDA.

Jackson, E. T. (2013). Interrogating the theory of change: evaluating impact investing where it matters most. *Journal of Sustainable Finance and Investment*, *3*(2), 95–110.

James, C. (2011). *Theory of Change Review. A report commissioned by Comic Relief*. Comic Relief.

Khan, A. (2011). *What is Theory of Change (TOC) thinking and its added value for social change movements?* (Working paper). *JASS Blog*.

Lawrence, K., Anderson, A. A., Susi, G., Sutton, S., Kubisch, A. C., & Codrington, R. (2009). *Constructing a Racial Equity Theory of Change: A Practical Guide for Designing Strategies to Close Chronic Racial Outcome Gaps* (Rep.). Washington, DC: The Aspen Institute.

Mackenzie, M., & Blamey, A. (2005). The practice and the theory: lessons from the application of a theories of change approach. *Evaluation, 11*(2), 151–68.

Mapping Change: Using a Theory of Change to Guide Planning and Evaluation (Issue brief). (2006). Grantcraft. Ford Foundation.

May, R. (2014). *Establish a Theory of Change* (Working paper). Biel: International Platform on Sport and Development.

Rogers, P. (2014). *Theory of Change, Methodological Briefs: Impact Evaluation 2.* Florence: Unicef Office of Research.

Stein, D., & Valters, C. (2012). *Understanding Theory of Change in International Development* (Publication). London: JSRP.

Taplin, D. (n.d.). *Theory of Change.* www.kstoolkit.org/Theory of Change. New York: ActKnowledge.

Taplin, D. H., & Clark, H. (2012). *Theory of Change Basics: A Primer on Theory of Change* (Tech.). New York: ActKnowledge.

Taplin, D. H., & Rasic, M. (2012). *Facilitator's Source Book* (Tech.). New York: ActKnowledge.

Theory of Change (n.d.). Zurich: Stiftung Zewo.

Theory of Change (n.d.). http://learningforsustainability.net/theory-of-change/. Accessed 28 June 2018.

Theory of Change – A Mesh Introduction (n.d.). https://mesh.tghn.org/articles/theory-change-mesh-introduction/. Accessed 28 June 2018.

'Theory of Change' for the UN Development System to Function 'As a System' for Relevance, Strategic Positioning and Results (Working paper). (2016). New York: UNDP.

Theory of Change – Guidelines (2013, February). Oslo: Bistandstorget.

Theory of Change and Program Design (Issue brief) (2016). New Haven, CT: IPA.

Theory of Change Summaries 2016–2019 (Working paper) (n.d.). Amnesty International.

Theory of Change Tool Manual (Rep.) (2005). Washington, DC: INSP.

Valters, C. (2014). *Theories of Change in International Development: Communication, Learning, or Accountability?* London: JSRP.

Valters, C. (2014, December 10). *Can Theories of Change Help Us 'Do Development Differently?'* http://asiafoundation.org/2014/12/10/can-theories-of-change-help-us-do-development-differently/. Accessed 28 June 2018.

Valters, C. (2015, September 15). *Four principles for Theories of Change in Global Development.* https://www.odi.org/comment/9882-four-principles-theories-change-global-development. Accessed 28 June 2018.

Van Es, M., Guijt, I., & Vogel, I. (2015). *Theory of Change Thinking in Practice* (Rep.). The Hague: Hivos.

Vogel, I. (2012, April). *Review of the Use of 'Theory of Change' in International Development* (Rep.). London: DFID.

Vogel, I. (n.d.). *ESPA Guide to Working with Theory of Change for Research Projects* (Tech.). London: ESPA.

Weiss, C. H. (1997). How can theory-based evaluation make greater headway? *Evaluation Review, 21*(4), 501–24.

Zand, D. E., & Sorensen, R. E. (1975). Theory of change and the effective use of the management science. *Administrative Science Quarterly, 20*(4), 532–45.

INDEX

Note: Page numbers in *italics* refer to figures and tables.